INHERITANCE

INHERITANCE

HERITAGE AND MEMORY IN
THE LEE VALLEY, COUNTY CORK

KIERAN McCARTHY

The History Press Ireland

Dedicated to those people who took the time to talk
about the cultural heritage within this book, opening up my own imagination.

First published 2010

The History Press Ireland
119 Lower Baggot Street
Dublin 2
Ireland
www.thehistorypress.ie

The History Press Ireland is an imprint of The History Press Group

British Library Cataloguing in Publication Data.
A catalogue record for this book is available from the British Library.

ISBN 978 1 8458 8972 2

Typesetting and origination by The History Press
Printed in Great Britain

Manufacturing managed by Jellyfish Print Solutions Ltd

CONTENTS

INNISCARRA DAM RETROSPECT

INNISCARRA NARRATIVES

ACKNOWLEDGEMENTS

A book such as this cannot be penned without the support, input, time and patience of numerous individuals. First and foremost, I would like to thank my friends and family for their ongoing support. My thanks to former editors Michael Carr and David Forsythe and their graphic team headed up by Johnny Lynch and Dave Ahern at the *Cork Independent*, where the sections of this book were first serialised. Thanks to The History Press Ireland for their vision and experience with this publication. My sincere thanks are also due to all those who gave insights, memories, guidance and multiple cups of tea:

Finbarr Crowley, Rooves Mór, Co. Cork
Peggy Looney, Coachford, Co. Cork
Neilie Twomey, Carrigadrohid, Co. Cork
Micheal and Nicky Quane, Coachford, Co. Cork
Joe Healy, Aghavrin, Co. Cork
Anthony Greene, Aghabullogue, Co. Cork
Andrew and Doreen O'Shaughnessy, Carrignamuck, Dripsey, Co. Cork

Peter and Ursula McSwiney, Dripsey, Co. Cork
Penny Rainbow, Nadrid House, Nadrid, Co. Cork
Kevin and Helen Feeney, Weigh Inn, Dripsey, Co. Cork
Anna Ryan, Dripsey, Co. Cork
Tomás Ryan, Dripsey, Co. Cork
Tess Begley, Dripsey, Co. Cork
Tony McCarthy, Blarney, Co. Cork

Eileen O'Connell, Model Village, Dripsey, Co. Cork
Helen, Jimmy, Elaine Kelleher, Dripsey, Co. Cork
Margaret Golden, Golden's Shop, Bishopstown, Co. Cork
Jimmy Noonan, Togher, Cork
Timothy O'Shea, Model Village, Dripsey, Co. Cork
Sadie O'Callaghan, Model Village, Dripsey, Co. Cork
Margaret Baker, Dripsey, Co. Cork
Margaret Barry, Cronody, Co. Cork
Patsy O'Regan, Dripsey, Co. Cork
Pat and Mary Carroll, Dripsey, Co. Cork
Martin McCarthy, Dripsey, Co. Cork

Leo O'Sullivan, Dripsey, Co. Cork
Cathal O'Leary, Cork City
Nancy O'Donovan, Vice-Principal, Sheila Desmond, teacher and Gerry Dineen,
Principal, Dripsey National School

Margaret Griffin, Griffin's Garden Centre, Lower Dripsey, Co. Cork
Oonagh and Kevin O'Mahony, Inniscarra, Co. Cork
John Manning, Innisleena, Co. Cork
Margaret Harrington, Gurteen, Co. Cork
Hennessy Family, Berrings, Co. Cork
Jackie Lenihan, Berrings, Co. Cork
Pat Reen, Berrings, Co. Cork
Sheila Healy, Ballinlough, Cork
Eamonn O'Mahony, Killeagh, Co. Cork
Betty O'Mahony, Killeagh, Co. Cork
John Burke, Faha, Co. Cork

Maurice Sweeney, Cork
Ferdie O'Halloran, Shanakiel, Cork
Donal O'Halloran, Bishopstown, Cork
Jack Sheehan, Togher, Cork
John and Mary O'Donovan, Beaumont, Cork
Malachy Walsh, Fountainstown, Cork
Diarmuid and Patricia O'Shea, Rochestown, Cork
Aileen Aeger, Ballincollig, Co. Cork
Margaret McAllister, Bantry, Co. Cork
Pat Murphy, Plant Manager, Cork Harbour and
City Water Supply Scheme, Cork County Council

Nora and Sheila Desmond, Ballyshonin, Co. Cork
Jane Quinlan, Model Farm Road, Cork
Donal Healy Cloghroe, Co. Cork
John Blair, Blair's Inn, Cloghroe, Co. Cork
Kathleen and Jack O'Leary, Cloghroe, Co. Cork
Annie Twomey, Ardrum, Co Cork
Charles Colthurst, Blarney, Co. Cork
Rory Sherlock, Galway
Helen Dodson, Galway

Con Healy, Inniscarra Community Centre, Co. Cork
Emma Dineen, Inniscarra Community Centre, Co. Cork
Dan Crowley, Coolatubbrid, Inniscarra, Co. Cork
Patrick Cronin, Gurteen, Co. Cork
Pat Healy, Ballyshonin, Co. Cork
John P. Hickey, Coolatubbrid, Co. Cork
Ann O'Mahony, Inniscarra Community Centre, Co. Cork
Eileen Collins, Inniscarra Community Centre, Co. Cork

George Williams, Canon's Cross, Co. Cork
O'Leary Family, Cloghroe Station House, Cloghroe, Co. Cork
Zwena & Peter McCullough, Tower, Co. Cork
Olwen Venn, Tower, Co. Cork
Joe O'Leary, Tower, Co. Cork
Madge Ahern, Tower, Co. Cork
Máire Geary, Cork City
Revd Ruth Jackson, Carrigrohane, Co. Cork
Jeffrey Good, Cork City

Catryn Power, Archaeologist, County Cork Council

Mary O'Driscoll, Northside Folklore Project
Stella Cherry and Dan Breen, Cork Museum
Dr Denis Lenihan, Department of Geography, University College Cork
The staff of the Cork City and County Archives
The staff of Cork City and County Libraries
The Irish Research Council for the Humanities and Social Sciences
Sean Kelly, Lucky Meadows Equestrian Centre, Watergrasshill, Co. Cork
Charlie O'Leary, formerly of Coláiste Chríost Rí, Cork City

...And to all my friends for showing me other signposts along the way, physically and metaphorically!

Kieran McCarthy

ABOUT THE AUTHOR

For over fifteen years, Kieran McCarthy has actively promoted Cork's heritage and its various communities. He has led, and continues to lead, successful initiatives through his community talks, city and county school heritage programmes, walking tours, newspaper articles, books, and his work through his heritage consultancy business.

In particular, Kieran has a keen interest in disseminating knowledge about the importance of local studies in Cork's primary and post-primary schools. Since 2003, he has annually co-ordinated the 'Discover Cork: Schools' Heritage Project', open to Cork City and County schools. The project focuses on celebrating, highlighting, debating and framing new and relevant approaches to Cork's cultural heritage for Cork's youth, teachers and the wider community.

For the past ten years, Kieran has written a local heritage column in the *Cork Independent*. He is the author of seven books: *Pathways Through Time, Historical Walking Trails of Cork City* (2001), *Cork: A Pictorial Journey* (co-edited 2001), *Discover Cork* (2003), *A Dream Unfolding, Portrait of St Patrick's Hospital* (2004), *Voices of Cork: The Knitting Map Speaks* (2005), *In the Steps of St Finbarre, Voices and Memories of the Lee Valley* (2006) and *Generations: Memories of the Lee Hydroelectric Scheme* (co-edited, 2008). In June 2009, Kieran was elected as a councillor (Independent) to Cork City Council. More on Kieran's work can be seen at www.corkheritage.ie and www.kieranmccarthy.ie.

Kieran McCarthy.

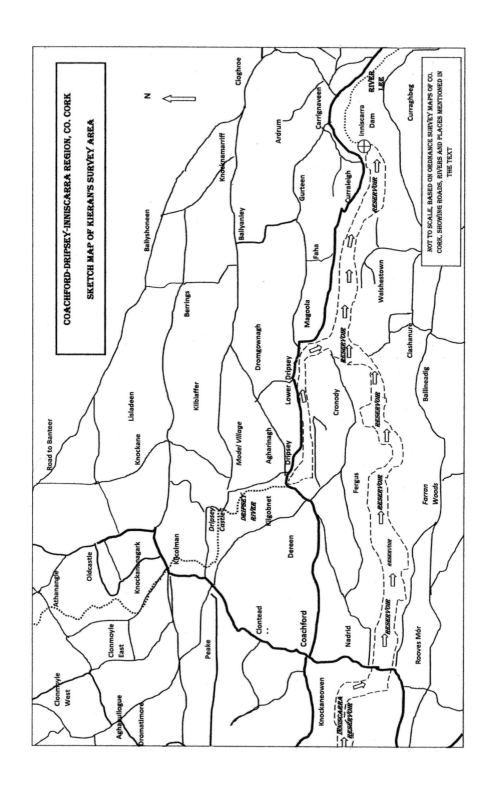

COACHFORD-DRIPSEY-INNISCARRA REGION, CO. CORK

SKETCH MAP OF KIERAN'S SURVEY AREA

N

NOT TO SCALE, BASED ON ORDNANCE SURVEY MAPS OF CO. CORK, SHOWING ROADS, RIVERS AND PLACES MENTIONED IN THE TEXT

Road to Banteer

Clonmoyle West

Aghabullogue

Dromatimore

Clonmoyle East

Peake

Athanangle

Oldcastle

Knockanaqark

Kilcolman

Knockane

Lisladeen

Kilblaffer

Berrings

Ballyshoneen

Knocknamariff

Ardrum

Cloghroe

Dripsey Castle

DRIPSEY RIVER

Kilgobnet

Model Village

Agharinagh

Dromgownagh

Ballyanley

Gurteen

Carrignaveen

Dereen

Dripsey

Lower Dripsey

Magoola

Faha

INNISCARRA

Dam

RIVER LEE

Curraghbeg

Clontead

Coachford

Nadrid

Fergus

Cronody

Walshestown

Clashanure

Ballineadig

RESERVOIR

RESERVOIR

RESERVOIR

RESERVOIR

Knockaneowen

INNISCARRA RESERVOIR

RESERVOIR

Rooves Mór

Farran Woods

INTRODUCTION

THE ARCHITECTURE OF INHERITANCE

Being the proud owner of a Honda 125 motorcycle had its advantages and disadvan-tages. Yes, I have felt every pothole from Gougane Barra to the City, felt the steepness of the valleyside of the Lee and was open to the changing seasons and the elements. Then there came a time for the bike to go to buy a bigger model. I have to say I felt sorry for the inanimate object I was leaving behind. In a sense, it was like losing a friend. That bike and I had spent eighteen months in the Lee Valley on fieldwork, exploring every byroad and by lane.

The old bike got me thinking about my journey down the Lee, and what I have learned, if anything. To begin with, this book is based on a series of articles that featured in the *Cork Independent* newspaper from October 2007 to June 2009 and it builds on my previous publications. Following the River Lee Valley from source to mouth takes one on a journey of forty-five miles from Gougane Barra in West Cork to the Lee Fields in Cork City. In that carved-out journey, I have delighted in the flow of the Lee, encountering its physical geography in a completely dif-ferent canvas to that of the north and south channel in Cork City. In essence, my decision to explore the River Lee Valley was informed by my love of physical and cultural geography. The project began as an exploration of heritage in the valley and to write about the key historical threads and memories within places that have evolved there. In addition, underlining my journey was the myth of St Finbarre walking from Gougane Barra to the area now occupied by Cork City. Those ideas still underpin my work but the further I travelled into the heart of the various par-ishes in the valley the more questions emerged to explore.

For me, the geography of the valley is still important and the more I journey in it the more I see how its landscapes and people are interlinked. I still get excited when I hear a new snippet of information, especially if is linked to a story I published a few weeks before. It's like finding a piece of a jigsaw puzzle that gives further meaning to the bigger picture. I suppose the whole journey is like an investigation of cultural heritage and debates how it is framed and how it survives in the busy globalised world. How do people's identities play out on the stage that is the valley? But my investigation has also led to vast research and I would like to think that my work aspires not only to celebrate people and place but to recover and renew an interest in local history and identity in not only the places I write about but also the people and places that receive the *Cork Independent* weekly.

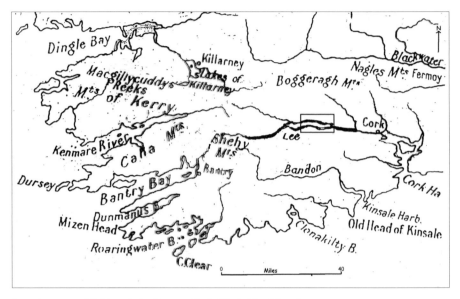

Location map of field study in County Cork (*Cork City Library*).

So unearthing the concepts of place-making play a huge part in my journey. I like the idea of culture not as something static but as something living, a process driving people and informing the decisions of the present. I have developed interests in ideas of legacy and how certain things are selected to be remembered and others disappear. Then in the valley I have marvelled at how the landscape has been transformed through ventures such as the Lee Hydroelectric and how it affected the population in terms of uprooting people, providing huge employment to the Cork region and creating new attitudes, mindsets and huge debates amidst communities, challenging them to change with the times. Then there is that notion of time. I marvel at the old black and white photographs showing families from 100 years ago and then marvel at the person showing me the photograph, who is the present day representative. The collision of the old and the new can be witnessed across the valley. Sometimes the contrasts are worrying but at other times, without them, the sense of living communities would be redundant.

I have thoroughly enjoyed the fieldwork component of my work. I have walked the land with my local contacts, chatting and negotiating fields and ditches and always revealing something striking. I felt like the proper explorer on many an occasion with my knapsack on my back with my notebook and camera, always ready to write or take a photograph. I have friends who call me Uncle Matt, the travelling fraggle from an old TV show *Fraggle Rock*, who always sent postcards back from where he was and offered commentaries on what he discovered. However, in my own journey, like Uncle Matt, there were times when I was destroyed by the rain, the mucky terrain and the countryside's briars as they cut into my clothes holding me for a couple of seconds as if to get my attention. The countryside slowed down the 'town mouse' or city boy element inside me – that notion that one must speed up and move through. I always remember the fields of maize and the claustrophobic feeling they gave me. All my guides went past the call of duty, giving me advice on how to negotiate the terrain. In addition many an afternoon's work ended in a cup of tea and a biscuit and more stories to be told setting me off on new tangents after just completing a task.

There are places in the Lee Valley that have stuck in my mind, like coming back from places such as Dripsey on these wintry days and witnessing amazing red sunset skies over Inniscarra Reservoir. I felt privileged to be viewing them. In fact, there are several signs that highlight the 'beautiful Lee Valley'.

Cronody townland on the banks of Inniscarra Reservoir, summer 2008.

There are the small delights in the little gems of landscape that one experiences in places such as Cronody Dovecote overlooking Inniscarra Reservoir near Dripsey. I have marvelled at the antique landscapes and the contrast of the standing stone and the satellite dish on a bungalow. There are ghostly presences and spooky atmospheres in the valley's ruined churches and graveyards.

But this book is more than an architectural record. The book is also more than a study of the rich language of images and symbols that are so inherent in rural environments. In fact, the many monuments on the local landscape could be described as part of a vast and varied open-air history book just waiting to be read.

This publication is based on explorations in the parishes of Aghabullogue, Inniscarra and Ovens on the northern valleyside on Inniscarra Reservoir, part of the course of the River Lee. The majority of the participants were met whilst traversing the parishes. Generally speaking, information in a library or on a map does not give you the tools for researching people and their attachment to place. Through fieldwork and talking to people, you can see that a community such as that in Aghabullogue parish or any other parish in Ireland evolved from leadership offered by individuals and families. People brought their own ideas and talents in forging a family space, which is then set in the wider community. It is interesting to note how the talents of a few can make a place or indeed reawaken one that is in decay. Some people's stories, especially in Aghabullogue parish, began elsewhere. In particular, the commercial possibilities of the region inspired many entrepreneurs and artisan families who settled in the region through the ages.

One aspect for certain is that the more I researched the places within the region or the more doors I knocked on, the more information came to the fore. What is also apparent is that everybody's view of the world is different. It could be an insider's view or an outsider's view, such as my own. For most people I met, heritage was a personal and collective experience focusing on their own roots. In fact, the historical data played 'second fiddle' to their personal stories. It has been interesting to see how stories and values have been handed down, and how each successive generation has taken it in turn to hold a torch for some element of the past in the present.

One recurring aspect is how much the region's cultural heritage runs metaphorically in 'people's blood'. There were a large number of people who noted, 'my father used to say' or 'my mother used to say'. That sense of inheritance is important and it is more than just honouring people. It conjures up debates about achievement and loss, and it is more than just recalling the memory of a few. For each person interviewed many more are represented through their life experiences. One is allowed to ponder on the power of the individual and their contribution to society, whether at a local or international level. The evolution of ideas can be mapped.

Maud Cotter, Dripsey, whose garden and attention to detail I always admired.

For the social scientist, the sense of inheritance poses questions for further study and debate, framing, enhancing and evolving old and new historical narratives. For the explorer, the sense of inheritance reveals a region of continuous creativity.

From fieldwork and interviews, the local people focussed in on several aspects of their locality's cultural heritage. Each person brought their own insights into their place and its roots, its identity and how it is perpetuated. Many of the themes talked about overlapped, signifying their importance to their lives and the community as a whole. It is difficult to place a weighting on the most important aspects. They all also link to ideas of landscape, mental imagery of the past, and concepts of memory.

So, *Inheritance* dabbles in the architecture of heritage and its interaction with life in the River Lee Valley. It does focus on a section of the Lee Valley, namely Aghabullogue, Inniscarra and Ovens parishes, but is not a definitive history of those regions. For me, the essence of the book is focussed on the beauty and structure of ordinary 'things' that one may take for granted but which highlight, debate and celebrate our cultural heritage.

This book is about a journey in seeking out the sense of place in the Lee Valley, a valley that has grasped my imagination and fails to let go. I have laughed, cried, wondered, been awestruck and got excited by my findings. The Lee Valley as a place has inspired in me a whole series of reactions. With all that in mind, *Inheritance* attempts to capture my explorations, the many moods and colours of a section of the Lee Valley, to contemplate new ways of seeing, to rediscover the characters who have interacted with it, the major events and the minor common happenings and to construct a rich and vivid mosaic of life by and on the River Lee. Above all this book is not about what we have lost but what we have yet to find…

Enjoy,
Kieran McCarthy

COACHFORD
TO DRIPSEY

1. COUNTRYSIDE, COACHFORD AND SACRED PLACES

We begin in Coachford, a village nearly sixteen miles from Cork City, which is an unofficial capital of mid County Cork. Coachford is a key place in the Lee Valley where the stories of human monuments past, present and future all collide to create massive contrasts. It is a place where changes in society and contemporary needs from the Stone Age to the Lee Hydro Electric Scheme to the modern houses next to Christchurch of the Church of Ireland are all evident. Place-making here is an ongoing process. Indeed my first impressions of Coachford I took from the 'souped-up' cars of several teenagers who were revving their engines as I drove home from the adjoining westerly parish of Aghinagh. I remember the cars vividly but also mentally recording the contrast of mid-nineteenth-century architecture of the village. It struck me that Coachford is a settlement in the Lee Valley where urban ideas have filtered in.

Looking at the Ordnance Survey map of the area, Coachford has developed at the meeting of four townlands, Nadrid (south-east), Knochaneowen (south-west), Monareagh (north-west) and Clontead Beg (north-east). The settlement also developed at the lowest crossing point of the River Lee. Life in Coachford has been influenced by the lie of the land, which Samuel Lewis in 1837 in his *Topographical Dictionary of Cork* described:

> The land, with the exception of about 150 acres of bog and waste, is of good quality and in a state of excellent cultivation, the system of agriculture has greatly been improved under the auspices of the resident gentry, and more especially of Messrs Colthurst, Good and P. Cross, who have been successful in raising green crops. Stone of good quality is quarried for building and for mending the roads, which throughout the district are kept in excellent repair.

Francis Guy, in his 1875 *Directory of County Cork*, pointed to Peake House, which was the residence of Miss Catherine Francis Lindsay and was a fine, strongly built mansion. It is noted as being erected in the seventeenth century and remodelled in the nineteenth century.

I was also intrigued to see in the archaeological inventory of the area that a standing stone is marked in Clontead More, just north of the village, and is still standing on a south-facing slope just over one metre high. The stone is not marked on the

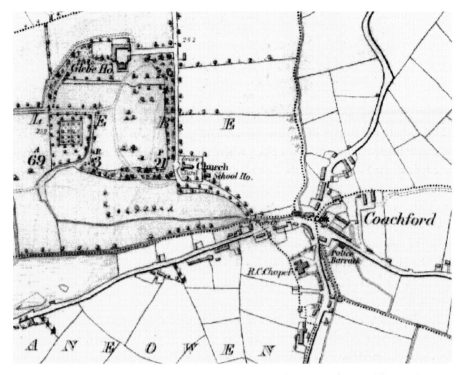

Section of 1836 Ordnance Survey map of Coachford. (*Ordnance Survey, Ireland*)

1842 or 1904 Ordnance Survey maps. Francis Guy in his section on Coachford in 1875 in his *Directory of County Cork* notes that the 'whole district to the north-west of Coachford abounds with stone circles, cromlechs, pillar stones, raths, holy wells and Danish forts'.

Belief practices have played a large role in the development of Coachford. In fact, the spires of the Catholic and Protestant churches are very prominent in the skyline as you enter Coachford from the Cork side. The Church dictated Coachford's growth as a settlement in the Lee Valley and aided in attracting residents to the area, developing a sense of pride of place. There were churches in this district as far back as the sixteenth century. The first notable structures were at Kilcolman and Aghabullogue. In the year 1584, the Protestant Bishop of Cork appointed John William Rhuwden, possibly a Welshman, as Perpetual Vicar of Kilcolman. Archdeacon Dee, on his visit to the site in the year 1615, found the church to be ruins. In 1618, the Bishop united Kilcolman parish to Aghabullogue, appointing John Odis rector of the two conjoined parishes. Aghabullogue became the parish centre in 1618 and continued to be the heart of Protestant life over the ensuing century. In 1669, Richard Synge was appointed vicar of Aghabullogue and Kilcolman. In 1674, he became Archdeacon of Cork and was succeeded by his brother, George, who served until his death in 1692 when he was succeeded by his nephew Edward. The Church of Ireland in Aghabullogue had a long and active ministry until its closure in the late 1800s.

In the year 1717, Robert Bulfell was appointed rector and vicar of Magourney. At that time Kilcolman still had its own parish identity, but on 22 June 1728 the two parishes were united under the name of Magourney. Robert Bulfell was the first rector. He was English, the son of a clergyman, but he was educated in Trinity College, Dublin. The Church lands were seventy acres in extent. It is also known a church was built. Charles Smith, antiquarian, in his *History of Cork* in 1750 describes a 'new parish church'. A Dublin man called Charles Phillips succeeded Bulfell. He was another Trinity graduate. Charles was aged fifty and unmarried when he came to the parish. Within two years, he married Catherine Vowell. On 16 February 1768, Revd Philips performed three marriages. Charles Shinkwin married Leah Gillman, Edmund Gillman married Ann Shinkwin, and William Sherrill married Anne Clarke.

In 1837 Samuel Lewis noted that Magourney church was enlarged in 1818 through the finances of a Protestant Board of Works, who were also known as the Board of First Fruits. The Board gave £200 towards the enlargement programme and also £224 towards the repair of the building. In the mid-nineteenth century a new Church of Ireland named Christchurch was built across the road, which was repaired and is now in private use.

Mind your step. The ruins of Magourney Church of Ireland church.

The contemporary Magourney Church of Ireland edifice is in a ruinous condition. The investigator in me noted that it has a west-east alignment. It has a large crenellated tower, surely one of the largest in the Lee Valley. There is evidence of a slate roof with pieces still in situ on the upper part of the tower. There are four large windows on the south-facing wall. In the north-facing wall, there is a blocked-up side door and window. There is evidence for a gallery through the presence of scaffolding or putlog holes. The probable timber stairs of the tower have disappeared.

I was conscious that this site is 300 years old. The site has grown in status through time and through collective respect, maintenance and regular visits by local people. The notion of time is reflected in the masonry of the encircling stone walls, which have been replaced and straightened over time. On the day of my visit, I was drawn to the architecture of the stone walls. There is a kind of poetry of contrasts in the stone. As material ruins, the different shapes and angles of the stones invoke a texture that is dirty and old but exciting and nostalgic at the same time. The cracks, scratches and indentations in the masonry reflect time like lines growing on an old hand. Those walls are aging and crumbling but you could feel they had an aura and a place in modern society.

To build the stone walls, emotion, effort and commitment had to be applied. Ruins can be talked about in terms of decay but also in terms of life. The walls in Magourney are a celebration of life. The walls showcase the past of golden ages, past crafts, traditional design. On one hand the ruins invoke loss but on the other they can also help recover identity and a sense of this place.

On the walls of the church we're told further stories of life as its benefactors and supporters are relayed to the visitor. In the former altar area, a cross marks the burial place of Herbert Webb Gillman who died in July 1898, the only son of Herbert Gillman. A plaque on the adjacent wall highlights that Herbert Webb's son Herbert Francis Webb Gillman was a member of the 'Council Madras'. He was born in June 1867. He died at Sinla, India on 23 November 1918 and was buried there. Another adjacent plaque highlights that the father of Herbert Webb Gillman died in 1877 and he is buried with his second wife, Sarah, daughter of Richard Neville Parker of Waterview. On the north-facing wall, a plaque memorial spans the years 1862 to 1888 and remembers the Crookes of Oldtown. Simon Davies Crooke died in June 1862. His grandson Simon Warren died in 1871 at the age of four years and nine months. His wife Jane Crooke died at the age of eighty-five.

Exploring the main graveyard, there are multiple unmarked stones, some of which have been recently exposed during a graveyard clean-up. There are several families with elaborate grave memorials. Not all of them can be read. Names and places can just be made out for the minority, as well as some of the ages. There are the plots of the Mahony family from Coachford and Inniscarra. The earliest of the Mahony stones remembers Patrick Mahony from Dripsey, who died in August 1837, aged nineteen.

Other individuals whose graves can be read are: Charles Field, died 1819; William Battelle, died 1830 at the age of twenty-six; Richard Walsh, died c.1869; Denis Sullivan, died 1873 at the age of nineteen; John Connor, c.1880; Johanna Varian, died 1893; William McSweeney, died 1908; Ellen McSweeney, died c.1945; John O'Keefe, died 1906; William Wiseman of Carhoo, Coachford, died 1919; Michael Murphy, Agharinagh, Dripsey, died 1975, buried with his wife Mary who died in 1927 and father Jeremiah who died in 1945, and Tadgh Crowley, Dromduv, Macroom, 1990.

There is a separate tomb on the southern side of the church ruins, that of Mary Laura Cross. She was born on 21 August 1840 and was the victim of the famous Dripsey poisoning case. Anthony Greene, local historian, in *The Coachford Record* for 1990 related that her husband was Philip Henry Eustace Cross who was a surgeon major in the British Army. He did service in the Far East, Africa and Canada. He married Mary (*née* Mary Laura Marriott) in Piccadilly, London in 1869. He was forty-four and she was twenty-eight. Returning to Canada, Mary had four children: Bob, Harry, Mona and Bess. The couple retired to Shandy Hall in Dripsey, County Cork where the fifth child, Etta, was born. The Cross family became members of the local gentry and were wealthy. Philip Cross had an army pension of £200 a year, ran a stud farm, was a cattle and sheep farmer and had a number of tenants. He also had inherited £5,000 from his father-in-law. His wife Mary had a small income from her brother and her father's will provided for ten yearly payments of £5,000.

In 1883, arising out of a dispute with a tenant, Philip Cross was boycotted by the local community. As a result, his stud business collapsed and his labourers left. By 1887, his wife Mary had become depressed and over time began to fear that she was dying of heart failure. At this time, Philip began to develop a relationship with twenty-one-year-old governess Effie Skinner, who was based at the local Caulfield residence at Classas. Mary's condition deteriorated and on the night of 2 June 1887, she died in much pain. Dr Cross made out the death certificate stating the cause of death to be typhoid fever and the duration of her illness fourteen days. She was buried in the Magourney Church of Ireland graveyard. Philip Cross went to London to see his children. Here also he met his Effie Skinner who at this stage was three months pregnant. Returning to Shandy Hall alone, rumours abounded with stories of the affair and that maybe Philip may have killed Mary Cross.

The rumours escalated and were taken seriously by District Inspector Tyacke of Ballincollig RIC, who wrote to the local coroner requesting that Mary Cross be exhumed. In the presence of Dr Crowley and Dr Charles Yeverton Pearson, lecturer in Medical Jurisprudence at Queen's College (now University College Cork), the body was dug up and taken to the courthouse where an inquest began. Small parts of the body were taken for scientific examination. Dr Pearson found traces of arsenic in the body. Dr Philip Cross was arrested and charged with the murder of his wife. He awaited trial in Cork Gaol. Several friends of the family and the local Coachford area gave testimonies. The combined evidence found Philip Cross guilty of murder and he was hanged on 10 January 1888.

The last Church of Ireland, the now revamped Christchurch in Coachford, a late-nineteenth-century structure, closed for service in 1988. It lies across the road from the earlier and now ruined Church of Ireland edifice. In 1994, the Quane family bought and renovated Christchurch.

Christchurch, Coachford.

Michael and Nicky Quane, residents of Christchurch.

Michael Quane grew up in Ovens in the 1960s. He attended the Crawford College of Art & Design in the 1980s. He is a stone sculptor whose studio is in Killumney. We can also indirectly attach Michael to the legend of St Finbarre's walk down the Lee. Michael has completed a number of commissions, one of which is a sculpted piece entitled *Figure Talking to a Quadruped*, which is in the President's garden in University College Cork (UCC). UCC's motto 'Where Finbarre [St] Taught, Let Munster Learn' could be applied to the great example of the tasteful renovation of Christchurch in Coachford into a house for the Quane family. Nicky, Michael's wife, is a botanist/medical herbalist and lectures on UCC's pharmacy courses and in several colleges of herbal medicine. She brought her own interests in botany to bear on the renovation and contemporary layout of the church and grounds. When I spoke to Michael, he noted:

> We liked the idea of living in a church. With architect Flor McCarthy, we worked in sympathy with the building, so that it appears like a home. The original structure is preserved. In one sense it is a house within a house, which is a unique approach. It doesn't have a spooky atmosphere. It has a rustic atmosphere on the inside – warm and relaxing. It does not have modern double-glazed building features – we do get plenty of air filtering through the stained glass especially if the wind is blowing from certain directions. The building does have timber cladding and insulation upstairs. When Nicky and I arrived, the stained-glass windows of the building were intact as well as the roof. Water was leaking through the cut stone. Much work was completed to bring it up to living standards.

The graveyard of Christchurch, which was opened in 1901, is now not in use but is intact and accessible behind the church. Valentia Island-born Anthony Greene has published articles on Coachford and has spent the last twenty years living in the area. He has amassed a vast knowledge on the people of Coachford, particularly those associated with the two Protestant churches, and he kindly offered to give me a guided tour of the churches themselves. What I found endearing about his discoveries was the way in which even the dead have a story to tell that adds to the identity of the region.

There are several unmarked graves, several graves that are vandalised, and some graves whose inscriptions are becoming weathered. Within the graveyard of the renovated Christchurch are several names of military men. Among those buried are Maj. Hubert Bernard Tonson Rye, Col. Trench, Gen. Cahill (whose wife Joan Cahill was a Catholic), Gen. Fitzgerald, Col. John Henry Newman who died in 1920, and Col. George Hawkes who died in 1959. George was one of three brothers who joined the British Army and all became colonels.

Christchurch graveyard, 2007.

Francis Henry Moblry Leader was in the Egyptian Army. His son was killed in action in France in August 1914. His wife was Agnes Letitia Leader. The granddaughter of Francis Henry married into the Jellett family, Huguenots and silversmiths from France who came to Ireland in the late 1600s.

Amy Clarke of the family of Clarke's Tobacco lived in Farren House, a site flooded out during the creation of the Inniscarra Reservoir in the 1950s. Despite being a multimillionaire, she is buried in a small grave. Her husband Tom Clarke was buried in Inniscarra in 1970. He was born in 1869 and died at 101 years of age. Their daughter Amy Marguerite Mathews died on 10 July 1924.

Ladies who are buried alone comprise Mary Dowden, who died in 1914 aged seventy-two, Mildred Wormold, Anne and Elizabeth O'Donoghue from Killinardrish, Wilhemina Hawkes Creed, who died in 1923, and Anne Mockwood. Anne's husband Mr Gillman is buried in the chancel of the other ruined church across the road.

Dafne Russell died in 1952. A cross lies across her grave. An interesting inscription can be seen, 'That God have mercy on my soul and man protect my dust, so long as doth a robin sing, this is my trust.' A sketch of a robin can be seen below the inscription.

The Lawless Pyne family were well known for their involvement in private banking in Cork. Caroline and Rebecca Lawless Pyne are buried in Christchurch graveyard. The rest of family emigrated to Queensland where relatives still exist. Margaret Anne and Robert Sutton died in the 1920s. My guide Anthony Greene informs me that all that is known about the couple is that they always sat in the church on the left-hand side, facing the altar, halfway down the aisle. An angel on an upright cross marks the burial spot of local doctor Abraham Cross Godfrey who lived in Broomhill near Godfrey's Cross. He contributed to the financing of the large stained-glass windows at the back of the church – the windows entitled *The Raising of Lazarus* and the *Daughter of Jairus*. In his will, Abraham left money to the poor of Coachford.

Three individuals are buried who, over time, were associated with the church itself. Revd Richard Hayes was rector of Christchurch, Coachford for thirty years (1880-1911). His son and grandfather were also clergymen. Thomas Carey was a verger of Christchurch and clerk of the local petty sessions. He died in 1940. His family members are buried with him; Anna died in 1947 and Edward in 1965. The last verger, John Buckley, who died ten years ago, lived nearby but his cottage is now demolished.

The burial place of Revd William Darling and wife can be viewed. They were the parents of the recently retired Bishop of Limerick. Mary Decima Tate, who was a direct descendant of Daniel O'Connell, and engineers Crossthwaite and Nichols are buried here. Crossthwaite and Nichols worked on the Cork–Muskerry line. The Good family from Crookstown are represented. The Levy family can be seen. The Levys moved from West Cork to Coachford to retire.

Mrs Linsay was the wife of 'Stuffy' Linsay. She was killed after the Dripsey ambush in 1921. 'Stuffy' retired from working in Northern Ireland to the Coachford area and expressed a wish to return to die in the North. His wish was unfulfilled and he died before his wife did. He was buried at Leemount.

Three-quarters of Ellen Fitzgibbon was buried in Christchurch graveyard. In her earlier years, she had a leg amputated because of diabetes. The leg was buried in Inniscarra. She lived in a house near Farren, which was destroyed by the Lee Hydro-Electric scheme.

Richard Mason Woodley died on 20 September 1904 and was a member of the Distinguished Service Order. He lived in Leades in Aghinagh and gave favourable evidence at the Dripsey ambush trial in early 1921, which resulted in two lads escaping the death penalty. He was married to Ailsa Margaret, who died in October 1926.

2. GROWTH OF A VILLAGE

On the approach road to Coachford from the Inniscarra reservoir side is the Catholic St Patrick's church. A plaque notes that the original church on the site dates to *c*.1840 and that the present church was renovated in 1990. There are three high crosses in churchyard dedicated to Revd Michael Irwin (died 1943), Revd Jeremiah Russell (died 1906) and Revd Daniel Coakley (died 1951). Another memorial in the yard is for the memory of Mary, who died in February 1887, beloved wife of John Murphy of Coolcullig.

Coachford does not appear in any late eighteenth-century map of County Cork or the Grand Jury Map of Cork in 1811. Coachford only seemed to grow as a settlement with functions from the 1820s onwards. The first edition Ordnance Survey map for the Coachford area in 1834 shows the two churches. A Protestant glebe house is shown just to the north-west of the church. Coachford Community College was founded in 1950 on the grounds of the glebe house. Just to the east of the church, a school house is marked. Today, directly across the road from Magourney church on the western side is Coachford National School. The present building dates to 1996. In addition, a terrace of four modern detached houses has recently been built just to the north of the grounds of the ruined church. The 1836 map also depicts a police barracks in the centre of the village and several houses built along the approach roads to the heart of the village crossroads.

Coachford, *c*.1900. (*Cork City Library*)

Guy's *Directory of County Cork* in 1875 depicts a lively village with a number of functions. Firstly, the mail arrived from Dublin at 5.30a.m. and left for Cork at 7.20a.m. The postmaster was Richard Burke. The national school teachers were Jeremiah Twomey and Ellen Twomey. The Church of Ireland teachers were Mr and Mrs McDonnell. The shopkeepers were John Buckley, Edward J. Murphy and Richard Burke. Mr Burke also had a vintners or public house. The other vintners comprised Mrs Forde, Charles Dinan and Michael O'Brien. A passenger car left for Cork at 8a.m. and returned at 7p.m. on Mondays, Thursdays and Saturdays. Timothy Connell provided the service. Coachford is noted as being six miles from the Kilcrea station on the Cork–Macroom Railway.

One of the most important factors in Coachford's development in the late 1800s was its association with the Cork & Muskerry Light Railway. Trains connect places and do add to creating new landscapes. The Muskerry Tram linked the disconnected countryside to the connected port city of Cork. The train gave access to the immediate hinterland. It quickened the transfer of goods between County Cork locations and the city. In a sense, its tracks symbolised the spread of industrialisation in this area of the northern valley side of the River Lee. Trains also create a sense of excitement and expectation about a place. Those are perhaps traits that still linger when one explores Coachford's geography and history. Coachford is still valued amongst Cork society as a place of importance. Perhaps the memory of the train line has indirectly created Coachford as a sacred space amongst the psyche of Corkonians?

Coachford railway station. (*Cork City Library*)

Cork–Muskerry
Light Railway
at Carrigrohane,
*c.*1900. (*Cork
City Library*)

The railway was also known as the Blarney Tram, the Hook and Eye, and the Muskerry Tram. It was financially successful and much used by locals. The Cork–Muskerry Railway was one the city's first narrow gauge lines. It was established with the help of the Tramways and Public Expenses (Ireland) Act of 1883, which enabled companies to obtain part or all of the finance to construct a line.

In 1883 preliminary meetings took place with prominent landowners, farmers and taxpayers to consider the possibility of establishing a light railway in the Muskerry area. On 13 October a meeting was held in the courthouse in Coachford between the interested parties and local ratepayers. The line was primarily built for tourists. It was to link Cork to the tourist town of Blarney and its historic castle. Supporters of the railway line also aimed to provide improved transport for locals with livestock and farm produce between the farming area north-west of Cork and the city, and for coal and minerals in the reverse direction.

In the early days of planning, engineer S.G. Fraser was appointed to inspect the area. The estimated cost was £65,000. On 24 April 1884 the project was investigated by the Grand Jury and recommended. Work began on the construction of the railway on 4 February 1887. Robert Worthington, who was a well-known railway builder, was the contractor for the thirteen-kilometre stretch, and the contract price was £59,000. The Blarney section was officially opened on 8 August, in time for the autumn tourist traffic of 1884. The journey took forty minutes at a speed of 6 mph on the road and 20 mph through the fields. The first-class return fare was 1*s* 8*d*, while the third-class fare was 10*d*.

The Coachford section was opened on 19 March 1888. Every day the first train for Coachford left Western Road at 8.30a.m. and the last train left at 5.30p.m. Trains left Coachford at 6.45a.m., 10.30a.m. and 4p.m. In all, the journey was fifteen and a half miles. The railway line started at a terminus at Bishop's Marsh adjacent to the Western Road. It was a single-storey building covered by a corrugated-iron roof with a long platform. The iron engine and carriage shed spanned three tracks. The first four miles of the line going west were very like that of a tramway. From the terminus the line crossed the south channel of the River Lee in Cork City via a small bridge leading to Western Road. The initial stops were at Victoria Cross, Carrigrohane and then north-wards to Leemount, Healy's Bridge and Coachford Junction.

The Cork and Muskerry Light Railway Section began at Coachford Junction and passed through Cloghroe, Gurteen, Dripsey, Kilmurray, Peake and Coachford. In 1893 a line was opened from Coachford junction to Donoughmore. The Coachford station had the usual offices with a single platform, loco and goods sheds turntable, livestock pens and two carriage sheds. The station house was built of corrugated iron with a canopy in front. There were ladies' and gents' waiting rooms. The stationmaster's office had a window with a slide facing the platform through which the tickets were sold. Several of the station buildings have survived and are now used as residences.

The railway had twenty-seven miles of track and the main line ran to Blarney. There were two branch lines, one to Coachford and the other from St Ann's, near Blarney, which followed the Shournagh Valley to Donoughmore. The Donoughmore Extension Light Railway also began at Coachford Junction and then travelled north-west, stopping at St Ann's, Burnt Hill, Gurth, Fox's Bridge, Knockane, Firmount and Donoughmore. Passengers had to change at St Ann's for a separate line to Blarney. The first-class fare was 2s 6d and third class was 1s 10d. The first-class compartment had padded seats covered in red velvet upholstery. In the third-class compartment the seats were of varnished wood and ran the length of the carriage. Whenever an impor-tant match was played in Coachford, great crowds travelled on the train. All the freight arrived by train: porter, whiskey, groceries, coal, and yellow meal for Coachford and Carrigadrohid. Pigs were carried to Cork by train for the city's bacon factory.

In 1924, the railway line was taken over by the Great Southern Railway. In the 1920s, the line began to lose passengers to the Southern Motorways Omnibus Company, who began to operate buses on the Western Road. The train was responsible for several minor accidents, especially ones involving horses. The only major incident occurred on 27 September 1927 when the 7.45a.m. train from Donoughmore collided with a steamroller. Two coaches were derailed but no one was injured. With the advent of the motor car, the railway lost its popularity and passenger numbers declined. On 29 December 1934 the last train ran on the line.

Sheila Moynihan and Ciara Merigan
at the former stationmaster's house,
Coachford, 2006.

In the early 1900s, the famous Irish photographer William Laurence photographed Coachford. Copies of these photos are still sold in certain shops in the area.
One popular image dating to *c.*1905 depicts a modern settlement but with rural
values. The intersection of the past and the contemporary is shown in a picture of a
thatched cabin and a telegraph boy. The boy's name was William O'Mahony. In later
years he became Coachford's postmaster. The thatched cottage in the postcard was
raised to a two-storey building in the 1930s and was occupied by the O'Mahony
family. William's daughter Peggy Looney is part of the fourth generation on her
mother's side to live in the same house in Coachford.

Using the postcard image and Guy's *Directory of County Cork*, we can recount
how busy a village Coachford had become in the early 1900s. The directory for
1910 provides evidence of seven grocers: Patrick Riordan, Ellen Sheehan, Timothy
Sheehan, Ellen Twomey, Timothy O'Callaghan, Jeremiah Hogan and Thomas Burke.
There were four vintners, comprising Thomas Burke, Hannah Dineen, Timmy
O'Callaghan and Mathew McDonnell. John Ahern was the bill poster, George
McNamara the victualler, William McSweeney the blacksmith, James Murphy the
carpenter, D. O'Keeffe the tailor and Billy O'Mahony was the harness maker (there

seems to have been two Billy O'Mahony's in Coachford in the 1930s, one young, who was the postman, and one older, the harness maker). Thomas Burke had the hotel and posting establishment, which dated back to the mid-1700s. The hotel was revamped in the late 1800s with ensuite bathrooms added in some cases. The hotel is also remembered on a plaque on the frontage of present-day Breathnach's Bar. Guy's *Directory* also notes that D. Foley was the manager of Coachford Co-operative Creamery Company, which was established in 1898.

Peggy Looney, who was born in 1936 and whose father William was shown in the postcard observes of the evolution of Coachford:

> Growing up in the late 1930s and 1940s, I remember them turning the train and the tip head where the train used to stop. Pat Horgan was the stationmaster. Mr Dan O'Connell was the train driver ... the line was a great place to play – you could walk to Peake on the old railway line.
>
> Coachford was an important village. It had everything in a small locality. The village green was in front of Jimmy O'Mahony's. My father had a bicycle shop in Coachford. He sold equipment for bicycles and repaired them. The village had a cooper who made barrels, a harness maker and a blacksmith. There were four public houses. There was a parish dancehall, which reopened in 1937 after having been closed for a time – the building was knocked down in 2004. There were two fair days – a pig fair on the last Wednesday in each

Above left: Peggy Looney, daughter of William O'Mahony, with Neilie Twomey, Bill Casey (who worked the Lee Scheme) and Judy Dineen, Coachford, 2006.

Above right: William O'Mahony, harness maker, early twentieth century, Coachford. (*Br M. Vianney*)

month and a cattle and sheep fair the previous Tuesday. The old showground is now the site of the GAA pitch. A branch of the GAA was formed in Coachford in 1885. Milk and cream could be sent direct via the Muskerry tram to liners in Cobh. The old courthouse is now the community house. My uncle Jerome O'Mahony was the village carpenter.

Joe Healy from the nearby townland of Aghavrin remembers Coachford to be a thriving village in the thirties in his book *When We Were Young Together*:

> Coachford was an integral part of our young lives. There was always something happening there; the hurling down in the enclosure (the GAA pitch now), dancing, concerts, Gaelic League classes in the Village Hall, etc. An odd evening when we would go hurling to Aghabullogue we would find out that some of the bigger lads were gone to Coachford practising for a game. The O'Learys, Donal Healy, Matt Noonan and Ned Murphy would be involved. Aghabullogue were doing well in the hurling fields and we followed them to the matches. When we got involved in the early forties we would practise in the GAA grounds in Coachford. We joined the teams in the early forties and got to know the lads – the O'Connells, Cooneys, Barry Murphys, Crowleys, Dineens, Sheehans, O'Riordans. Many great friends had spent many hours hurling in the enclosure or travelling playing other teams. Very few went forward for second-level education then. In the minor team (under eighteen) we played on in 1942 only three players went for secondary school. Most lads either went farming, working at a trade or into the Dripsey Woollen Mills.

Joe Healy was born in Clonmoyle, just to the north of Coachford. Now living in Aghavrin, he is the youngest son of Thomas John Healy and Abina (*née* McCarthy). The family is reputedly the sixteenth generation on the family farm, having originally come from Donoghmore. He was educated in Rylane National School and spent a short term at the North Monastery in Cork. He played hurling with Aghabullogue and Muskerry teams and with Canovee in football during the forties and early fifties. He won the Tenor Competition and was awarded the O'Shea Cup at the Feis Maitiú in 1950. He was a member of the Aghabullogue Hunt and rode with the hunt for thirty years. He is a founding member of Coachford Young Farmers' Club (which later became Macra Na Feirme). In 1984, he wrote the *Story of Aghabullogue GAA*. In recent years, in association with Coachford Historical Society and Community Council, he has published *When We Were Young*, a personal account of growing up in Aghabullogue, Coachford and Rylane. He also composes and has published songs on local places in local historical journals and the Cork *Holly Bough*.

During my fieldwork with Joe Healy in Coachford, he noted with pride that his grandfather John Healy was involved in canvassing with the local MEP in the 1880s to gain financial support for the building of the Muskerry Tram. He also told me that his father Thomas John Healy and grand-uncle Michael Healy were very involved in the Coachford Agricultural Show, which ran between 1892 and 1928. Thomas was show secretary for a number of years whilst Michael was a show director. The show was held on what are now the Aghabullogue GAA grounds in Coachford, near Rooves Bridge.

It is hard to ignore Joe's perspectives on twentieth-century Coachford. His book *When We Were Young* is now out of print but provides an important record of life within a section of the Lee Valley. His record is perhaps of an Ireland that is also disappearing as the effects of our Celtic Tiger economy have not only changed the landscape in terms of infrastructure but also morals and attitudes in society. Today, one can boast that Coachford is still a convenient place to live – just twenty-five minutes from the city.

Another related aspect of modernity is Coachford's proud links to theatre and pantomime. Former curate Fr Sheehan was very active in promoting plays in the 1940s. Fr William Buckley took over from 1956 to 1962 and produced several pantomimes. The venue was the local parish hall. It came to a halt when Fr Buckley was transferred. He died as parish priest of Midleton in October 1982.

3.   THE HERITAGE OF THE LAND

Man will always be seeking new ways and new inventions, but the culture and the people of the past should not be forgotten, as they have brought us to this day.

Joe Healy, Aghavrin, County Cork

I was drawn further north into Aghabullogue parish to Aghabullogue village by the myth of St Finbarre. Folklore has it that St Olan, the patron saint of the parish, was Finbarre's confessor. There are aspects of education and spirituality legacy here, more so than in anywhere else in the Lee Catchment area. Indeed, as one explores the area St Olan's Well and the Ogham Stone are unmissable.

During my wanderings, I was drawn to the topography of Aghabullogue, the canvas on which the cultural geography unfolds. The southern extremities of the area form the immediate northern valleyside for the Lee. The parish of Aghabullogue extends from the Lee near Coachford northwards for a distance of seven miles, as far as Rylane. The northern portion includes the villages of Aghabullogue and Rylane. Knochnagour and Annahinny Hills enclose a broad saucer-shaped basin, which is interspersed with numerous heights, bogs and sheltered plantations. All those sites combine to provide a variety of scenic attractions. The Dripsey River crosses through the heart of the parish and enters the Lee at Dripsey. The Delehinagh River flows south near Aghabullogue and enters the Dripsey River at Peake. In cross section, the rivers have created a very distinct 'ridge-trough' profile. The roads are all steep and the valleysides of the Dripsey River seem to tip the traveller, or draw him to the water. The narrow streamed valley also exposes the underlying sandstone rock and in a sense gives access to the heart of the parish.

The ridge and valley character in Aghabullogue provides a rich sheltered environment for crops and the out-wintering of cattle. There is great variety in County Cork landscapes of scenery, slope, altitude, soil structure, drainage patterns and exposure to wind, rain and sun. This is very evident in the area extending from Aghabullogue to Dripsey, where the bedrock is purple mudstone and red sandstone with rock depth ranging from two to five metres. The topsoil at the higher elevations comprises peaty podzols with brown podzols over most of the Dripsey River catchment area. Compared to the raw landscape of the western portion of the Lee Valley in Uibh Laoghaire, in Aghabullogue the sense of smoothness is present, its rolling fields showing that the land was carved more by rivers and human activity than by glaciers. Certainly, at the end of the last ice age 20,000 years ago, moving glaciers would have affected the land but not to the extent of the western half of the Lee Valley where the effects which still can be seen.

In local folklore, Aghabullogue (or Achadh Bold) has many meanings, testament to the fact that the area's story has suffered a form of memory loss. It may mean 'the field of the bags or sacks' or 'the fields of the caves or the swellings'. In terms of early settlement in Aghabullogue parish, there is a distinct Bronze Age presence; settlement markers from 5,000 years ago in terms of Fulachtaí fia, or cooking sites, are located near the rivers. The famous Bronze Age hoard found in 1907 at Mount Rivers is now kept in the National Museum. Then we fast forward to *c.* AD 600 to the legend of St Olan and the first development of early Christian churches in the area. There is a high concentration of ring forts – six are marked on the Ordnance Survey map within five miles of Aghabullogue village. The townland name Old Castle reflects the presence of two ring forts in that area, which still can be seen as low oval mounds.

Aghabullogue's history is linked to the land. The land has provided and continues to provide employment in farming and industrial pursuits. Dairy farming is an age-old tradition in County Cork. Farmhouse dairying was at one time very intense. Churning took up valuable time in the household for several days of the week. The tradition of milk production was handed down through the generations, which has, in a sense, preserved the heritage of the land. At one time, the link between land and people was much stronger. Farmers supplied markets in local towns. Butter roads, with farmers carrying homemade butter bound for the Cork Butter Market, were well utilised.

Dripsey River, Clonmoyle townland.

Clontead House.

The Co-operative Wholesale Society was founded in 1854 in England. In time its aspirations of co-operation amongst farmers filtered into Ireland. In 1894, the Irish Agricultural Organisation Society was founded with co-operation as its central aim. In 1899, the first co-operative creamery was founded in Dromcollagher, County Limerick. By the year 1900, there were 200 co-operatives in Ireland. There were four creameries opened in Aghabullogue by 1916 (Kilcolman and Coachford in 1898, Rylane and Aghabullogue in 1916). Today the presence of Dairygold Co-operative Society Ltd in Coachford is the thread that connects the past, present and future, in terms of the inherited importance of the land.

Heading north from Coachford, the R1619 road bound for Mallow gently slopes and follows for a time the dismantled track of the Muskerry Tram. This is the townland of Clontead, or Cluain Teide. Teide means a plateau or a plain on a hill, so Cluain Teide means 'plain of the flat-topped hill'. In 1944 the Irish Tourist Association recorded a dolmen in Clontead More, half a mile from Coachford, in the farm of Mr Dan O'Halloran. It consisted of a single boulder weighing three tons and lying flat in the corner of the field. Legend has it that the giant Mushera threw it from his lair on the Mushera Mountain and the marks of his fingers could be seen. The site is marked on the present-day Ordnance Survey map as a standing stone. Further north on the right is Clontead School, which opened in 1958 but has closed in recent years.

The Aghabullogue district was a popular centre with the wealthy classes and the large number of nineteenth-century country residences that can still be seen testify to this. Approximately twenty buildings that could be classed under the heading of mansions exist in the parish. The buildings in plan and outward appearance display certain Georgian characteristics such as a plain façade, tall windows, a roof sloping back with small slates, and noticeable absence of hood mouldings over the doors.

In 1837, Samuel Lewis in his *Topography Dictionary of Ireland* gives interesting insights into the changing cultural landscapes at that time in Aghabullogue parish. He notes:

> Numerous large and elegant houses are scattered over the parish: the principal are Clonmoyle, the seat of C. Colthurst, Esq.; Ahavrin House, of Capt. T.E. Crooke; Leeds, of E. Woodley, Esq.; Cooper's Ville, of W. Warsop Cooper, Esq.; Deelis, of R. Fuller Harnett, Esq.; Mountrivers of N. Whiting, Esq.; Kilberehert, of R.B. Crooke, Esq.; The Cottage, of Pyne, Esq.; Rock Ville, of T. Radley Esq.; Ahavrin Cottage, of the Revd I. Smith, and Carrigadrohid, of the Revd Pierce Green, P.P.

Clontead House was built *c.*1840 and was owned by the Gillman family up until the First World War. After the war, the family sold out for safety reasons due to the ongoing violence across the country from 1916 onwards. Clontead House was the residence of Herbert Webb Gillman (1832-1898), a one-time President of the Cork Historical and Archaeological Society, an author of several historical articles and a Member of the Royal Society of Antiquities. Clontead House is now owned by the Long family.

Three miles north of Coachford near Peake there was once a monument, which stood in a field near the road. It was a plain ivy-covered rectangular tower, which at one time appeared to have had a stone roof. Known as the Trafalgar monument, it was approximately eight feet square and twelve feet high. It was erected by Captain Colthurst of the British Navy who fought at Trafalgar. He wished to commemorate the victory near his home. His residence was Dripsey Castle. From my fieldwork, it would now seem that the monument has disappeared.

Turning left at Larchfield Crossroads and following the sign for Aghabullogue, one encounters the old ticket office of Peake Station. Peake Station was the first station on the Hook and Eye line. The ticket office, an ornate but dilapidated building, has survived in the car yard of Jimmy Buckley. Further on is the gate lodge for the Cork–Muskerry train, which facilitated the train crossing the road on its journey eastwards. The lodge has completely changed and now has a modern house design.

Former Peake ticket house.

Passing through Peake, or An Phéac (a peak), one passes the Dew Drop Inn, now owned by the Ring family. Across the road is the collapsed structure of Dinneen's Public House, which was burnt down in recent years. A yeomanry barracks existed in Peake at one time for the convenience of soldiers stationed in the area. The current large premises of Moremiles Tyres occupy the demesne of the Big House of Clonmoyle, which is now in ruins. The Colthursts of Ballyvourney reputedly built it in the late 1700s. In the mid-1800s, Harry Leader occupied it and he introduced a local furze mill for the fattening of pigs. Harry Leader is noted as having been an engineer in Egypt and applied his experience in local irrigation schemes, most of which failed.

Leader's Folly was a part of the local irrigation scheme and was an impressive aquaduct across the Dripsey River. Now hidden amongst the overgrowth, the general structure was erected about the year 1860. Twelve piers supported a water chute intended to irrigate the land across the valley. The highest pier was eighty-five feet high. Some of the piers have been dismantled in the last century for building purposes. The water was piped for a distance of two miles cross-country. It was then fed into the chute and conveyed across the valley from Old Castle to Clonmoyle. It is said it did not operate for very long. Mr Harry Leader was a philanthropic type of individual and very often the object of his experiments was to provide employment for the poor people of the locality.

Ruins of Leader's Folly.

An amusing story is told of the erection of Leader's Folly. Masons were first employed for the building of the piers but their work was deemed unsatisfactory. Mr Leader finished the project by direct labour. He employed several labourers and also accepted a number of boys who were on a juvenile rate of pay. One of the youths wore his father's hat and pants and was classed as a man. Soon all the boys were in their fathers' clothes and received the adult rate of pay without question. Mr Leader financed his schemes from a mortgage on his property. It was discovered after his death that he had no title to the land and the bank lost approximately £20,000.

Climbing the western side of the Delehinagh River Valley and still bound for Aghabullogue, Peake House can be viewed. Of early-nineteenth-century appearance, it has an east-facing entrance of five bays and a central door with semi-circular fanlight. It was once the premises of the Lindsay family but is now owned by the O'Sullivan family.

Just entering the Aghabullogue village district, one enters the townland of Dromatimore or Drom a'Tighe Móir, 'hill-back of the big house'. Dromatimore is an unusual style of house and is different in style to the Georgian house. It has a mixture of castle and Georgian forms. On stylistic grounds, it resembles a structure built in the late 1600s. It has three storeys of sandstone and a turret in the centre of the buildings on the northern and southern sides. Kevin Murphy presently occupies the dwelling.

4. AGHABULLOGUE'S UNIQUE GAA MEMORIAL

Much has been written on the history and impact of the GAA movement in Irish society since its inception in 1884. At the entrance to Aghabullogue village there is a plaque denoting the importance of the GAA to enhancing community life and the sense of place in the parish. During my travels in the Lee Valley catchment area, it is the only GAA memorial in a public space that I have seen. The inscription reads, 'Erected in proud memory of Aghabullogue Hurling Team 1890, Cork's First All-Ireland Champions.' The local GAA branch published a centenary programme in 1990. Within, the historical research by Jerry Buckley, Anthony Greene, Ted Long and Seamus O'Donoghue illuminates the players of that significant event and brings the names and stories associated with the meaning of the memorial alive.

Trainer Revd Andrew O'Riordan was the seventh of twelve children. His parents were William O'Riordan and Mary O'Keeffe, Fair Lane, Mallow. Born on 14 November 1852, Revd O'Riordan went on to be ordained in Maynooth in July 1877. He served three years in the Diocese of Liverpool and became curate in Banteer in August 1880, Ballyvourney in 1885 and Aghabullogue in 1887. He served in Aghabullogue until his death in 1907. He was President of the local hurling club.

Cork's First All-Ireland Winners, 1890. Back row, left to right: J. Buckley, D. Linehan, D. Looney, D. Drew, D. Lane (Captain), J. Hinchion, J. O'Connor, T. Twomey, M. Morgan and P. Buckley. Front row, left to right: P. Riordan, J. O'Reilly, T. Kelleher, D. O'Sullivan, T. Good, Revd Fr A. O'Riordan CC, D. Morgan, E. O'Reilly, J. Linehan, J. Kelleher, J. O'Sullivan and P. O'Riordan. (*Aghabullogue GAA*)

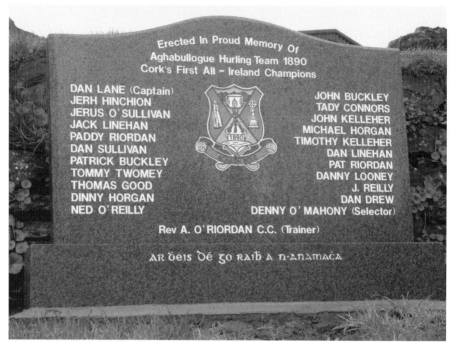

Erected In Proud Memory Of
Aghabullogue Hurling Team 1890
Cork's First All – Ireland Champions

DAN LANE (Captain)
JERH HINCHION
JERUS O'SULLIVAN
JACK LINEHAN
PADDY RIORDAN
DAN SULLIVAN
PATRICK BUCKLEY
TOMMY TWOMEY
THOMAS GOOD
DINNY HORGAN
NED O'REILLY

JOHN BUCKLEY
TADY CONNORS
JOHN KELLEHER
MICHAEL HORGAN
TIMOTHY KELLEHER
DAN LINEHAN
PAT RIORDAN
DANNY LOONEY
J. REILLY
DAN DREW
DENNY O'MAHONY (Selector)

Rev A. O'RIORDAN C.C. (Trainer)

AR ꝺeis ꝺé ꝃo RAIꝅ A n-AnAmAċA

GAA memorial, Aghabullogue.

John Buckley lived in Peake, where he was porter in Peake Railway Station. He was the goalkeeper on the 1890 team. He had two sons, John and Jimmy, and a daughter Janie. John died in September 1935.

Patrick Buckley was born in Peake in 1857. He was a shoemaker by trade. He married Julia Twomey and had five children. He and his family lived at Coolacullig. He made the sliotars used by the team. He was also a noted bowl player. He died in August 1939.

Tady Connors was born in Toureen, Rylane in 1864. He lived at Aghavrin and worked for Captain Crooke. Tady had five children: Paddy, Bill, Johnny, Kitty and Nora.

Dan Drew was born on 5 November 1862 to Con Drew and Hanora Mahony. He was a ticket collector on the Muskerry Railway. He lived at Henmount. The Drew family had a great tradition of an open house, featuring music and dancing. Dan was killed tragically at Donoughmore Junction when he fell between two train carriages.

Thomas Good was born on 12 February 1870 to Thomas and Mary (O'Mahony) Good. He became a harness maker in Coachford, living at Knockanowen. He was a relation of William O'Mahony, the harness maker in Coachford.

Jeremiah (Big Jerh) Hinchion was born on 23 December 1865 at Cottage, Clonmoyle, the third of six children of John Hinchion and Eliza Forrest (of

Blarney). He married Johanna Ahern in 1898 and they had six children. He died, almost crippled with arthritis, in 1938 and is buried in Aghinagh. Local historian Joan Hinchion is Big Jerh's granddaughter.

Dinny Horgan was one of three pairs of brothers on the team. The Horgans lived in Carhue Upper on the Hawkes estate. Like his brothers he emigrated to London, where he played with London Irish. He captained the London Irish team that beat Redmonds in the All-Ireland Final of 1901.

Michael Horgan was the brother of the famous Dinny, and like his two brothers Dinny and Dan, became a member of the London Irish team.

John Kelleher was born on the family farm at Cahirnafulla. He married into the O'Connor family in Ceapnagown. They had three children, Patrick, Cis and Mary Jo.

Timothy Kelleher lived in Carhue and was one of a family of six. He died in March 1944.

The captain of the team was Dan Lane who was born on 7 March 1862 to Dan Lane and Mary Coakley on the family farm at Tullig. All his brothers and sisters emigrated to America. He had five sons and two daughters. One son, Tim, emigrated to Boston at the age of sixteen.

Jack Linehan was born on 29 October 1864 to Patrick Linehan and Julia Murphy. He lived and worked with the local doctor, Dr Tim Crowley.

Dan Linehan was born on 5 January 1860 to Patrick Linehan and Julia Murphy. He was a brother of John Linehan (Jack). He lived near the pump in Peake. He worked at Dripsey Castle for the Bowen-Colthurst family.

Danny Looney was born in 1870. His family lived in Coolinea, Danny went to America and never returned. He was accidentally killed whilst attending to a boiler. The Looneys of Coachford are related to Danny.

Edward John O'Reilly was born in Blarney in 1868. He emigrated to San Francisco about 1900, joined the American Army and fought in the Spanish–American War. After his military service he went to night school, qualifying as an attorney. He married Peg Cullinane of Macroom and they had two children, John and Agnes. In the San Francisco earthquake of 1906 the family home was destroyed and the cherished All-Ireland medal was lost.

Jerus O'Sullivan lived in Clonmoyle. He left Ireland in 1894 after participating in the Peake Tournament. After leaving home, Jerus travelled across the American continent and on to Alaska in search of gold. He died in Seattle in December 1941.

J. Reilly was born on 12 May 1861, his father being Daniel Reilly and his mother Bridget Crowley. He lived at Bowens' Lodge (near Dripsey pond) and he drove a carriage for the Bowen-Colthurst family. He married Julia Hill of Peake and had no family.

Pat Riordan lived in Aghavrin. Pat married twice, first to Annie Lynch and secondly to Kate McCarthy.

Paddy Riordan lived in Clonmoyle. He was the oldest man on the team. He had nine children. He died in 1919 during the great flu epidemic.

Dan Sullivan lived with a bachelor uncle and an aunt named Hallissey in a hunting lodge called Larchfield House until the middle of the 1800s. Dan's wife was Mary (*née* O'Leary). They had seven children: John, Brigid, Ellie, Minnie, Jim, Hannah and Daniel. Evicted from Larchfield, Dan went to live in Passage West where he worked in the boatyards. Most of the family emigrated to London. Dan died in 1912 and was buried in Coachford's Magourney graveyard.

Tommy Twomey, 'The Master', was a teacher first in Tullig and later in Aghabullogue. He lived in Kilcoleman before his residence in Aghabullogue was built. He died in 1923.

5.   A LAYERED PAST

Aghabullogue parish has been textured by its long past of creativity, conflict, belief systems, emotion and technology. Indeed with these overlapping layers of history, one can identify how communities like Aghabullogue have evolved. Communal and individual studies are useful in piecing together the broader view of how local human landscapes came into being. Communal efforts such as St John the Baptist church and the GAA memorial in the village of Aghabullogue are important, if only to recharge the sense of pride that exists in the region.

The individual level of research is also important in unravelling the local aspects of human history and experience in Aghabullogue. We can survey the attitudes of present-day residents by interviewing them and drawing on their knowledge of their world. Joe Healy in his book *Aghabullogue, Coachford and Rylane* talks about the importance of the village pump in the 1930s and 1940s. Sinking the pump was the work of Dan Lynch from Rylane. All the work was completed with pickaxe and shovel. Circular holes were made into the ground. Rock was usually met about six metres down and then a charge of gelignite was placed into the hole in the rock and blown up. This blast usually brought up the water.

Joe and May Healy, Aghavrin, 2007.

Healy family *c.*1939. Back row, left to right: Jack Healy, Olan Healy, Michael Healy, Mary Healy (Joe's mother, *née* McCarthy) and Ned Healy. Second row: Abina Healy, Jane Healy and Thomas Healy. Front row: Joe Healy and Cal Healy. (*Joe Healy*)

Dan Healy owned the pub on the southern side of the village and was a reputable harness maker. His stitching of leather was deemed a work of art. Joe's father Thomas always made sure he looked after the cobs' harnesses, as the cob and trap was the mode of transport for going to Mass, funerals, journeys to the train, visiting relatives, etc.

Next to Dan Healy's premises on the upper side was another pub owned by Dan Buckley. Dan looked out for the local community by not serving drink to anyone who could not cope with large amounts of it. Dan Healy also owned the post office and shop. The shop stayed open til dusk and according to Joe Healy it was very handy if you had a spare penny for sweets. There was another shop in the Upper Square in the village, which was owned by Mary Jerry (Murphy).

Aghabullogue Creamery was acquired by the Dairy Disposal Board as well as other creameries in the Muskerry area. During the 1930s, the Creamery manager was Tom Geaney who also managed the Co-op Store, which was run by shareholders. A creamery served as a type of information centre. It helped farmers with the intake of milk, supplying of animal feedstuffs and groceries. The cream was transported to Coachford Creamery for buttermaking. The creamery is long gone and modern houses now stand on the site.

Joe Healy remembers a time when commodities such as fertilisers and feedstuffs would be delivered to farmers in jute bags. There was a loft on every farm for keeping oats, and it would have been filled at threshing time for livestock feeding and for the storing of seed, wheat and oats for the coming season. No barley was grown at that time and it did not become popular until after the Second World War. Barley needed more lime in the soil than wheat or oats did. The use of lime was very labour intensive, as it had to be drawn from a limekiln by horse and butt. It was then put out in heaps in the field. The lime lumps were slaked down with water, which made it into powder, and then spread with a shovel.

Aghabullogue village gives title to the parish and was probably the principal hamlet of the area in earlier times, but the actual basis of its interesting name is now lost to time. Today, Aghabullogue is a small settlement comprising a number of modern houses, John Cremin's Foodstore, a national school, the Roman Catholic church of St John and an associated small graveyard for former parish priests.

The Church contributes significantly to the early history of Aghabullogue parish. Just north of the present village is the townland of Coolineagh or Cúilín Aoidh, 'Hugh's Recess'. Now bisected by a roadway, that area was an important early medieval ecclesiastical site in the catchment area of the Lee. It was associated with St Eolang (Olan), who according to hagiographical tradition, or the tradition of studying saints, was St Finbarre's teacher. The site is noted in the various biographies of St

Aghabullogue Village from Oldcastle townland, the site of the hunter trial course.

Finbarre with regard to how the monastery of Cork gained control over it. The era 'early medieval' refers to the period AD 600 to AD 1177. The origin of these sites can be attributed initially to the fifth-century mission of St Patrick who strengthened the concept of Christianity in Ireland especially in the northern half of the country. Ecclesiastical sites in early medieval Ireland varied in size from small, isolated hermitages, as in the case of Skellig Michael, County Kerry, to the monastic-type cities like Clonmacnoise in County Offaly. The majority of these sites were located on the better agricultural land with more or less the same distribution pattern of that of a secular ring fort. Closeness of a ring fort may have provided access to the wider national trade routes. Padraig O'Riain, in an article on Aghabullogue in *Cork: History and Society*, points to the presence of a bivallate ring fort (two banks and two ditches) near Dromatimore at the south-west side of present-day Aghabullogue.

The ecclesiastical site of St Olan is frequently recorded as a parish church in later medieval documents. The O'Cremins of Aghabullogue are mentioned as the ecclesiastical families of the barony of Muskerry in the sixteenth century. The surviving remains consist of a relatively modern church within a rectangular graveyard. A segment of the original circular enclosure can be traced in the south-western quadrant of the site.

Today, the fragmentary remains of two successive Church of Ireland parish churches of Aghabullogue survive in the graveyard. Of the earlier St Olan's church, which was initially built about 1690, the the sod-covered remains survive. Built in 1838, the later church building stands immediately to the north of an earlier church with the eastern gable wall and part of the south wall surviving. In 1838, an ogham stone was found built into the earlier church. The southern wall of the later church was built on the line of the northern wall of the earlier church. The extant gable has a tall pointed central window embrasure.

In the graveyard is St Olan's Cap, an upright stone measuring five feet high with ogham inscription. A second stone was placed on top of it (now cemented in place) and was the subject of interesting fertility rituals. It was alleged to be an 'an unfailing object to have in your house in childbirth cases and was also used for other female illnesses'. The associated rituals were occasionally the cause of official clerical disapproval, leading to its removal at one stage in the nineteenth century. Today when one views the stone, it is clear that it has been much rubbed by human hands.

A standing stone called St Olan's Stone is traditionally said to mark the grave of St Olan, patron saint of the parish. It was located to the north of the graveyard but moved to within the graveyard c.1985. It has two depressions on its upper surface, believed to be St Olan's footprints. It was one of three stations; the others were St Olan's Cap and St Olan's Well.

Left: St Olan's Cap.

Far left: Ogham stone adjacent St Olan's well.

St Olan's graveyard, located in the townland of Coolineagh just north of Aghabullogue, was once the site of an early Christian monastery. It is now of sub-rectangular shape and is enclosed by a stone wall. There are many eighteenth and nineteenth-century inscribed headstones. The earliest dates to 1794. There are also some low, uninscribed grave markers, which provide evidence of a famine plot.

St Olan's Well is located on the side of the road between Aghabullogue and Rylane. It is enclosed by a circular stone-built structure with a small opening facing east. A plaque records that rounds are paid each year on 5 September, the feast day of St Olan. Mass is also celebrated on that day at the site. The Kelleher family of Clonmoyle has recently cleaned up the well and its surrounds.

An eight-foot-tall ogham stone stands adjacent to St Olan's Well. The stone was discovered in a drain nearby and placed in its present position. Ogham is the earliest written source of the Irish language. For the most part it records Irish personal names on memorials or territorial standing stones. Ogham is an alphabetic writing system and the first real evidence of Irish scholarship and learning used to record names. Its script comprises strokes cut on, across and either side of a line.

The oldest known ogham inscriptions date from the fifth century to about the seventh century. From the seventh century AD, those studying poetry and grammar particularly used ogham. That tradition survived into manuscript work in the eighth and ninth century. The inscription on the ogham stone next to St Olan's Well is nearly complete. It reads 'Madora MaQi Deag'. There is evidence that the inscription is connected to the Clann Deag, a family who lived hundreds of years ago in the region.

The ogham stone at St Olan's Well is one of a total of 260 ogham stones that can be found in southern Ireland in the counties of Kerry, Cork and Waterford. The recently refurbished ogham stone corridor in University College Cork forms the largest collection of such inscribed stones on open display in Ireland. The collection was commenced *c.*1861 and its most recent addition was in 1945.

Nearby is Athanangle Bridge, from Ath an t-Aingeal or 'Ford of the Angels'. Legend has it that a dispute between St Lachteen and St Olan occurred over parochial territories. St Lachteen, believing that a portion of his territory had been wrongfully obtained by his fellow missionary, is supposed to have remarked that 'there will always be a robber at Aghabullogue'. St Olan, realising that his neighbour was difficult to deal with replied, 'Donoughmore will always have its mad dogs'. Legend has it that the dispute had to be interrupted by angels – hence Ath an t-Aingeal.

With regard to the evolution of the Roman Catholic Church in Aghabullogue, Samuel Lewis in his *Topographical Dictionary of Ireland* in 1837 notes:

> In the R.C. divisions, this parish [Aghabullogue] is the head of a union or district, which comprises also the parish of Magourney and a moiety of Aghinagh and contains two chapels situated at Aghabullogue and Magourney: the former is a large and handsome edifice, in the pointed style of architecture, with a broad, flat castellated bell turret. The parochial school for boys and girls is built on the glebe adjoining the church, and is endowed by the rector with the entire plot of glebe: there are also two hedge schools in the parish.

St John the Baptist church in Aghabullogue still stands next to the local national school. In the graveyard of the church on the southern side is the lone burial place of Revd Jerome Dennehy PP, 1951-52. On the northern side is the grotto, which was erected in 1931. There, further Celtic crosses mark the burial places of former parish priests, such as Revd Andrew O'Riordan, who died in 1907. He was twenty years in the parish, plus he was President of Aghabullogue Hurling Club. A branch of the GAA under the parish title of Aghabullogue was formed at Coachford as far back as 1885, and two years later, on the opening of the Cork–Muskerry Railway, a monster tournament comprising thirty-three teams, both in football and hurling, was staged at Coachford. The Hurling Club erected the cross for Revd O'Riordan. The other Celtic crosses on the church grounds mark the final resting places of Revd Patrick McAuliffe, PP, 1906-1921; Revd Michael Ahern, PP, 1921-1928; Revd D. Barrett, PP, 1928-1935; Revd Denis Barrett, PP, 1952-1973, and Very Revd Canon John Finn, who died on 1 April 2006. Fr Donal Roberts, PP Aghabullogue, and Revd Tim O'Connor CC Coachford, are the present clergy. A modern Roman Catholic church named St Olan's exists in Rylane just two miles north of the old ecclesiastical site.

6. FADING MEMORIES

Connected with this past, and standing now as mute witnesses of the history of the peoples that have occupied the county, there still exist all over its surface, the remains of structures and other objects raised by the successive races. Probably any one resident in a country district could mention off hand dozens of such objects within a circle of ten miles round his residence.

Herbert Webb Gillman,
Aghabullogue parish resident and member of the
Cork Historical and Archaeological Society, 1891.

Extending from the north to east of Aghabullogue Village lie the townlands of Clonmoyle West and Clonmoyle East. Clonmoyle or Cluain Mhaol means the 'bare meadow'. Clonmoyle Mill is a mid-nineteenth-century corn mill on the western bank of the Dripsey River, two miles north of where the river meets the River Lee. Like Bealick Mill near Macroom, the story of Clonmoyle Mill is bound to the Great Famine and its effects locally. Indian Meal was first imported into this country in 1847. The foreign product was imported free of duty with the result that huge cargoes were dumped at the ports. Numerous small mills were erected around the countryside about this period for the purpose of meeting the increased demand for the new meal. Clonmoyle Mill is thought to have been built between 1846 and 1854. The actual year is uncertain, but one of the grinding stones is said to be a replacement from another mill and is dated 1856. Mr Charles Colthurst of Ballyvourney first operated the mill.

The mill was worked from a millrace off the Dripsey River. The wheat was first kiln dried and then ground. There was over 120 years of continuous production in Clonmoyle Mill up to the 1960s when they closed. John Young & Sons Ltd were the last owners and they lived in Clonmoyle House in Peake. The surviving, ruined rectangular four-storey gable-ended structure is of sandstone construction. The floors have collapsed in on each other but much can still be seen. The paddles of the water wheel have been removed and the water now just flows over the bare wheel. The wheel pit within the building survives and houses a cast-iron 'breast shot suspension' waterwheel. A surviving inscription notes the makers' names as J. Steel & Son, Vulcan Foundry, Cork. Two connecting 'line shafts' powered two pairs of French burr millstones on the first floor, which are now in a collapsed position in situ. One gets the impression at this site that it would not take much effort to just lift everything up and slot everything back into position.

Above left: View of the front façade of Clonmoyle Mill.

Above right: Interior ruins of Clonmoyle Mill.

Within a mile to the south-east of Clonmoyle Mill in the townland of Kilcolman lies another hidden gem – the ruins of the Protestant Kilcolman church and graveyard. Kilcolman or Cill Colmáin (church of Colman) was named after the patron of the Diocese of Cloyne. Kilcolman was the principal Protestant church in the Aghabullogue area up to the beginning of the 1600s. The earliest record for Kilcolman church dates to 2 July 1584, when John William Rhuwden was appointed vicar. William Sheyne was vicar in 1591 and John Oldis in 1615. However in the year 1615, the building was in ruins. By 1717, the church had been rebuilt. At that point in time, Kilcolman and Magourney churches were the key Protestant churches in the area and formed the hearts of two separate parishes. In 1717, Robert Bulfell was made vicar of both churches on the death of his predecessor Revd Jones. Bulfell was born at Hawshead, England, and studied at Trinity College Dublin before being ordained a priest at Cloyne in December 1714. He was vicar of Kilcolman and Magourney from 1717 to 1755. During Robert's tenure, in June 1728, the parishes of Kilcolman and Magourney were united in the Diocese of Cloyne. Revd Robert Bulfell died in 1755 and left £10 to the poor of Magourney.

Dublin-born Trinity graduate Revd Phillips was vicar between 1755 and 1777. By 1774, Kilcolman church was in ruins but the vicar Charles Phillips was still taxed in the King's books at £2 per annum. On the death of Philips, Samuel Rastal from Cambridge was rector from 1777 to 1780. From 1780 to his death in 1781 he was precentor of St Patrick's, Dublin, and Dean of Killaloe. From 1780 to 1798, Simon Davies was rector of Kilcolman and Magourney. Born in Burdanstown in County Cork, he was also a Trinity graduate, and from 1772 to 1795 he was a vicar in Macroom. Mary, one of his two daughters, married into the local Leader family. Simon Davies died in 1798 in his post. At that point in Brady's account, the documented history of Kilcolman is scant. We do know that by the year 1805, there were fourteen Protestant families in Magourney. Hence there was a Protestant population of fewer than 100 people. Kilcolman is not mentioned in Samuel Lewis's *Topographical Dictionary of Ireland* in 1837 but by that point, Magourney church had become the principal Protestant church.

In piecing together the fuller picture of the development of the Church, the ruins of Kilcolman must be viewed. It lies in tillage atop a hill with access across fields. It is a striking building on the landscape overlooking the Dripsey River. The roughly D-shaped graveyard is enclosed by a stone wall (approximately sixty metres north to south by fifty metres, east to west). The church and graveyard are in a seriously ruined state. This was the one graveyard in the Lee catchment area that I visited where I felt an air of sadness, as nature takes back the site. Memory is fading here.

The surviving rectangular church at the centre of the graveyard has an east–west alignment (sixteen metres in length and seven metres in width). Closer survey reveals that there are two phases of developments. The eastern wall, the eastern end of the southern wall and the northern wall are remains of an earlier church. Evidence of rebuilding can especially be seen at the eastern end of the southern wall. A later wall overlies the earlier wall. The earlier wall only stands to just above

Fading memories: the overgrown graveyard of Kilcolman church.

foundation height. Three tall windows survive on the north-facing side.

The graveyard is no longer in use. There are many rows of low uninscribed grave markers. The extant inscribed headstones in the western section of the graveyard are from the nineteenth and twentieth centuries. Many of the inscribed headstones are nearly unreadable. The dates of death are difficult to view. Those that do exist are important to record for the sake of future generations and researchers of the Dripsey area. One grave from the late 1800s marks the resting place of Nora O'Connor and Michael O'Connor. J. Hickey of Aherla created the tombstone. Other graves comprise that of Johanna McCarthy, Coolcullig (died 1870s), Cornelius O'Leary from Blarney, and John Sullivan and Julia O'Sullivan from Rylane (who died in 1939). A large family plot notes the resting place of members of the Caroll family. John Carroll died on 5 August 1916, aged forty-nine years. His father Tom Carroll died at Hayfield on 18 November 1889, aged sixty-two years. Tom's wife Mary died on 14 January 1917, aged eighty-two years.

Within the overgrown interior of the church is the grave of Julia Carey (*née* Sullivan) and family from Ballycunningham, Donoughmore. Other graves include those of the Long family from Knockane near Berrings and the Lynch family from Coachford. There is also a tomb, which is overgrown and open. The inscription is unreadable. This may be the grave noted by the *Archaeological Inventory of Mid Cork* as dating to 1807. In the southern side of the graveyard, there is uneven ground – evidence from the fallen masonry of the church – which is now overgrown. The ruins of Kilcolman church and graveyard are sad to witness but there are so many sites like them across the countryside. The problem is what do you do with them, let them decay or try to keep them?

7. STRONGHOLDS, SOUTERRAINS AND DRIPSEY CASTLE

Carrignamuck Castle (generally known as Dripsey Castle) is impressive. It stands on a solid rock of old red sandstone, near a bend of the River Dripsey and about a mile from the village of the same name. The meaning of the name is 'Rock of the Pigs'. It is said to have been so called because of a pass by the river near it, where pigs, domesticated or wild, used to be killed. The castle forms part one of a chain extending from Blarney to beyond Macroom – all formerly in the hands of the Lord of Muskerry – of the MacCarthy clan. The castle and the adjacent Georgian house still lived in reflect habitation going back over 500 years. Change in terms of living standards and aspects of continuity in settlement are very much evident here. In fact we can detail the development of settlement here all the way back to the fifteenth century. Whilst researching Drispey Castle, an earlier and nearby settlement site came to my attention through the work of late-nineteenth-century historian Herbert Webb Gillman.

Knockanenagark (or Cnocan na gCearc) means 'hillock of the hens or the grouses'. The area is popularly known as Henmount. Seven hundred years ago in that townland, there was a ring fort of a type unusual in the county and was not, as is usually the case, a circular rampart of earth enclosing and rising above a level floor inside the rampart. Instead, the fort consisted of a mound of earth nearly circular, about sixty-three feet diameter at its base, sloping upwards, about ten feet vertically, to a level platform of about forty-eight feet diameter, which formed the floor of the fort. There were traces of a moat around the back of the mound. With a wooden stockade about its sloping face the place would be very defensible. This fort was known locally as the 'Mote' and may have been the early equivalent of Dripsey Castle. There are no other mottes in the area and one has to travel to North Cork to find the nearest one. Mottes are generally associated with the early fortifications of Anglo-Normans in the 1200s, who may have breached the area during their colonisation of Ireland. However, my theory in this instance is that that the MacCarthys must have lived in the area in some fort (the motte) before they built the castle. They would have been aware of the shape and form of contemporary castles and may have adopted the Norman style for building castles.

The motte was on a plateau about thirty feet above the bed of the River Dripsey, which flowed 100 yards off on the south-west side. The mound mainly consisted of the river gravel and fine sand. It is probable that in former geological times the plateau formed an 'inch' or flat meadow by the bank of the river, which must have flowed at that period at the level of this plateau.

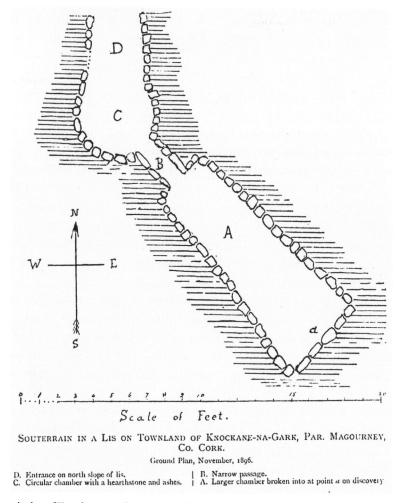

SOUTERRAIN IN A LIS ON TOWNLAND OF KNOCKANE-NA-GARK, PAR. MAGOURNEY,
Co. CORK.

Ground Plan, November, 1896.

D. Entrance on north slope of lis.	B. Narrow passage.
C. Circular chamber with a hearthstone and ashes.	A. Larger chamber broken into at point *a* on discovery

Gillman's plan of Knockanenagark souterrain. (*Cork City Library*)

When Herbert Webb Gillman visited the site in November 1896, about a third
of the body of the mound had been already scraped away by sand diggers. It was
during their work that the souterrain was discovered. When cutting the gravel the
workmen met a vertical wall built of rough field stones. It faced south-east and was
of a shape something like the letter D inverted. The wall was about six feet wide
and six feet high, surmounted by a flat slab of stone at the top. Breaking an opening through this wall they found that it formed the end of a chamber, which they
opened up and cleared out for a length of six to eight feet.

Mr Kelleher, the occupier of the land, consented that the building should be fully examined in a systematic manner and he and his brother assisted actively in the investigation. The result was the discovery that the building consisted of a chamber connected by a narrow and short passage with a smaller circular chamber. A fragment of bone was found in the wedge-shaped Chamber 1. Chamber 2 was not fully explored as it was blocked with sand and stone. The walls in both chambers were blackened due to burning. Some charcoal and burnt clay were found in Chamber 2 and surrounding a flat flagstone, which Gillman suggested was used as a hearth. No visible surface trace has survived. The site was completely removed due to quarrying in 1937.

As an aside, Knockanenagark is also noted for St Gobnait's Well and Stone. According to oral tradition St Gobnait paused here to drink water on her way to Ballyvourney. The townland comprised the site of her well and the marks on the stone edge show the imprints of her knees. The deeper depression where she placed her hand was used to place offerings. Rounds were performed here until the early to mid-1800s. It was also known as Abbey's Well. The well has been destroyed and the stone moved from its original site.

If one takes the story forward in time to around AD 1450, we find that in that year the MacCarthys built a superior fortification downstream at Carrignamuck. The exterior of the castle/tower house is in an admirable and impressive state of preservation. The structure presents the appearance of a rectangular tower or keep with a rectangular flanking tower projecting from the east wall. Before the era of cannon, a tower such as this relied upon its passive strength for defence. If well provisioned, it would defy the attack of an enemy that did not have military engines. The active defence of the tower was directed chiefly from its battlements. The loops in the walls of Carrignamuck are so constructed that they are of no use for close defence, their purpose being the admission of light and air and there are no arrangements for a flank defence.

Atop the castle, the battlements do not overhang the walls and therefore there are no machicolated openings through which missiles could be shot on the besiegers. There is also evidence of a 'bretashe'. This was a gallery of timber put up when a siege was expected, which ran around the walls outside the battlements and was supported by struts and covered in a sloping roof. The western and southern faces of the castle show, at the level of the battlements walk, numerous holes where the beams may have rested originally.

The exterior face has a slight batter or slope for weight distribution and also for defensive purposes. It was usual to have a walled structure known as a bawn around tower houses. The Carrignamuck enclosure was divided into two parts, one around the castle itself and the other stretching down to the river bank over the steep ground to the north and east sides of the castle. The extent of the bawn cannot now be ascertained.

The entrance to the castle or keep is in the east wall. On the left of the entrance the mural gallery has been solidly built up, probably in anticipation of a siege. The basement floor is not levelled as the rock still protrudes. The room was a storeroom and a kitchen as evidenced by a chimney and hobs on either side of a fireplace. There are forty-six steps of a circular staircase. The rectangular block structure contains a main chamber at each level. There is a small section projecting from the tower, which contains the stairs and smaller chambers. Great provision was made for sanitation and cleanliness in this semi-military building. There is evidence of garderobes or toilets. A rectangular shaft for taking away waste runs inside the length of the northern wall and finishes in the basement.

The window embrasures in the main chambers are square set, covered by segmental vaults. Hence, much light was allowed to come through. Window openings elsewhere in the tower have splayed and lintelled embrasures. The amount of light getting into these areas of the keep was minimal and so this was probably part of the overall defensive scheme of the tower.

The walls are not strong. The thickness of the wall is hampered by mural galleries in the basement and on the first and second floors, all vaulted. In addition, any of the garrison leaving his post on the battlements would have to pass by the two sides of the principal sleeping chambers and probably could not evade detection.

8. THE LEGACY OF THE MacCARTHYS

Carrignamuck Castle was one of the strongholds erected by the Lords of Muskerry, chiefs of one of the three great stems into which the MacCarthy clan divided at a period before they erected stone castles. The first of the third stem was Dermod Mór MacCarthy, a son of Cormac MacCarthy Mór of the main line. Dermot was born in the year 1310 and in 1353 was acknowledged or created the first Lord of Muskerry by the English. The lands passed down to the ninth Lord of Muskerry, Cormac McTeige MacCarthy Laidir, who succeeded in 1449. He was a great builder and financed the construction of Blarney Castle, Carrignamuck and Kilcrea. It became the custom for the Lords of English lands to place some relative in each of their castles. Cormac Laidir's own brother Eoghan, the chosen relative (tanist), was stationed at Carrignamuck.

Carrignamuck Castle.

English interest in Munster was much weakened by the Wars of the Roses and Irish clans took many English castles. In the barony of Muskerry, the English settlers paid Cormac MacCarthy £40 per annum for protecting them from rebellious native families. Cormac was wounded and died during a quarrel with his brother Eoghan. He was buried at Kilcrea in 1494. The clan set Eoghan aside and did not appoint him the tenth Lord of Muskerry but gave the honour to Cormac's son Cormac Oge (1447-1537).

The sixteenth century was a further period of unrest in Munster, disturbed by feuds between rivals of the House of Desmond and by the rebellions against the sovereign power. A long-standing feud existed between the Earls of Desmond and the MacCarthys. In 1521, the head of the Fitzgeralds, James Earl of Desmond, burst with a powerful force into Muskerry and ravaged and burnt and destroyed until Cormac Oge led out an army against them. The opposing forces met near Mourne Abbey. It was after this that in 1528, Cormac Oge attended parliament as 'Lord of Muscry'.

The MacCarthys managed to hold their own during the sixteenth century, saved from the fate of the Desmonds, whose vast territories of over half a million acres were confiscated at the close of the century. In 1542, Teige MacCarthy, the eleventh Lord of Muskerry was one among eight chieftains of the country who made an 'indenture of submission' to the Crown, in which they agreed to refer all disputes between themselves to a commission of arbitration appointed for Munster, and consisting of the Bishops of Cork and Waterford, instead of appealing to the Brehon Judges.

In the 1570s, the fourteenth Lord of Muskerry, Sir Cormac McTeige MacCarthy, was rewarded for his allegiance. He kept his lands and received large grants of confiscated property. The lord had access to up to 3,000 men. Sir Cormac consented to adopt the royal device for passing down family property – the surrender of his lands including Carrignamuck into the hands of the sovereign and to receive the same back by a re-grant. The Crown rent was two hawks, or £6 13s 4d.

Shortly after the granting, on 4 August 1580, Sir James Sussex Fitzgerald, youngest brother of the Earl of Desmond, made one of a series of regular attacks hoping to rob cattle from the barony of Muskerry. Donal MacCarthy, the Lieutenant of Carrignamuck, assembled an army and attacked and completely defeated Sir James, with the loss of 150 of his men. Sir James was wounded in the fight and was captured by a blacksmith, who hid him in a bush until the fight had ended, and then delivered him. Sir Cormac ordered the confinement of James in Carrigadrohid Castle, three miles to the south-west of Carrignamuck. Soon after, the captive was surrendered to Sir Warham St Leger, Commissioner for Munster, who had him tried for treason. On his conviction Sir James was executed. His head and limbs were affixed to one of the drawbridges that led into the walled town of Cork. Donal MacCarthy, the lieutenant, was mortally wounded during the battle, by an arrow that struck him under the right ear, and penetrated six inches into his neck. He died some time after.

Donal's death raised the next brother, Callaghan, then of Castlemore, to the title of fifteenth Lord of Muskerry. A year later in 1585, Callaghan had passed the lordship to his nephew Cormac Mór MacDermod MacCarthy. In 1588, Cormac attended the English parliament as Baron of Blarney and because of the unsettled political atmosphere in Ireland in the following year he surrendered his lands to the Crown and obtained a re-grant.

The problems arising from English colonisation in the late 1500s continued into the early 1600s. Many Irish Catholics felt a strong resentment towards the Crown. They refused to accept the new Protestant religion and as a result small and violent rebellions were common. It was at this time that Cork became known as the 'rebel county'. By the late 1500s, two Irish chiefs, Hugh O'Neill and Red Hugh O'Donnell were waging all-out war against Queen Elizabeth. In 1600, O'Neill marched to the south of the country, reaching Inniscarra, five miles west of Cork. Here, he met with southern chieftains Florence MacCarthy, Lord of Carbery and Donal O'Sullivan, Lord of Beara. A campaign against English forces was proposed. However, while O'Neill was in the south, 7,000 English foot soldiers and 800 horsemen invaded Ulster. O'Neill was forced to temporarily abandon his campaign in the south and returned north to a struggle of varying fortunes.

In 1601, the Lord of Muskerry, MacCarthy of Carrignamuck, raised an army to assist the Lord President of Ireland, Sir George Carew in his fight to squash the rebellion by Hugh O'Neill and O'Donnell and to avoid Spanish involvement. The MacCarthys accompanied the Lord President in his march to Tipperary to find O'Donnell and then returned to Kinsale to engage in the battle against O'Neill outside the town.

The country remained unsettled after these events, and it appears that Carrignamuck residents engaged in some of the disturbances. They secured the usual pardon, one issued in March 1603 in favour of 389 Muskerry persons including Callaghan McTeige McCormac MacCarthy of Carrignamuck and Shilie McTeige McOwen, his wife. Callaghan, by his pardon, kept his lands and manor.

In 1616, Cormac, the sixteenth lord, died and was buried at Kilcrea, the last lord of his family to be buried there. His eldest son, Cormac Oge McCormac MacCarthy, succeeded the deceased lord. He was to become the seventeenth Lord of Muskerry. He was born in 1564 and was fifty-two years of age at his accession. He was educated at Oxford and in 1628 Cormac Oge was created Viscount Muskerry and Baron of Blarney. The title Lord of Muskerry was changed to Viscount Muskerry. His eldest son was Donogh MacCarthy, eighteenth Lord of Muskerry (or now Viscount Muskerry). He was born in 1594, being forty-six years old at his accession.

Carrignamuck House.

King James I ruled until 1624, a time of prosperity for the walled town of Cork but also a time of uncertainty for the civil administration of the land. He was replaced by his son Charles I. Fearing another Spanish–Irish attack, Charles attempted to win the support of Irish Catholic landlords. He rejected the Oath of Supremacy, to which Roman Catholics objected on religious grounds, in favour of an Oath of Allegiance, which the Catholic landlords swore in return for three annual subsidies of £40,000. Influential Protestant families, such as the Inchiquins and Broghills, publicly questioned Charles's strategy. They launched a letter campaign to persuade the monarch to change his approach, but their pleas were ignored. Over time, this situation had a detrimental effect on the financial and social position of the Protestant settlers in Cork. Many Protestant landlords deemed Charles's support of Catholicism wrong and felt the work of conversion that had been completed in the preceding years was being unravelled. Viscount Muskerry and his army were destined to play an important part in the rebellion of 1641.

Viscount Muskerry was one of the first to take up arms, mustering several thousand Irish. In April 1642, a decision was taken under the leadership of Viscount Muskerry to blockade the walled town of Cork and in August 1642, it was decided to besiege the prominent English castle of Liscarroll in North Cork, and the castle was won back after thirteen days by pro-Crown supporters.

By January 1649, the parliament of Charles I had turned against him and his own MPs ordered his capture and execution. Britain thus became a republic. The Parliamentarians sent a force to Ireland to suppress any pro-Royal sympathy. The new Lord Lieutenant of Ireland, Oliver Cromwell, led the army. He arrived in Ireland on 15 August 1649 and immediately took control the town of Drogheda after a bloody massacre. He then proceeded to Wexford and Ross and sent out small contingents into the Munster countryside to take note of any Royalist military activity.

In May 1650, Lord Broghill commanded 2,000 Cromwellian foot soldiers and 1,600 horses and defeated the Irish at Macroom, where he took the castle of Carrigadrohid. With their sights on Carrignamuck Castle, the besiegers planted their cannons on a low hill at the opposite side of the Dripsey River and made a breach in the east face of the castle in the outer of the double walls on that side. It is said that it was from the grounds of the contemporary Meeshal House that Lord Broghill bombarded Carrignamuck Castle around the year 1650. After the capture of Carrignamuck in 1650, Cromwellian soldiers occupied the castle for some time.

What became of the Carrignamuck family between this and the Restoration of Charles II in 1666 is unknown but the family of Lord Muskerry did not immediately lose all the property. Lady Muskerry was allowed to remain on some of the lands in Muskerry and was not one of those transplanted into Connaught. King Charles II was restored in 1666 and with him Lord Muskerry, Donagh MacCarthy, was returned. Two years later in 1668, he received the further title of Earl of Clancarty.

In 1683 a new Catholic King ascended the throne, King James II. The English parliament objected to the new monarch and offered the throne to the Dutch prince, William of Orange. James was forced to flee to Ireland and in March 1688 he arrived at Cork and incited the people to rise up against the Protestant monarch. When King James landed at Cork on 12 May 1688, he was received by Donough, the Fourth Earl of Clancarty. In the spring of 1689, William led an extensive army to Ireland to restore power.

The Earl of Clancarty and his regiment were taken prisoners in September 1690, when Cork City was captured by the army under the Earl of Marlborough. The Earl was confined in the Tower of London, but escaped to France in 1694. His estates, valued then at £200,000 a year, were among those confiscated. All his lands, including Carrignamuck, were sold by public auction by the Hollow Blade Company in

Current occupants of Carrignamuck House, Andrew and Doreen O'Shaughnessy.

Dublin in November 1702. The Book of Postings and Sales is still extant. The forfeited estate of Donagh, Earl of Clancarthy, in the barony of Muskerry and County of Cork, was a fee-simple estate, consisting of farms and lands amounting to 223 acres 'with 6 cabbins, a castle, and a corn mill, worth £8 per annum'. Sold for £300, the purchaser was George Rogers of Cork. He paid for one-fifth of the lands in money and the rest in debentures.

Charles Smith, in his *History of Cork* in 1750, noted that a Mr Beer inhabited the castle. Some years later, the property passed to the Colthurst family, relatives of the present Colthursts of Blarney Castle. Dripsey Castle became in time part of the Bowen-Colthurst estate through the marriage in 1777 of Jane Bowen to John Colthurst. By that time, the old castle had been abandoned as a dwelling place. The present and elaborate mansion was built around 1746 by the Colthurst family. The front of the building has been considerably altered. The residence is true to Georgian style, with sash windows, basements and high ceilings.

In 1866, the Bowen-Colthursts restored the castle. At that time, the present slate roof, fireplaces in northern wall, and a wooden front door were inserted. It was the birthplace of J.C. Bowen-Colthurst who murdered Sheehy Skeffington in Dublin in 1916. Captain Colthurst was court-martialled and found guilty but insane. The family were boycotted, as a result of which they sold out and settled in England. Currently the house is the property of Andrew and Doreen O'Shaughnesssy.

9. MAKING THE CUT: DRIPSEY PAPER MILLS

Dripsey, or An Dripseach, can be translated as 'muddy river'. The region was one of the most industrialised areas in the south of Ireland in the late eighteenth and early nineteenth centuries. The tiny village of Dripsey once boasted a paper mill, a cheese factory and one of the last original working woollen mills in Ireland. It is just south of the village that the Dripsey River joins the River Lee (or Inniscarra Reservoir).

The industries contributed to the development of linear settlement extending over a mile along the road to Cork. Dripsey village began in the townland of lower Dripsey and grew with the development of paper mills by local man Jimmy Batt O'Sullivan. He was a well-established and esteemed manufacturer in the last decades of the 1700s.

The O'Sullivans were part of the Industrial Revolution in the late eighteenth century, which was slowly changing the way certain industries were carried out across the country. New ideas for manufacturing certain goods more quickly and more cost effectively filtered into Cork and led to the growth of several secondary industries. Among the more profitable industries that saw an escalation in profit margins were brewing, distilling, corn milling, tanning, engineering and the manufacture of items such as linen, wool, glass, paper, and gunpowder.

There were approximately fifty paper mills in the country in the 1770s and 1780s and over 50 per cent of these were located in or near Dublin. In the 1750s, there were approximately six mills in southern Ireland, most of which were located in and around Cork City. The city provided the paper mills with a plentiful supply of rags and the waste fibres from the linen and cotton industries could also be used.

The rivers flowing into the Glanmire Valley in County Cork became the focus of paper-making in the region. By 1841, there were eleven paper mills in the Glanmire area. The Lavitts, a Huguenot family, built one of the first paper mills in Glanmire in the first decade of the 1700s. Subsequently, they let the mill to a paper maker named Bond in 1713, who in turn let it in 1763 to the stationers, Phineas and George Bagnall. In the 1760s the mill had a manufacturing capacity of 40,000 to 50,000 reams per annum.

Dripsey man Jimmy Batt O'Sullivan served an apprenticeship in Bagnall's Mill and rapidly rose to the job of foreman. Jimmy was educated at a local hedge school in Dripsey and then at Fr Reddington's Academy on the eastern side of Great Island. His growing knowledge of the Glanmire paper industries and his interest in paper manufacture led O'Sullivan to set up five mills in the area. As a Catholic, he benefited from the Catholic Relief Act of 1782, which permitted Catholics to purchase and inherit land and property. Sullivan soon became the largest paper manufacturer in the whole country, owning mills at Dripsey, Blarney, Beechmount, Towerbridge and Springhill. His exports were sent to England and comprised writing, printing, lapping and tea paper.

In the 1700s, O'Sullivan manufactured in association with James St John Jeffries, son of the man who owned Blarney Castle and estate before the Colthursts. Jimmy Batt O'Sullivan was connected to a cotton mill, linen mill, mills that turned out sheeting, camp equipment, sail cloth and bagging, and finally paper mills, both hand and machine operated, including one at Healy's Bridge, run by his father, Bartholomew. O'Sullivan reputedly opened Dripsey paper mills in the year 1800 and installed the most modern machinery, which was the invention of a Frenchman named Didot. (France in the mid to the late 1700s was the most advanced country in paper making in Western Europe.)

In the early years of operation, it is known that O'Sullivan invested £50,000 in his mills at Dripsey and Blarney in contemporary machinery. In 1807, Fourdrinier machines were installed in Dripsey Paper Mills. The machine made paper in continuous sheets, constituting a large change from the process up to then of sheets only three feet long and one and a half feet wide. The machinery was perfected at Fourdriniers of London. A machine could produce five to seven times as much paper as a vat (handmade process) and at a lower cost. The Dripsey Mills were the first to use the machines in Ireland and there were just under a dozen firms in England doing so. Dripsey was at the cutting edge of technology in paper manufacture.

Paper mill at Butlerstown, County Cork. (*Cullen, 1971*)

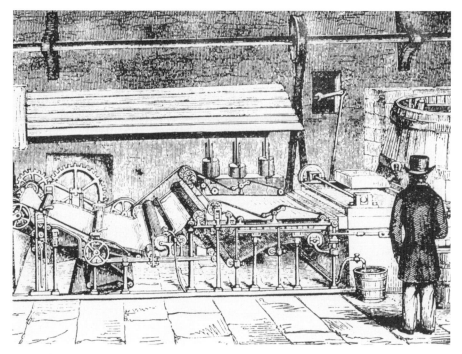

View of paper-manufacturing machine, c.1830. (*Shorter, 1971*)

In the beginning of the 1800s, the total Irish output of paper was one twentieth of that in England, and came from about one tenth the number of mills. By 1824, many machines had been set to work in key English paper-manufacturing firms. Their total output exceeded that of the handmade manufacture, with 14,500 tons as against 12,000. Over the next twenty years, it was the machine that would take over and outcompete many of the small firms who could not afford to change over to machinery.

Much of the Dripsey paper was exported to England. The mills were the first to manufacture ruled paper. The sap of the red willow, a tree that grew in abundance on both banks of the Dripsey River, formed the main colour constituent of the formula O'Sullivan used for lining paper. Jimmy Batt O'Sullivan devised a colouring process for the Bank of England notes made at Dripsey for the Treasury in London. In 1804, he was producing watermarked paper.

Dripsey Paper Mills was reputed to be one of the largest paper mills in Ireland. It had six vats, six presses and three waterwheels. It gave employment to 400 people. O'Sullivan brought over English and Scottish workmen to work in the mills who had experience in the English paper-making industry.

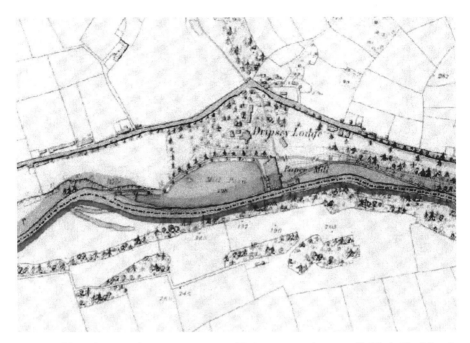

Section of first edition Ordnance Survey map of Dripsey area and paper mill. (*Cork City Library*)

In the early 1800s, Jimmy Batt O'Sullivan had stables on a farm beside Dripsey School. About the year 1812, he leased a farm of 207 acres at Agharinagh, just west of the mills, known as The Acres. Through his farming ventures, O'Sullivan became a member of the Royal Agricultural Society and brushed shoulders with the upper echelons of society. In 1813, O'Sullivan held a large ploughing rally and invited many guests to a big party. He used the occasion to encourage the owners of Big Houses to replace linen tablecloths with his continuous sheet paper coloured and decorated for that purpose. The Dripsey complex attracted the attention of some of the contemporary and leading political and civil figures, including the Lord Mayor of London, Sir Christopher Magnay. The Magnays had property interests in Ireland and at the time had an office at Winthrop Street, Cork.

The economic downturn of the late 1810s after the end of the Napoleonic Wars resulted in O'Sullivan selling off Dripsey Mills and other industrial assets. By 1817, Dripsey Paper Mills were owned by Reeves & Co. who were in turn bought out in 1823 by Sir Christopher Magnay, Lord Mayor of London in 1822/1823. The change-over resulted in industrial unrest at the mills and serious damage to the machinery. World steam-locomotive builder George Stephenson and his son Robert visited Dripsey Paper Mills in 1823 to inspect the damage. The replacement parts were bought from Stephenson's Newcastle factory between December 1823 and August 1827. The Stephensons designed the first steam locomotives.

Dripsey Paper Mills are shown in the first edition Ordnance Survey (Ireland) map of Cork in 1836. As the Lee Hydro-Electric Scheme submerged the site in the early 1950s, the map is a very important document in reconstructing the industrial complex. An extensive mill pond is shown. Mill buildings are clearly depicted. The River Lee formed the southern boundary of the industrial complex. Across the six acres, in addition to the mill building, there were stone-built passages, store houses, dams and water conduits, fed from a large pond to the west of the mill. The pond was a back-up from the dam on the Dripsey River close to the paper mills and to this day the pond field directly in front of the present Dripsey National School is often referred to as Blackpool Field. There were two entrances, one for the many carters who brought rags daily to the mills, the other to the administrative block.

The carters, on entering the eastern entrance, travelled along a passage on which there were several gate pillars and storehouses before they reached the boiler house. At the western end the three-acre pond in Blackpool Field fed a big millwheel at the mouth of a long millrace. Blackpool was the nickname given to the village of mainly mud-wall houses that cropped up in the townland of Agharinagh immediately west of the paper mills and housed many of its workers. There were also some stone-built houses in the three-quarter-of-a-mile stretch of 'Blackpool' along the main road, and a hedge school. There were also some scattered houses on the other side of the road. Closer to the paper mills there was one authorised public house and two shebeens.

The peak period in Irish paper making coincided with the decades of the 1820s and 1830s. In 1837 there were fifty-seven paper mills in Ireland and fifteen of those were in County Cork. Cork manufacturers focused on high-quality paper. The largest manufacturers were Jenkins & Reeves in Blarney, Hodnett of the Sallybrook and Riverstown Paper Mills, Magnay of Dripsey, and Phair at Butlerstown. They all had warehouses in Cork to take advantage of the large paper market in the city. Around 1830, Matt Twogood took over Dripsey Paper Mills.

Samuel Lewis in his *Topographical Dictionary of Ireland* in 1837 (p.260) noted:

At the western extremity of the parish of Iniscarra are the Dripsey paper-mills, belonging to Messrs Magnay & Co., and situated in a deep and well-wooded glen; the buildings are of handsome appearance, and the works afford employment to a number of persons, varying from 70 to 100; in the manufacture of large quantities of paper for the English market. In another part of the parish is a small stream, which turns the Cloghroe boulting-mills, which are capable, when there is a sufficient supply of water, of producing 140 sacks of flour weekly.

In 1846, Mr Alfred Greer took over the Dripsey complex. Alfred was a Quaker merchant who was born in Dungannon in County Tyrone. His first wife was Helena Carroll but on Helena's death he married Peggy Bowen-Colthurst in 1853. They resided in Dripsey House, which lay adjacent to the paper mills. Soon afterwards, he converted to the Church of Ireland. A large number of family papers survive in the Public Record Office of Northern Ireland, Belfast. A photograph of the family outside Dripsey House and solicitor papers survive.

At one time, it is said that around 400 people worked in Dripsey Paper Mills. That is a sizable community, a large portion of which would have lived in the Dripsey area. Each person would have had his or her own personal story on living and working in Cork. Unfortunately the stories are lost. A wages book dating to the mid-nineteenth century or Alfred Greer's time (and recorded by Dripsey historian Tim Sheehan) gives the following selection of names of the workers in Dripsey Paper Mills:

William Barrett, Richard Beastley, Andy Blake, Frank Blake, William Blake, Con Brennan, Frank Brennan, John Brennan, Mary Brennan, Michael Brennan, Pat Brennan, Dan Brien, Paddy Brien, Tade Carty, Jerry Carthy, John Carthy, Michael Casey, W. Castlewood, Con Corcoran, Denis Cronin, Jerry Crowley (by two), Jerry Cronin, Ned Coleman, Jerry Coleman, Jerry Dilworth, Tom Drummy, John Hall, Tom Hall, Pat Hallassy, Con Haly, John Haly, J. Haslewood Mary Healy, Con Hegarty, Jack Keeffe, Owen Keeffe, Jerry Leary, Dan Long, John Long, Mary Long, John Magee, William Mahony, Peter McCarthy, Denis Murphy, Jerry Murphy, John Murphy, William Murphy, Richard Nagle, Dan Reilly, Jerry Reilly, John Ring, Frank Roche, James Roche (by two), Con Sullivan, Joe Sullivan, Pat Sullivan, Thade Sullivan, Timothy Sullivan, Joe Sweeney, Ned Sweeney, John Twomey and Tom Twomey.

Output trebled in the paper industry in the 1830s and 1840s. However, paper production had become more mechanised and the smaller mills that made handmade paper could no longer compete with the mills that used continuous paper-making machinery. The number of mills in the country dropped dramatically during the 1840s. By 1852, all eleven mills in the Glanmire Valley had ceased operation. There were only three mills in the county left, at Dripsey, Towerbridge and Transtown. Many mills closed because manufacturers were unwilling to invest in new technology. The local market limited the development of new markets. Hence paper mills in Dublin and England were better placed and prepared to serve the larger markets.

In 1851, there were only twenty-eight paper mills surviving in Ireland. Many of the early mills were small and had been situated in rural areas. They were forced to close with the larger ones surviving in or near urban areas and close to suppliers of raw materials. A total of twenty-two of them were in and around Dublin City and Liberties, whilst the remaining six were located in Transtown, Dripsey and Towerbridge. There was one mill in Galway and one in Clare. According to the census returns for the 1850s, there were, at this time, 751 people employed in paper manufacture in Ireland compared with 713 in 1841. The numbers employed had dropped to 402 by the year 1861.

John Francis Maguire, in his description of the 1852 Cork National Exhibition, stated that Dripsey Paper Mills exhibited cream or ivory notepaper. Charles Gibson's *History of Cork*, published in 1861, records:

> Paper is manufactured at Dripsey by Mr Alfred Greer who has also another coarse paper mill at Glenville on the Bride, distant ten miles from Cork. The excise duty paid on the paper manufactured at these mills averaged during the last five years between £9,000 and £10,000. Mr Allen has paper mills for the manufacture of brown, sugar and tissue paper on the Shournagh near St Ann's, Blarney and Mr Phair has one at Butlerstown, Glanmire, near Cork.

Dripsey Paper Mills continued to function for several years following 1861, and on the death of Alfred Greer the factory was operated by his son Mr A. Greer. In Henry and Coughlan's *Directory of Cork* for 1867, the Greer warehouse was based at 10 and 11 Academy Street, Cork City and was one of nine paper warehouses in the city. During the 1860s, British Government excise duty on the manufacture of paper strained the financial position of Dripsey Paper Mills. Shortly afterwards, during an overhaul of the plant, one of the heavy iron bearings was accidently broken. Sufficient capital was not available for the cost of replacement and so about 1880, the once flourishing Dripsey Mills closed. Large stocks of paper were on hand, however, and for a few years longer they continued to supply some of their old customers. For the Cork Industrial Exhibition of 1882, Messrs A. Greer & Co. Ltd are listed as having an exhibit of paper from their Dripsey Mills.

Dripsey Paper Mills closed about the year 1880. By 1885, the total number of paper mills in operation in Ireland was nineteen, and by 1900 the number had fallen to nine. The Irish paper-making industry suffered because of the paucity of capital in a country with a comparatively low standard of living. The disturbed political situation and the general decline in population from 1840 onwards were also factors.

As for the original owner of Dripsey Paper Mills, James B. O'Sullivan lived a wealthy lifestyle for a number of years in 1820s London, where he died after spending a period in a mental hospital. His son William Kirby O'Sullivan, who was born in Dripsey in 1822, survived him. A specialist in chemistry, W.K. pioneered the development of the sugar content in beet long before sugar factories were thought of in Ireland. He was at one time Professor of Chemistry at the Catholic University and in 1872 was appointed President of Queen's College Cork (now UCC) in succession to the first president, Sir Robert Kane. W.K. O'Sullivan held the position until his death in 1890.

Linking back to Dripsey Paper Mills, with the demand for scrap iron during the First World War, most of the paper-making machines at Dripsey were scrapped for armament purposes. Portions of the buildings were later converted into a cheese factory under the management of Miss Peggie Bowen-Colthurst of Dripsey Castle. Peggy was the youngest of the four children of Robert Bowen-Colthurst. The other children were Mary, Jack and Robert. Educated at Oxford University, she was awarded a degree in 1904. She returned to Dripsey to help her family on the farm. The family farm comprised 300 acres at Dripsey Castle and Demesne, a farm at Cronody, and the Greer property, which came into the Bowen-Colthurst possession on the marriage of her mother. For a number of years, Peggy grew flax on the land and stored it in a portion of the paper mill. The enterprise was not successful. There are still fields in Dripsey known as the flax fields.

The risk of food shortages arising from the outbreak of the war induced the British Committees of Agriculture to ensure supplies were met. One of the key issues met was the need to replace the male labour force, which had gone to the front line in France to serve military service. During her college days Peggy Bowen-Colthurst had an association with the committees. She was asked to assist in the food campaign by training English 'land girls' on her farms in Cork. She began a cheese factory at the then-idle paper mill. The nearby Dromgowra farm was ideal for dairying and a place to train land girls. The farm buildings and residence at Dromgowra were enlarged to accommodate the girls. Roofs from some of the old paper mills were used in the Dromgowra farm reconstruction, which was carried out under the supervision of Jack Walsh, a carpenter of Magoola.

Several farmers in the area became regular suppliers. Others supplied Coachford Creamery or made butter at home. An English woman named Miss Breth became chief cheese-maker. Her assistants were Miss Horne, also from England, Miss Grebon from Mayo, Miss Gibbons from Mayo and Miss O'Hara from Galway. There were around twenty girls in all. Those involved were the first women to wear slacks in the area. There were also staff and local hands employed on the farms. John Mullane was chief ploughman at Dromgowna and on the Cronody farm. Mr Sutton was the farm steward. The principal markets were in England, in particular Liverpool, Manchester and Birmingham.

Peggy's brother was Captain Jack C. Bowen-Colthurst of the Royal Irish Rifles, who was stationed in Dublin during the 1916 Easter Rising. He ordered the execution of Francis Sheehy Skeffington and two journalists, Mr Dickson and Mr McIntyre, and personally shot a teenage boy. The British authorities, both military and civil tried to downplay the event by court-martialling the Captain in June 1916 on whom they pronounced a verdict of insanity. The entire Bowen-Colthurst family fell into disfavour with the Sinn Féin movement. After the reorganisation of the Volunteers in 1919, active reprisals were taken against the family in Dripsey. Farmers were asked to discontinue supplying milk to the cheese factory and employees at Dromgownagh were asked to resign. Despite threats, the boycott was not fully carried out.

Employees of the farm were intimidated and assaulted, and on the night of 14 August 1920, the farmyards of suppliers to the cheese factory were visited and the milk churns smashed with pickaxes. The cheese factory closed. Shortly after the forced withdrawal of supplies, the Dripsey Cheese Factory, Dripsey House, Dromgowna House and Dripsey RIC Barracks were burned as acts of reprisals. Soon afterwards, Dripsey Castle and farm were sold and the Bowen-Colthurst left Dripsey and Ireland. They had been landlords for over 300 years in the Cork region.

In the time that followed, the cheese-maker Miss Grebon removed some vats, drums and barrels to a house some distance away where she restarted the cheese-making. She employed some of the staff of the Bowen-Colthurst venture. It continued for two years before it closed. Peegy Bowen-Colthurst took over the 300-acre farm, known as Brickwall Farm at Layer-de-la-Haye, Essex, England. Later in life, she married her cousin Arthur Greer. She died in May 1970 at the age of eighty-eight.

As for the ruinous structure of Dripsey Paper Mills, at the outbreak of the Second World War, scrap-iron merchants again got busy and completed the work began by their predecessors in selling off the scrap metal. Up until the early 1950s, the buildings were partly standing. The old mill shaft was the only portion intact. It was a tower completely clad in ivy. In the mid-1950s the Lee Hydro-Electric Scheme covered the entire site with water, immersing its history into the depths of Inniscarra Reservoir.

10. REBUILDING MEMORY: DRIPSEY AND THE CORK WOOLLEN MILLS

One institution that does appear consistently when researching Dripsey is the woollen mills, whose history stemmed from the early 1800s to the 1980s. Again, its past is scattered but its memory can be partially rebuilt.

Cork woollen manufacturers in the late 1700s were primarily craftsmen who made wool by hand. The basic process in the manufacture of the various types of woollen cloth can be divided into four stages: preparation, spinning, weaving and finishing. The financial fortunes of the many manufacturers suffered when English manufacturers mechanised their spinning processes in the 1790s. Hence, there was a series of economic fluctuations in the history of the Cork woollen industry. Attempts were made at mechanisation. In 1795, a Cork manufacturer called Kemp was the first to introduce new technology to Ireland.

At the turn of the 1800s, economic depression arising from Home Rule brought about a severe decrease in the market for textiles in the Cork area. The Napoleonic Wars brought a boom in the coarse woollen industry. There was an acute demand for uniforms. In 1800, around 2,500 people were employed in the industry in the city. There were 457 looms in operation and a total of forty-one employers in the city at the time who were master manufacturers. Blackpool and its environs was the

Dripsey Woollen Mills in the early twentieth century. (*O'Shaughnessy family*)

principal weaving district in the city. The O'Mahony family owned the largest firm operating in Blackpool during the 1790s. The family was involved in the woollen industry since the mid-eighteenth century. They carried out the entire process of manufacturing, from fleece to finished cloth.

By 1822 there were just under 1,000 people working in the Cork woollen industry, compared to between 2,500 and 3,000 at the end of eighteenth century. Those that invested capital in their industry survived the economic downturn. The manufacturers who established new mills outside the city during 1820s and 1830s comprised Crofts (at Grenagh), Craig (at Coole), Nicholls (at Glanmire), Lyons (at Glanmire) and O'Mahony (at Blarney).

An enterprising local group whose names have been lost to time created Dripsey Woollen Mills sometime around 1830. Flannels, friezes and rugs were produced by hand up until the Great Famine. Financial difficulties beset the enterprise and Coachford Benevolent Society took it over. The society comprised a number of locals including: Major John Bowen-Colthurst; J.H. Colthurst; Dr Barter; H. O'Callaghan; H. Minhear; J. Rye Coppinger; H.Cross; T.Cross; Dr Godfrey; Mr McMahon; T. Golloch; S. Croole; J. Good; Mrs Weistead; Mr Carther, and Revd H. Johnson.

In the post-Famine era, the Fielding family, who owned mills in County Cork, took over the business. In 1875, Mr D. Lynch came into possession of the mills, which were up to then of relatively small dimensions. The products were sent to Lynch's establishment in Macroom. In 1881, the blankets, flannels, rugs and winceys manufactured were adopted as standard samples for contracts in the North Dublin Union. Numerous other unions and institutions followed suit. The firm's success was much aided by the exhibitions of 1882 and 1883 in Dublin and Cork respectively, at both of which the exhibits of the firm obtained prizes. Arising out of financial success, the concern was turned into a limited liability company. The buildings were considerably enlarged to cope with the growing business and in 1883 most of the old buildings were taken down and a fine spacious structure was built.

By 1875, the mills had become the enterprise of D. Lynch. An article in the *Cork Examiner* in December 1888 tells of a visit by a group named Southern Industry, who reveal several important insights into the set-up of the mills. All the operatives and foremen employed were locals and self-trained. The visiting group asserted that the firm possessed some of the most modern machinery in use to perform the varied processes, from the washing and dying of the raw wool to the finishing of the beautiful tweeds, serges, friezes and blankets. They further noted:

Here are to be seen the busy looms and great intricate, self-acting spinning machines, 100 feet long, on one flat; and on the next are the carding, condensing, and different finishing machine; while in separate apartments are the wool and cloth steam-dyeing machines.

In a large outer detached shed within the complex, the 'dyeing, washing, fulling, teasing, etc.' was carried out. The motive power was from an abundant supply of water from the Dripsey River, running just by, which turned a powerful patent turbine. Steam was also available as an auxiliary backup. The wool used was almost exclusively Irish home-grown. As regards design and export, Southern Industry stated that:

> …the designs in their splendid cheviot tweeds are novel and excellent, and a variety of fancy colours, some quite brilliant, are used therein. They do a large trade throughout Ireland, especially in the Northern and Midland counties, and they have orders at present for four months in advance, so that the difficulty generally seems to be to keep supply up to the demand.

Dripsey Woollen Mills was not alone in having modern machinery. By the end of 1800s, Cork was the principal focus of the mechanised woollen industry in Ireland. By 1897, there were twenty-seven factories in County Cork involved in the different processes within the woollen industry. The total number employed was between 2,000 and 3,000 people. The county was the principal centre within the woollen industry in the country. The larger mills in the county were: Martin Mahony & Bros. Ltd, with 15,000 spindles and 100 looms; O'Brien Bros., St Patrick's Mill, Douglas, 5,000 spindles and 135 looms; Crofts & Co., Sallybrook Mills, Glanmire, 1,000 spindles and 29 looms; Cogan & Son, Midleton, 1,500 spindles and 20 looms, and Dripsey Woollen Mills, 1,600 spindles and 16 looms.

In 1903, Andrew O'Shaughnessy purchased Dripsey and reorganised its specialisation into quality woollen goods. The O'Shaugnessys descended from Daithí, the last pagan King of Ireland, their sept producing several Kings of Connaught. The home of the clan was at Kiltartan in County Galway on the border with County Clare. The seventh-century St Colman, son of Duagh, established a monastery on land given him by his cousin King Guaire. The chieftains were buried in the monastic centre, which contains an elaborate round tower. The site was of such importance that in the twelfth century it became the centre for a new diocese. It is now incorporated into the Diocese of Kilmacduagh (Church of the son of Duagh). The coat of arms of the family, two lions upright against a castle, a knight's helmet, and a hand holding a spear over it, is based on the symbolism on the shield of Diarmuid O'Shaughnessy, buried at Kilmaduagh. The motto of the family is 'Fortis et Stabilis' anglicized as 'Strength and Stability'.

In the mid-twelfth century, the family chieftain Seasanach was part of the eighth

Roger O'Shaughnessy II,
b.1583-d.1650. (*O'Shaughnessy family*)

generation descended from Daithí. It is recorded that Seasanach held 16,800 acres at that time. O'Seachnaigh is anglicised as O'Shaughnessy. It was during that time that the name O'Shaughnessy stuck to the different family chieftains that followed. The lands were dispossessed during the reign of King Henry VIII. Dermot O'Shaughnessy surrendered his lands, but showing his allegiance to the Crown, he got his lands re-granted.

A portrait of Sir Roger II O'Shaughnessy (1583-1650) hangs in Dripsey Castle House. He was made a freeman of Galway in 1611. In the early 1630s, Sir Roger II was embroiled in a land issue. Titles were sought by the King's Lord Deputy of Ireland, Thomas Wentworth, from Irish chieftains in order to have lands legally theirs. Roger went to London to plead his case before King Charles I. Thomas Wentworth ordered his arrest along with his two companions, Martin and Darcy. Roger and Darcy were imprisoned in Dublin Castle for a time. They attained their release through the political pressure of the Earl of Clanricarde in Galway, a family connected to the Anglo-Norman colonialists, the De Burgh. After his release, Roger lived for a time in a castle near Timoleague Abbey with his second wife.

By Cromwellian times (*c.*1649), the O'Shaughnessy land was split amongst the family. Oliver Cromwell dispossessed much of the lands. After the Restoration of King Charles II in 1660, 2,000 acres were returned to Sir Dermot III O'Shaughnessy for services rendered to the monarch during his exile in France. The remaining lands in County Galway were declared forfeit after James II's defeat at the Battle of the Boyne in 1690. Some migrated to France and were involved in the wine industry. They became known as the 'wine geese' and even became aristocracy. William O'Shaughnessy was a captain in the army of Louis.

However, from the Cromwellian confiscation many of the family members moved to and settled in South Limerick and North Cork. They brought with them a rich tradition of how to grind corn and weave cloth. However, their wider contribution to Cork and Limerick society is impressive. They were scientists, engineers, knights, Lords, Bishops, clergy, statesman, politicians, MPs, ambassadors, entrepreneurs, athletes, sportsmen, barristers and solicitors. An O'Shaughnessy branch settled in Charleville and Denis O'Shaughnessy established a woollen mill at Ballyhea nearby. The Ballyhea branch in turn spread to Coolbane near Freemount, the Liscarriol area, Kiltane, Ballagh, Clonbanin, Dromina, Dripsey and Coachford.

Andrew O'Shaugnessy was born on 28 July 1866 into Coolbane Mills, Freemount, near Kanturk, County Cork. He was the second son of Andrew and Ellen O'Shaughnessy. In a lecture later in life, Andrew (junior) eloquently put it that 'I was born within the sound of the mill wheel.' His father died when he was fifteen and he was asked to help with the mill in Freemount. The mill was one of five O'Shaughnessy mills in North Cork. He decided to emigrate to America and spent several months there. He came back to Ireland but shortly went back to the States again to attend business school in New York. He spent his twenty-first birthday in the 'Big Apple'. By that time America had produced very talented inventors, such as Thomas Edison and his electric light and Alexander Graham Bell and his telephone.

Andrew was described in later years as a man of vision and foresight, traits that were forged during his stay in America. After absorbing some American business and manufacturing ideas, he came home and rented an old mill at Newmarket, which he converted into a creamery in 1895. He soon added six central creameries. Apart from Newmarket, those comprised Mitchelstown, Coachford and Knockulty, and Mullinahane in County Tipperary. He also established twenty-four branches to add to his Newmarket concern, thereby creating a chain under the name of the Newmarket Dairy Company in 1904. In ensuing years, Andrew added Bridgetown Flour Mills, Sallybrook Woollen Mills, Kilkenny Woollen Mills and Dripsey Woollen Mills to his operation.

In 1903, Andrew O'Shaughnessy purchased Dripsey Woollen Mills from Mr Charles Olden, who was then a senior partner of the firm of Atkins & Chirnside &

Co. An article in the *Cork Sun* on 16 May 1903 on Dripsey Woollen Mills discusses Andrew O'Shaughnessy's early contribution at that time. Any business involves time and effort to make it a success. In 1903, there were a small number of workers, approximately twenty-one, employed at the mills. They included Hannah Brennan, Nora Browne, Pat Clohessy, Nano Falvey, Johnny Healy, Mickie Lynch, John Magner and his mother Neilie, Dan Horgan, Micheal Horgan, Maggie O'Mahony, Kate O'Mahony and her sister Julie, Abbey O'Mahony and her sister Nora and brother Denis, Nora O'Carroll and her sister Kate and her father Dan, and Jeremiah Sullivan. The foreman and tuner was Denis Kelleher (Sheehan, 1972).

Eleven years later, on 30 March 1914, the *Cork Examiner* printed a feature on the Woollen Mills with pictures. The commentary claimed that the mills were a 'progressive concern' and that they were a 'lesson to Ireland'. A walk through the factory showed many departments peopled with workers. Staff numbers by the year 1914 were at seventy-five at Dripsey and twenty-five at the branch factory at Sallybrook. Some of the workers were housed nearby in neat, well-ventilated cottages. They paid a nominal rent and there was a spacious garden attached to each house. Several of those houses still survive today. The *Cork Examiner* piece of 1914 noted that:

> During working hours the people work well, for they are clever and willing, they are
> thoroughly respectable and very different to those in the ranks of the weavers of West

Above left: Andrew O'Shaughnessy (b.1866–d.1956) in later life. (*O'Shaughnessy family, by Irish painter Seán O'Súilleabháin*)

Above right: The O'Shaughnessy family, *c.*1913-1914; included are Andrew and his wife Margaret Mary Casey (from Kiskeam). The children comprise Aileen, Andrew, John Michael, Edward, Patrick James, Mary, Lily, Mark, Kathleen, Pearl and Síle. (*O'Shaughnessy family collection*)

of England towns. There is a freedom in their employment, although there exists thorough discipline in the factory, but as the staff are conscientious, efficient and are in most cases inhabitants of the district, trained in the Dripsey factory to do the neatest work in the shortest way, the strain of stress of management never falls on the craftsman.

The mills doubled in area over the first decade of Andrew O'Shaugnessy's ownership. By 1914, all of the machinery and departments were covered over by roofs. The old waterwheel was now high and dry and leaning against a wall. The waterpower was made the most of by installing turbines. That power was only generated by a national engine-suction gas generator, which was linked up to the main shaft with the turbine.

All the machines where close attention was needed, such as the 'Dolcrosse looms', were under a flood of light, coming from overhead and side windows. Every possible care was given to the Dripsey manufactures in all their stages, whether it was in the choice of wool or the other production areas. A great percentage of the wool was bought locally. The 1914 report went on to describe the manufacturing process:

There were the stores where the fleece fresh from the sheep was stored. There were the areas where the wool is cleansed, dyed, dried over steam jackets, carded, spun into warp wool and woof (the technical names of the thread on the length or across the piece). Each of the new looms had high speed shuttle and turned out rapidly the best of woven materials.

Above left: Staff at Dripsey Woollen Mills, March 1937. (*O'Shaughnessy family collection*)

Above right: Section of the staff gathering, June 1958. (*O'Shaughnessy family collection*)

Above left: Aerial view of Dripsey Woollen Mills, *c*.1980. (*O'Shaughnessy family collection*)

Above righ: Andrew O'Shaughnessy, Dripsey Castle, 2007.

During the *Cork Examiner*'s visit, they noted that in the stockrooms were piles of all descriptions of tweeds of all colours ready for despatch. The tweeds were sent out to the houses of William Dwyer in Blackpool and T. Lyons on South Main Street, who were extensive purchasers. Messrs Todd was the principal purchaser in Limerick, whilst there was large support for Dripsey manufactures from drapery houses in Dublin, Manchester, Leeds and London. Further afield, houses in Canada bought large amounts. The Chinese trade also bought beautiful light tweed. The ladies' dress materials made a great show of patterns and colours; especially fascinating were the varieties of the famous 'Kathleen Ni Houlihan' dress materials.

The directors of the mills in 1914 were Andrew O'Shaughnessy, R.N. Colthurst and William Cronin. William Cronin was a long time working in the woollen trade. He graduated at the well-known and prosperous factory of O'Brien Bros. in Douglas and for some years worked at Clayton's in Navan. He was manager of Dripsey Woollen Mills. It is also stated that the foreman, not named, also worked at O'Brien's. In 1922, the number employed at Dripsey Woollen Mills was sixty and the mill had fourteen looms and three carding machines, as well as a plant to produce its own electricity. By the year 1938, there were 180 workers employed across the range of processes from wool sorting to finishing

During the early years of consolidating Dripsey Woollen Mills, Andrew developed a passion for improving and preserving old residences of character. He resided in several locations in Cork and its hinterland during his long life, living in sixteen different houses altogether. Six or seven were local dwellings. He lived in Peake House, Riversdale House near Rooves Bridge, Windsor in Rochestown (now the Rochestown Park Hotel), and Mount Pellier in Douglas (now demolished but once located in Donnybrook). He spent a lot of time in the Italianate-designed St Raphael's House in Montenotte. In 1923, Andrew O'Shaughnessy was elected as a TD for the Cork Borough (where he remained until 1927), winning the fifth and last seat for the Progressive Association. During his term as TD he went with Alfred O'Rahilly to the International Labour Conference in Geneva. Mr Maurice Healy, prominent Cork solicitor and brother of the famed Tim Healy, first Governor-General of the Irish Free State, once publicly described Andrew as the 'most far-seeing man he ever knew'. Early in 1928, Andrew became one of the founder members if the then new Irish Catholic weekly newspaper *The Standard*. He also associated himself with the Juverna Press, Ltd. As a TD he lived in Dundrum, Dublin where he bought a flour mill called Dock Mills. He later lived in Kilkenny and eventually made his home at Dripsey Castle.

The 1930s and '40s coincided with economic decline in Ireland. That was due to the Wall Street Crash and Ireland's 'Economic Wars' with Britain. In 1931, Andrew's son John O'Shaughnessy, fresh from academic and technical training in Galashiels in Scotland, took over as managing director of Dripsey Mills. To keep the company afloat and profitable, he rationalised the concerns of the mill. He closed the Sallybrook Mills at Glanmire and took on board ten of the employees from that branch. By 1954, the mills had grown to fifty-four looms and eight carding machines. The numbers employed rose to 160 with an annual wage output of £40,000. The woollen industry was being brought to a very high peak.

Andrew O'Shaughnessy (b.1866 - d.1956) had five daughters and six sons. His son Andrew took over management of the Kilkenny Woollen Mills and settled in that city. John took over management of Dripsey Woollen Mills and lived in Dripsey Castle, while Michael inherited a family farm in Carrignamuck, Coachford. Edmund became a medical practitioner and settled in County Wicklow, Patrick moved to Spain, and Mark spent a good many years in England.

John O'Shaugnessy, on the death of his father in 1956, took over the running of Dripsey Woollen Mills. Andrew, his son, now lives in Dripsey Castle. Andrew was born in 1932. He grew up around Dripsey and went to school locally. He notes:

As a child, I worked with the guys on the farm, worked with the cattle and horses; everything done by horse; watering and feeding … we went ferreting at the weekend and snaring and catching rabbits. At twelve years of age, I went to boarding school at Glenstall Priory, County Limerick. In 1950, I worked at the Dripsey Mills in the wool store and worked through the departments. I also spent three nights a week in Sharman Crawford Tech. studying textile technology. I went to UCC in 1951 to do a B.Com. and furthered my studies of textiles when in 1954, I went to a textile training college in Scotland.

Dripsey Woollen Mills were renowned for the quality of their produce and their worldwide reputation. They were specialists in ladies' and gentlemen's apparel cloths, furnishing fabrics, curtaining and upholstery, blankets, travel rugs, and knitting yarns. They became a household name more in terms of blankets and rugs. The Dripsey blanket was well known. Dripsey Woollen Mills specialised in highly designed cloths. Fashion consultants were employed from European cities of London, Paris and Leeds.

Almost 90 per cent of the products were for export, mainly to Paris and London. They also exported to Italy, Holland, Greece, America, Canada, Japan, Australia and New Zealand. Among its customers were such fashion names as Kenzo, Dior, Cardin, St Laurent, Aquascutum, Burberry, Simpsons and Austin Reed. They also processed orders for Rodler, Specifique, Roger Mahr, Celine, Christian Aujard, Claude Barthelemy, and Paul Smith. Andrew recalls, 'Kenzo invited me to go their show in Paris. Kenzo was a very famous Japanese designer. Our fabrics were in those shows as well as other fabrics from mills in Europe … they were in a sense paying a tribute to Dripsey.'

In Dripsey Woollen Mills, weaving was brought to its highest peak. The company won eight gold medals at the Sacramento Trade Fair in the 1960s. Andrew remarked that one of their biggest boosts was seeing a Dripsey Woollen suit worn by Princess Diana, who was photographed by *The Times* of London wearing the outfit. Of the other factors in the success of the mills Andrew asserts:

> My father used to say that nobody had business in the woollen industry unless they were dedicated … my father John devoted his life to it … there are so many variables … our slogan was 'quality, style and durability' … we took the raw fibre to a finished product. Each stage is a study in itself. A huge tribute has to be paid to the heads of our departments, to the staff who took a pride in what they were doing. In the 1940s and 1950s, there were 166 people working in the mills … the mills became an all-family venture. Locals had generations of family members going there. The local people working in the mill were proud of its achievements … the mills provided much-needed employment and slowed down emigration in the wider region.

Dripsey Woollen Mills processed a high proportion of Irish wool as well as fine wools imported from Australia (Marino wool) and New Zealand. They also met the high standards of Bayer of Germany in the manufacture of Dralon fabrics, which they initially made in 1965. They also manufactured Woolmark and Dralon furnishing fabrics, which are flameproof and used widely in public buildings. They were commissioned to make curtaining materials to furnish the Cork Regional Hospital.

An article in the *Cork Examiner* by Evelyn Ring on 12 April 1982 charted the decline of the mills. There was a continuing contraction of the milling craft, particularly within the EEC. In 1982, there were forty-five men and twenty-five women employed at Dripsey Woollen Mills. In Evelyn's article Andrew argued:

> Many of our good customers, particularly in this country have literally disappeared and we find that our major customers in London and Paris are ordering less fabric than we would normally expect. The greatest problem to be faced by Irish clothing industries when competing abroad was inflation, now almost double that of most European countries. Already mills in Britain are folding up while other struggling textile industries are finding themselves in unsteady and dangerous economic ground.

Sadie O'Callaghan (*née* Corcoran) lives in the Model Village, Dripsey. She was born in South Berrings in 1931. One of the many interesting aspects about Sadie and the mills is that she was captured on camera by local man Denis McCarthy tidying up on the last day of operation in 1988. The photograph is an important artefact in piecing together the great legacy of Dripsey Woollen Mills. The mills had made a huge contribution to local and national industry, but they also changed local people's ways of life. From my experience of talking to people, the mills rejuvenated and strengthened the sense of pride of place and ancestry that is today very much inherent in this area of County Cork.

Sadie worked in Dripsey Woollen Mills in the 1950s and early 1960s. She got married and had a daughter called Eileen. Sadie returned to work after raising Eileen and remained working in the institution until the mill's closure in 1988. She was employed initially as a cloth looms piece weaver and worked intensively as a blanket weaver making cellular blankets (blankets with holes in them) and curtains. Her husband was Michael O'Callaghan who worked in the spinning department. Sadie finished up as a cone winder.

In the weaving shed, Sadie remembers a number of local people working with her: 'Baby' Mary Murphy; Johann McCarthy, Lower Dripsey; Mrs Eileen Nolan; Nora May Lumbert; Jer Galvin; Mary Forde; Johnny Crowley, and Pat McElroy. She

Above left: Sadie O'Callaghan of the Model Vilage, Dripsey.

Above right: Sadie O'Callaghan sweeping up on the last day at Dripsey Woollen Mills in 1988. (*Denis McCarthy*)

also remembers the harpers Paddy Farrelly, Timmy McCarthy and Joe McCarthy. Her supervisor in early years was John Birmingham, who lived in one of the mill houses. Joe O'Callaghan replaced him as the man in charge of the looms. Dan Maher eventually took over the position. Sadie remembers the noise of the machines in the mills. She can recall the thirty-six looms working in 1963, and the four working in the end in 1988.

In 1988, Dripsey Woollen Mills were sold off and bought by a receiver. Today, what are left are just the memories. The main building is demolished. Ruined sheds stand without their roofs. Some of the buildings are still slated. Dripsey Woollen Mills certainly warrants further study, especially exploring the working community of the mills over the O'Shaughnessy legacy. The story of the woollen mills marries ideas of change and continuity, tradition, local and regional identity, globalisation, place-making, art, experience and memory. These strands combine to create not only the modern Dripsey area but also mid-Cork.

11. A GUN AND ITS STORY: DRIPSEY AMBUSH MEMORIAL

This gun was taken from a British Major, who was subsequently killed by me in the year of 1920 and was used in many an encounter against the British Armed Forces who ravaged our land for over seven hundred years. This gun, with thousands of others, was captured from the British by the young men of my generation who forced the British to surrender on the 11th day of July 1921, thus succeeding where generations of brave and gallant Irish had failed, to win the freedom we enjoy today. Other Irishmen will yet win our complete freedom.

A Gun and its Story; presented by Frank Busteed, Commandant
6th Battalion, Cork No.1 Brigade IRA to his grandson Brian O'Donoughue.

Another important thread in Dripsey's past is the ambush memorial. As the Irish War of Independence advanced, the movements of British troops throughout the country were tabulated and where it was noticed that convoys were maintained on a regular basis between any two points, suitable preparations were made for an ambush on the route. In this way, it was calculated that a convoy of three lorries of soldiers would proceed from Macroom to Cork on 27 January 1921.

The planning for the Dripsey Ambush came in the aftermath of the Burning of Cork and Sean O'Hegarty, Brigade No.1 Officer in Charge, was anxious to see armed reprisals carried out against the auxiliaries throughout the command area. The Dripsey Ambush was largely planned by O'Hegarty, Busteed and Jackie O'Leary, but Flying Column Commander Busteed was in charge. Following a detailed discussion on the topography and contour points of the area, it was decided that a site at Godfrey's Cross midway between Dripsey and Coachford was the most advantageous location for an ambush. There was high firing ground on the near side, and an open stretch on the off side would expose the soldiers to the full fire of the attackers. The auxiliaries passed the site regularly every Friday evening. When the men of the 6th Battalion were taking their places at the ambush site, the locals, who knew of the proposed action, were leaving work early to avoid being caught up in the conflict. The children in the local national school in Coachford were sent home early on the instructions of the parish priest Fr Auliffe.

Positions were taken up, but the military did not depart on that day owing to some technical delay at Macroom. The ambushers, anticipating that the convoy would probably proceed within twenty-four hours, decided to remain overnight at their posts. In due course, this information passed between the locals and was brought to the attention of Mrs Lindsay of Leemount House, Coachford, whose sympathies were known to be with the English authorities.

Mrs Lindsay decided to inform the military at Ballincollig, and without further delay ordered her chauffeur named Clark to drive her to the local barracks, a distance of about twelve miles. Not far from her house she came upon the local Roman Catholic curate Revd E. Shinnick, informed him of her purpose, and requested that he advise the ambushers to abandon their project. Passing through the ambush cordon without hindrance, she safely reached Ballincollig and accurately described the position to the Commanding Officer of the Manchesters who were stationed there.

Meantime, Fr Shinnick approached the attackers, and without stating the source of his information, informed them that the military were now aware of their plans. He suggested that they retire from the spot as quickly as possible. The ambushers, thinking that this was simply a move on the part of Fr Shinnick to have bloodshed avoided, decided to remain at their posts. At Ballincollig, full preparations were made for a surprise attack, and a strong military party arrived at Dripsey Bridge about 3p.m. There they divided into two sections, one group advancing along the byroad towards Peake, and the remainder proceeding along the main road to Coachford.

The Peake road party was able to approach the ambushers from the rear, and both sections opened fire simultaneously. The ambushers, now on the defence, were armed, but were outranged by the service rifles of the military and decided to retire under cover of a rear guard party of six men. In the early stages of the encounter it was discovered that the military had made one tactical error by not also closing in from the west or Coachford side. Taking full advantage of this oversight, the main body of the ambushers quickly slipped through the gap in the attack, and with nightfall approaching, they were soon clear. Their comrades remained at their posts. However, there came a point where there was no alternative but to surrender. Ten men were arrested. The British troops confiscated sixteen shotguns with 101 rounds of ammo, four rifles with thirty-three rounds of ammo, three revolvers with eighty-six rounds of ammo, and six bombs. From Dripsey, they were conveyed to The Barracks, Cork City.

The sentence of death was passed on five men, who were executed on 28 February 1921, exactly one month later. An immediate sequel to the encounter was the arrest of Mrs Lindsay and her chauffeur by the IRA who notified General Strickland, Commanding Officer, British Military Forces in the South Coast, that if the five men be released, Mrs Lindsay's life was safe, but in the event of their execution, then there would be no alternative but to take similar action with Mrs Lindsay. Her residence at Leemount was burned down as a further reprisal. Mrs Lindsay's family then left the country and resided in England.

Dripsey Ambush Memorial on the Coachford–Dripsey Road.

The man heading up the ambush was Captain James Barrett. He was born at Killeen, Donoughmore on 29 June 1880. He was employed by the Cork and Muskerry Railway Company and was stationmaster at Firmount for nearly two decades before his death. He was Captain of Aghabullogue Football team. He joined the Donoughmore Company of the Irish Volunteer movement in 1914. He was Quartermaster within the 'C' Company of the 6th Battalion Cork No.1 IRA Brigade. He was wounded in the leg at Dripsey, taken prisoner and brought to Cork Military Barracks. His leg was amputated but he died shortly after. He was buried in Donoughmore.

The five men executed were all members of the 6th Battalion Cork No.1 IRA Brigade. Jack Lyons was born at Clonmoyle near Coachford in 1895. He joined the Volunteers in 1917. He was a member of Aghabullogue 'D' Company. He was one of the lookouts for the ambush. Timothy McCarthy was born at Monavanshara, Donoughmore on 2 January 1900. He was educated at Firmount National School and was inspired by his teacher J. Murphy to develop a love for the Irish language. Timothy worked for the Gaelic League and other national organisations of the Nationalist tradition. He was a member of 'C' Company in the 6th Battalion.

Thomas O'Brien was part of 'E' company in the 6th Battalion. He was born in upper Glanmire, County Cork, in 1900. He resided at the Model village and was employed at Dripsey Woollen Mills. He joined the Irish Volunteers in 1918. He was involved in an attack on Blarney Barracks and the ambush of British Military forces in Inniscarra. He was a keen hurler and played with Inniscarra junior hurling team. He was wounded and captured at Dripsey.

Daniel O'Callaghan was born at Model Village, Dripsey in 1899. He joined the Irish Volunteers in 1917. He was a member of Inniscarra Hurling Club and played for them in 1919. With the Volunteers, he was involved in attacking British forces at Inniscarra and an attack on Blarney Military Barracks. He was a member of 'E' Company. Patrick O'Mahony was born at Derry, Berrings on 23 September 1896. He joined the Irish Volunteers in 1917. He was involved in the attack on Blarney and Carrigadrohid Police Barracks and an attack on Inniscarra. He was a member of 'C' Company.

Mrs Lindsay had been kidnapped by the 6th Battalion for leverage to free the captives. However, on their execution, and after careful discussion with General Headquarters in Dublin and a Brigade meeting at Blarney, the decision was taken to execute Mrs Lindsay and Clarke, her chauffeur. In early March 1921 they were shot by a firing squad consisting of six Volunteers under the command of vice-commandant of the 6th Battalion, Frank Busteed. The Lindsays' House at Leemount suffered an arson attack. On the night of 12 March 1921, four British intelligence officers, accompanied by a party of twelve other ranks, raided the Busteed House in Blarney reputedly looking for Frank. The existing narrative notes that Frank's mother Mrs Busteed was pushed down the stairs in the attack, broke her back, and died a day later. Frank avenged his mother's death by tracking down and killing the perpetrators. Those events bring the ambush, its organisation and subsequent narrative to the psychological level. What was it like to shoot in a disciplined and dispassionate manner? It must have had a deep emotional toll on all those men and women on both sides who were deeply involved in the War of Independence.

Frank Busteed was the second in command of the 6th Battalion Cork No.1 Brigade, IRA in 1921. In November 1920, Sean O'Hegarty, OC of the Cork No.1 Brigade appointed him commander of an active service unit (Flying Column) attached to the battalion. Frank Busteed was involved in the city Volunteers between 1920 and 1923 and had also been involved in numerous ambushes and operated in the Cork–Macroom area.

Born on 23 September 1898 in Kilmuraheen, Doughcloyne, Frank grew up in Blarney. He was of Protestant background and though brought up Catholic, professed atheism and was socialist in outlook. His mother Norah's strong nationalism was a significant influence. During terms in prison between 1919 and 1920, he was taught

Irish by scholarly inmates. He had an enquiring mind and was well read. Two of his brothers were raised as Protestants by their paternal grandmother in Passage West; Frank and another brother were raised as Catholics by their mother in Blarney. Yet he remained on good terms with both sides. An example of this was in 1921 when one of his brothers, who was a sergeant in the British Army stationed in Blarney, warned him of a forthcoming raid on his house to arrest him, allowing Frank to escape.

Immediately after the end of the Civil War, Frank was still involved in operations but had to leave the country and he escaped to the United States with three of his comrades. In New York, he settled, married, started a family (he had six children in all during his life) and started his own business – ice cutting and delivery. In the mid-1930s the family decided to return to Ireland, with Frank eventually taking up a post as Captain in the Irish Army during the Emergency (1939-1946). They also had their own business in Cork. Frank was actively involved in organizing new Fianna Fáil cumanns in the city. Later in the 1960s, he was afforded Labour Exchange Manager in Passage West. He kept in contact with many people in the Blarney–Donoughmore–Inniscarra–Dripsey area over the years, and he attended the unveiling of the Dripsey Ambush Memorial in 1938, as well as many of the commemorations and the fiftieth anniversary in 1971. Frank Busteed died in 1974.

Above left: Frank Busteed, Captain in the Irish Army, 1939-1946. (*O'Donoughue family and Cork Museum*).

Above right: Frank Busteed's revolver is part of the Frank Busteed memorabilia housed in Cork Museum. (Kieran McCarthy, courtesy of the O'Donoughue family and Cork Museum).

Frank Busteed's memorabilia was donated by his grandson Brian O'Donoghue to the Cork Museum. It consists of a revolver with an attached inscription and a picture of Frank as a young man with two other Volunteers with rifles in their hands. There were two medals submitted. One was an Anglo-Irish War medal (also known as the Black and Tan medal because of its colour). Anyone active in the War of Independence between 1 April 1920 and 11 July 1921 was awarded the medal by the Irish Government in 1941. The second medal presented to the museum was a fiftieth anniversary medal (1971) of the War of Independence.

Dripsey Ambush Memorial has a number of levels of study, whether one is talking about the general historical narrative, the effects on local and national memory, or the meanings of the physical memorial – the obelisk. In a sense, you could get quite taken up by the entire package. You could romanticise the entire ambush event, but at the end of the day, the memorial remembers real people and real events. It is a past that is not only linked to annual commemoration ceremonies but also to what we as Cork people have inherited.

Today, the bend on the road and the overgrowing hedgerow seem to tunnel the traffic past quickly. Indeed, one could pass the Dripsey Ambush Memorial without seeing it, but it does mark the site of the ambush. A slender limestone obelisk, created by Seamus Murphy, commemorates the Dripsey Ambush site. The extant memorial forms part two of the ambush narrative; it commits individuals, events and actions to public memory. At a basic level, the ambush memorial is a stone sculpture that helps and enhances the fading story. However, there are a number of levels operating. The monument is a shared memory that shaped a local generation of its time but also the time that was to come. The monument is in the public realm and so also sells the concept that the public memory shaped a nation. There are also the intentions of the commissioning body, who advised the sculptor on form and the people on how to venerate it. Then there is the level of the private memory that shaped the individual artist. Everyone involved in the production brought and continues to bring their own experiences and ideas. So if you look at all those factors, the meanings of a carved piece of stone become varied and complex.

From the late 1920s to the early 1970s, hundreds of memorials commemorating the events of 1916, as well as subsequent conflicts and the First World War, were erected throughout Ireland. The creation of memorials was not state led. It was only in the mid-twentieth century that the Irish Government set aside £14,000 each year to commission artists to embellish town halls, post offices, custom houses, streets and market squares with symbols of the Republic of Ireland. In the 1920s, 1930s and 1940s, it was local committees who organised collections of subscriptions for local memorials. A multitude of projects took many years to come to fruition.

Questions of who should be remembered and in what spirit were important. Land had to be attained from landowners, churches and local governments. Artists, architects and masons had to be approached. The majority of committees comprised the surviving men of IRA brigades, battalions and their relations.

The earliest memorial committee was formed from a Cavan IRA Flying Column in 1922. They erected a cross to a member of their company who had died in May 1921. Brigade committees raised monuments in prominent locations in towns such as Tullamore, Cavan, Athlone, Galway, and Enniscorthy, and Republican plots in cemeteries such as St Finbarre's Cemetery in Cork City. Battalion committees set up memorials to mark ambush sites where they had lost men. There is a large concentration of memorials in County Cork – Dripsey, Kilmichael and Macroom.

The first Dripsey Ambush memorial was a simple wooden cross, which was erected by friends and relatives of those who died. Anne MacSwiney, a sister of Terence MacSwiney, unveiled it in 1924. A committee of locals and members of Dripsey Pipe Band was formed to consider a larger memorial. Jimmy O'Mahony chaired the committee, Jeremiah O'Callaghan was secretary, and the treasurer was John O'Brien. The other members comprised Brian O'Connors, John O'Connell, Denny O'Connell, Harry O'Brien, John Michael O'Brien, Jerry Noonan, Matty Galvin, John Murray, Henry O'Donoghue, Bob O'Donoughue, John Byrne, Tadgh Twomey, Ernest Leonard, Michael O'Mahony, Genie Lantry, Brian Riordan and Jim Noonan. The speaker at the unveiling of the new memorial in 1938 was Mick Leahy of Cobh who was a prominent member of the Cork Brigade No.1. The wreath maker was Jack Sexton of Blarney. The sculptor chosen was Seamus Murphy.

Between the years 1938 and 1963, Corkman Seamus Murphy produced several War of Independence memorials. He was a stonemason who was well established in his studio in Blackpool by the 1930s. In fact, he worked in that area for over fifty years, gaining not only a regional reputation for the quality of his stonework (carving and lettering) but a national and international one as well. In 1964, he became Professor of Sculpture of at the Royal Hibernian Academy. In the international arena, he exhibited his work at the World Fair in New York in 1939.

Seamus Murphy bridged the gap between the fine-art sculpture, the stonemason and the stone-working tradition in Ireland by revitalising all three elements. He created memorials that looked like First World War monuments. He employed a limited vocabulary of forms and symbols. The aspects of military, religious, cultural and funerary elements were present without one dominating and insisting on its message. Seamus wished to avoid the language of Republicanism and the themes of bitterness and hopelessness associated with the Irish Civil War. He wanted to express a more vibrant Ireland.

Above left: Seamus Murphy's ornate script on the Dripsey Ambush Memorial.

Above right: Seamus Murphy in the 1930s. (*Murphy family and Cork City Council*)

In 1938, Seamus Murphy designed Dripsey Ambush Memorial. It is a truncated obelisk, just over sixteen feet high, decorated with a plain, raised cross, which is allowed to punctuate the outline of an obelisk. On the front Seamus carved a large two-edged sword in relief. The 'sternness' of those simple images was reduced by the decoration on the Cross – guard of the sword and curved edges of the base of the monument.

At the broader base under the point of the sword, the incised inscription, of a bold and simple form, is composed in Gaelic and executed in old Gaelic script. The entire monument is raised on a series of steps and backed by a thick wall of evergreens. Seamus's other prominent memorials commemorating the Irish War of Independence can be viewed in Midleton, in Bandon, at Leemount near Carrigrohane, the Republican Plot at St Finbarre's Cemetery, Cork, the Thomas Kent Memorial in Collins Barracks in Cork City, and the Gaol Cross Memorial in the city.

12. NADRID AND THE GRACIOUSNESS OF THE PAST

There are several notable sites that should be mentioned if you survey eastwards along the sides of Inniscarra Reservoir from Coachford to where the Dripsey River meets the Lee. The townlands near the river by Rooves Bridge are Leemount and Knockanowen ('Cnocán Eoin' or 'Owen's Little Hill'). The name Eoin may refer to St John the Baptist or an apostle. The name of the townland of Classas is from the Irish word 'Clais' which means furrow, hollow, glen or valley. William Laurence, 100 years ago, captured the tranquil mood of the river when he took a photograph of an older lady sitting on the riverbank near Rooves Bridge. The title of the photo is 'A View of the Lee at Classas, Coachford, County Cork'. It seems that it was taken on a summer's day as the lady is wearing a sun hat and is dressed elegantly. Another woman is shown further downstream standing on the riverbank. An early-nineteenth-century house called Riversdale still exists in Classas.

The old coach road, which is now the R619, crosses the Cork–Coachford road in Coachford and intersects the townland of Nadrid, from Nead Druide or 'starling's nest'. It might also mean Nead Druid or 'Spot of the Enclosure'. Nadrid House is a 250-year-old Georgian house standing in five acres of mature gardens by the edge of picturesque Inniscarra Lake.

Nadrid, about eighteen miles upriver from Cork City in the Lee Valley, was originally owned by a family called Matthews, part of the extended Clarke tobacco empire clan. It is a mid-sized country Georgian home, two storeys over basement. The house is unusual for a Georgian residence in the way its facade is asymmetrical; not only is the door with its columns and fanlight off-centre, but the windows are not symmetrically placed.

Beyond the Georgian entrance there is an outer hall with a black slate fireplace and fuel store with an arch to the larger inner hall, and this has an imposing staircase and a forty-two-bulb chandelier. The drawing room has an Adam-style fireplace, with one window facing south over the water and another looking east over a croquet lawn, and there is a patio door to the garden. There's also a sitting room looking south and west, with a marble fireplace and a solid-fuel insert stove, and again a patio door to the gardens. The ground floor has a dining room with a small fitted serving kitchen, a main kitchen with units in cherry and a cloakroom with a bath and WC. The stairs return houses a cloakroom/linen press. Off the main landing there are five bedrooms. Two have en suites, and there is also a main bathroom and a separate WC. Down in the basement, there is a billiard room, boiler room, laundry, sauna and gym and stores. Outside, Nadrid House has a courtyard, incorporating a caretaker's house and a bell tower.

View of present–day Nadrid House.

Penny Rainbow, present owner of Nadrid House.

The present owner, Penny Rainbow, has sensitively renovated the building, as she puts it, to 'blend the graciousness of the past with the comforts of the present'. She informs me that it was the Clarke family of Clarke's tobacco who built the house. The house was one of three Clarke properties in the area. The Clarkes possessed 1,800 acres encompassing huge amounts of farmland and forestry. Their lands stretched across the River Lee and took in the Farran Wood area as well. As a result of the direct access to the river, they had fishing rights as well as hunting and shooting rights. In the early 1900s, a daughter of one of the Clarkes, Amy Marguerite, married Captain Horace Lionel Mathews. They spent a long time in India with the British Army and returned to take over the running of Nadrid House. The couple nurtured the estate, which became renowned for its eleven acres of gardens. At one time, ten full-time gardeners were employed. The Mathews family also employed many other people in Coachford.

During the early 1950s, the ESB placed a compulsory purchase order on Nadrid House. As part of the Hydro-Electric Scheme, the site of the house was initially planned to be flooded. When it was not destroyed, the Mathews leased the building back from the ESB. Part of the deal encompassed the giving of Farren Wood to the Irish State on the proviso that people in Nadrid and Coachford should not pay to use the amenity. The appearance of pay booths at Farren in recent years has led to some discontent amongst local people regarding the honouring of that agreement.

In 1965, Horace Lionel Mathews died and his wife Amy retired to Scotland. Dan O'Riordan, who worked for many years for the Mathews, was given the house to mind. When Amy Marguerite Mathews died in 1984, she was buried with her husband in Christchurch graveyard. Her papers and family effects were buried on the grounds of Nadrid House. Dan, through living in the house for so long, officially became the owner. He later sold it on to Ann and Dave McCarthy. At that stage, Dan had been living in the house for sixty years. The new occupants lived in it for sixteen years and did a lot of work in restoring the house to its former glory.

In 1999, the occupants, Mr and Mrs David Noonan, sold up and bought another property in West Cork. In 2000, English-born Penny Rainbow, who has an interest in old properties, bought the house and began to consolidate the conservation work of the previous residents. Subsequently she turned the structure into a successful guest house. At present the house is undergoing further conservation work, work that is being very tastefully completed. Exploring the adjacent yards and out buildings is like stepping back in time. Penny informs me that the location scouts working on the film *The Wind That Shakes the Barley* visited and considered the use of those buildings for the film.

13. CROSSING BARRIERS: CAPTAIN KENNEFICK MEMORIAL

> Every townland in Ireland has its own history and this, in many cases, is a history in miniature of the times through which the residents have lived.

> Herbert Webb Gillman, 1895.

Following the road east from Nadrid House, which is just to the north-east of Rooves Bridge, is a monument to the memory of Captain Timothy Kennefick who died on 8 September 1922, a casualty of the Irish Civil War. Aged twenty-nine and a member of the 1st Cork Brigade of the Irish Republican Army, he was travelling in a lorry going to the funeral of his mother in Cork. He was captured by the Free State Army and killed. His body was found in a field and removed to Coachford courthouse. The information released at the ensuing inquest noted that he was badly beaten up. He was from Lady's Well Hill, Blackpool, Cork, and was buried in the Republican plot in St Finbarre's Cemetery. In later years, his son and daughter are said to have emigrated to America. In 2005, the Kennefick monument was restored and over 300 people turned out to see it unveiled. It is rare to find such a monument commemorating the Irish Civil War in the Lee Valley. There are predominantly more War of Independence memorials than those which note the ensuing and bloody Civil War. The Cork consciousness has been selective in that regard and it would be an interesting study in itself to map out and study the various meanings of memorials dedicated to that era of Irish history.

Tony McCarthy is secretary of the memorial committee that represents broad Republican interests without being party political. Tony points out during our chat that the Irish Civil War is central to Irish history. However, very little work has been completed on the subject – probably due not only to the political split that incurred but more importantly due to the raw emotion arising at that time out of many deaths caused on both sides. It remains a topic to be negotiated with care. Tony notes that, 'The Civil War story should be told, so that at least we can come to terms with what happened and move on from that.'

On a Sunday drive five years ago, a friend asked Tony McCarthy to visit people home from America, the children of Timothy Kennefick, Tim and Ellen, both in the late autumn of their lives. Corkman Tony was drawn to their story and sympathetic to the basic memorial, which recorded the death of their father and his part in the Irish Civil War. As Tony chatted to the Kennefick family on that Sunday afternoon,

Above left: Timothy Kennefick Memorial, 2007, Nadrid, County Cork.

Above right: Commemorative committee members pictured at the Celtic Cross monument in Honour of Captain Timothy Kennefick. Left to right: Dermot O'Leary, Paddy Casey, Timmy Looney, Ted Meaney, Tina Dennehy, Pat Twomey, Matt Healy, Patrick and Phil Looney, John Desmond, Michael Church, Sean McSullivan, Patricia and Tony McCarthy. (*Tony McCarthy*).

the facts on the stone and especially the question of who Timothy Kennefick was came to life. With their imaginations fired, Tony and others assembled a committee and began to work on perhaps improving the Kennefick memorial in line with the wishes of the Kennefick family.

Timothy Kennefick was born the sixth of nine children to Michael and Katherine Kennefick in Cork in 1893. In 1914 he lost one brother due to an accident. Timothy's father passed away in 1916, and his mother just five days before his own life was taken. In fact, he was *en route* to her funeral when he was captured and killed.

Timothy had married Ellen Enright on 19 July 1919. The family lived upstairs at the Pier Head Inn in Blackrock, where he was a bar assistant. The Inn stands to this day, although with updated furnishings. This was where his daughter Kathleen was born. In his early twenties, Timothy Kennefick left the operation of the Pier Head Inn for full-time IRA duties. He learned to drill, to camp, to march and to scout. He moved his family over to the Lady's Well Hill, where his mother lived. Captain Timothy Kennefick was involved in the Anglo-Irish War until the truce was called in July 1921. The Treaty was signed on 6 December 1921 and the first shot of the Civil War was fired on 28 June 1922. The Civil War lasted until May 1923. Families split and friends parted. Captain Timothy Kennefick took the Anti-Treaty side during the Civil War, similar to Tom Barry, Dick Barrett, Liam Deasy, Dan Breen, Richard Russell and Liam Lynch. Every known Republican was swept into prison. The houses of people who had sheltered and nursed and helped the very men in power, when they were irregulars themselves, were raided and ransacked by day and by night. Young men were taken out of their homes at the dead of night; they were tortured and murdered by the roadsides or on the tops of mountains.

Picture of Timothy Kennefick, *c.*1920. (*Tony McCarthy*)

Timothy Kennefick was always an active man, and rose to the position of Captain. During the month of September 1922, tension was very high in the Cork area after the August ambush of Michael Collins at Béal na mBláth. Timothy was billeted out near Ballingeary when he got news of his mother's death. He was a passenger in Mr Seamus Cotter's lorry making his way back to Cork for the funeral when they were apprehended by Free Staters at Mishells Gates. According to the evidence presented at an inquest after Timothy Kennefick's death, Emmett Dalton was the Commanding Officer over thirty Free State officers on Friday 8 September 1922. They had three lorries and an armoured car. Mr Seamus Cotter, the owner of the truck, and Mr Herlihy, another passenger, were allowed go free. Timothy was arrested and put into a caged truck.

The full party then travelled on towards Coachford where all thirty-one Free State soldiers had breakfast at Thomas Burke's Restaurant. The prisoner was left in the caged truck while the party was in the restaurant. After breakfast some of the Free State soldiers got into the caged truck and travelled towards Dripsey. They turned right and stopped at Oldtown. The inquest concluded that it was there that the Free State soldiers tortured and murdered Timothy. He had several marks on the face, two broken teeth, and bullet wounds to the head. The groups then returned to join the rest of their party in Coachford. An inquest was held by coroner J.J. Horgan at Fr Gilligan's house in Coachford on Monday 11 September 1922, on the circumstances surrounding the death of Timothy. The following was the verdict of the jurors:

> We find that Captain Timothy Kennefick was wilfully murdered at Nadrid Coachford on Friday 8 September 1922 by a party of Free State troops and we bring in a verdict of wilful murder against the officer in charge of the Free State troops at Coachford on the morning in question and that the cause of death was shock and haemorrhage due to laceration of the brain caused by bullet wounds. We extend to his wife and relatives our sincere sympathy in their bereavement.

A little boy was born shortly after Timothy was murdered. Ellen and the children moved shortly afterwards to the east coast of the United States to carve out a new life. Over eighty years later, the commemoration committee of the Kennefick memorial collected funds to revamp the monument. A high cross replaced the stone-inscribed slab, which can now be viewed at the side of the monument. Finbarr McCarthy of Denis McCarthy, Mallow Road, sculpted the piece and it was unveiled on 4 October 2006.

14. CRONODY OF THE SWEET APPLES

Moving eastwards along Inniscarra Reservoir one travels into the townlands of Fergus West and Fergus. Fergus (or Feargus) highlights the 'Home of Fergus' who lived around AD 600. Feargus was the grandson of Tighernach and became a holy man who reputedly lived with St Finbarr at his monastery at Corcach Mór na Mumhan or the 'Great Marsh of Munster' (now the City of Cork). Oldtown House in Fergus West was another country house, but is now an overgrown two-storey ruin.

Further east is the townland of Cronody or 'Corra Noide', which means 'Stone Enclosure of the Church'. In the late 1800s, Fr J. Lyons from Kilmichael argued that Cronody is said to have formed part of the outfarms of Inishleena Abbey, which was located in Inniscarra. Later, in 1895, Herbert Webb Gillman, who was vice-president of the Cork Historical and Archaeological Society, penned an article in the society's journal entitled 'History of a Townland in Muskerry, with Glimpses of Country Life'. Gillman lived in the Coachford area and there is a monument to his memory in Magourney Church of Ireland church, amidst the ruined altar area. He died in Sinla in India in 1918.

In his 1895 critique, Herbert Webb Gillman outlines a comprehensive history of Cronody townland with aspects of the past and the contemporary investigated. The article is based on a visit to Cronodymore on 28 December 1894 with Mr Cross Hawes Fitzgibbon. His father was Mr Epinetus Fitzgibbon, a well-known antiquary from the Inniscarra area. The grandmother of Epinetus was Anne Cross, a resident of Cronody who also shared with him much information on the history of the area. Herbert Webb Gillman also mentions and draws from the historical work of Fr J. Lyons, a learned parish priest from Kilmichael.

In the early 1600s, the Cronody area belonged to the McCarthys who had their manor house on the opposite bank of the Lee in the parish of Aglish. They owned vast lands on both sides of the Lee. The representative of the family around the year 1636 was Cormac McDermod McTeige McCarthy. In that year, he sold for £600 the townland of Cronodymore and the impropriate tithes (Church of Ireland property) of Aglish to Richard Hawes, an English settler. Hawes also leased adjacent land from Cormac in the Rooves area, stretching from Rooves Bridge southwards to Knockshanavee. The transactions were all open contracts, having nothing to do with forfeitures.

The Hawes were not the earliest settler family in the south. Richard Hawes also acquired land in Bandon and several other townlands. He married Elinor Elwell, the widow of a family who were among the initial Bandon settlers. She already had a daughter, Mary Elwell. Richard Hawes and Elinor had no children. Hence when he died, in his will he left to his wife all his lands in the barony of Kinalmeaky and some lands to his tenant Robert Colthurst in the parish of Carrigrohane. Cronodymore was bequeathed to Mary, the stepdaughter, on the provision that she could not marry too early, that is before the age of eighteen and with the consent of her mother and the overseers of his will. If his wishes were not met, the land was to go to the poor of the parish of Kilbrogan (Bandon).

With full consent Mary married Philip Cross, the second son of Epinetus Cross of Carrigrohane Castle. In later years the Cross family were involved in the drainage of Cork's marshes and development of eighteenth- and nineteenth-century Crosses Green. Philip Cross is said to have been an officer in the local policing forces who met Mary on a salmon-fishing excursion on the River Lee. The couple inherited all the Hawes lands and lived in a residence near Blarney. Mary died in 1684. During those years, Hawes Cross supported the English and Catholic King James II and eventually had to flee from Cork.

The only son of Mary and Philip Cross was Philip Hawes Cross. On 15 September 1716, he married Elizabeth, the eldest daughter of Henry Baldwin of the Mount Pleasant family. The newly married couple settled down on Cronodymore overlooking the River Lee. Elizabeth Baldwin was deemed a great builder and is credited with the renewing or rebuilding of the mansion. The building was reputedly built from stone from Inishleena (Innisluinga) Abbey, a religious building flooded during the Hydro-Electric Scheme.

Cronodymore House, just south of Dripsey, was of a rectangular plan, sixty feet long in the front facing south and twenty-five feet deep. It was three storeys high with a chimney standing up at each of the four corners of the structure. The site appears on the Ordnance Survey map of the area in 1844 (sheet No.72). The building was a roomy structure for its day. The current structure was built over 100 years ago more or less on the site of the previous house by Tom Murphy, the grandfather of the present resident, Margaret Barry.

Cronody also bears the native addition of Coradh-noide-na-n-abhall-milish, 'Cronody of the sweet apples'. Apple trees at one time abounded all over the townland. In Herbert Webb Gillman's article on Cronody in 1895 in the *Journal of the Cork Historical and Archaeological Society*, he noted that the apple trees of a wilder kind were grown nearer to the Dripsey River. Sweeter apples were grown in the lawn area. Cider was made from the sweet apples and in a good year twenty hogsheads of cider would be made. None of the liquor was ever sold. It was all drunk on the premises. During Herbert Webb Gillman's visit in 1895, Mr Murphy, the resident farmer of the land, opened some old stone buildings in the rear of the ancient dwelling house. Masonry vats were discovered in which the cider was made. There were half a dozen of them, each five feet square and four feet high, ranged along a wall. Each vat had a masonry drain, which probably held a wooden shoot, tending towards the house. A quantity of the remains of glass bottles over half an inch thick was found under the fallen masonry.

Perhaps the most notable structure in Cronody today and an unusual feature in the Lee Valley is a dovecote or pigeon house. Overlooking the reservoir and in very good condition, it is a roofless and circular stone-built structure. Herbert Gillman noted that the building was weather slated on the outside. Some of the nails and a few slates could be seen on his visit but none survive today. The pigeon house has been dated to *c*.1716, the same time Cronody House was erected. Measuring approximately five metres in diameter and six to seven metres high, the entrance of the dovecote has a round-headed door ope on the southern side. The masonry of the interior walls is random rubble and comprises slabs of sandstone carefully built upon each other. A collection of fifteen rows of nesting boxes can be seen. Herbert Gillman in 1895 noted that each row contained thirty holes making 450 nests in all. The nests are in the shape of an 'L'. Each nest entrance is large enough to put in your arm. The bend in the 'L' gave good shelter for the nest. Gillman observed that that the nests were visited twice a month for the young birds and pigeon pies must have formed some of the dishes provided by the residents of Cronody for their guests.

Above left: The Dovecote or pigeon house, Cronody.

Above right: Interior of Cronody dovecote.

In the latter half of the last century the owner of Cronodymore kept a superior breed of carrier pigeons. Those that were trained and put into use had a small silver label on their necks. They were used for bringing news of racing events from England. Mr Ford of Dripsey village told Mr Gillman of the long distances the birds travelled. They bore news in the time of Ford's great-grandfather who was interested in horse-racing events. Doncaster in Yorkshire is mentioned as one of the points from which the birds started.

Herbert Gillman's 1895 article also notes that along the southern part of Cronody and underneath a rocky ridge overhanging the River Lee was a plantation of trees called 'cuill-shana-Hawes' or 'the wood of old Hawes'. On a site on this ridge and commanding a pleasant view of the winding of the river, Elizabeth Hawes built a tea house in which guests were treated to tea and an occasional small dance. The foundations of this house were extant in 1895 but are non-existent today. The ruins measured twenty-two feet facing the river by twenty feet inland. There was a window overlooking the river view and a fireplace and chimney in the west wall.

On Mr Gillman's visit in 1895, west of the pigeon field was a deer park. The upper parts of the deer park walls were gone in 1895 and presented the appearance of neat but ordinary field with fences of the stone and earth kind. One tall pier still stood in 1895 marking the entrance to the deer park. Not far from this gate, on a boreen leading to the avenue and near its junction with the latter, was the site of another gate. That gate bore the name of Geata-na-Sciúrsachta meaning the 'scourging gate'. This seems to have been kept (and used) for the benefit of trespassers on the deer park.

A story is told that a servant of MacCarthy of Cloghroe came to the place with a mare on business. The Cronody folk fostered the breeding of good horses. MacCarthy's man trespassed in some unauthorised way on the deer park and was promptly tied up and received an allotted number of lashes. His master, to whom he complained on his return home, did not like how his servant had been treated. The next day, dressing himself in servant's clothes, he presented himself with the same mare again to the then Mr Cross of Cronody. Mr Cross bade him go away but MacCarthy said Mr Cross should be off first. A fist fight ensued and Mr MacCarthy, who was a powerful man, overpowered Mr Cross. It is said that the scourging gate fell somewhat into disuse after this episode in its history.

15. TRACKING EAST: TOWARDS DRIPSEY VILLAGE

Tracking the R618 from Drispey Ambush Memorial to Dripsey village, we pass a number of noteworthy sites that also inform the identity of the region. First is a crossroads named Godfrey's Cross, named after Dr Thomas Godfrey who lived in the nearby Broomhill House, now the property of Ernie Murphy. Margaret (Peg) Brennan lives at the Cork end of Dripsey village. She recalls her father Michael chauffeuring for Mrs Godfrey. On occasion Michael was also sent north to Barrahaurin in the Boggeragh Mountains, North Cork to get turf for the family. Together with other staff he harvested it, set it out to dry and put it in the turf bunker. The Godfreys were remembered for their large gardens and elaborate out-houses, the designs of which are not of the typical vernacular style. The extant buildings are large and more imposing structures than the norm.

On Dr Godfrey's death, a portion of his investments was distributed amongst the poor widows of all denominations in the local parishes. That included food, material and about £3 every Christmas for a period of time. Christchurch, the home of the Quane Family in Coachford, has a stained glass window to the memory of Thomas B. Godfrey's daughter Maria Rubie. In a 1915 postal county directory, Mrs A. Creed was living in Broomhill with Dr Abraham Cross Godfrey (buried in Christchurch grave-yard, Coachford). In the early twentieth century, the property Broomhill was sold to Philip Murphy. Relatives of the Godfrey family now live in Canada.

Postcard image of Shandy Hall, Dripsey, c.1920. (Br Vianney, Presentation Brothers, Cork)

Further east is the impressive Georgian mansion of Shandy Hall. The plaque above the door notes that the dwelling was constructed in 1758. It was the residence of the notorious surgeon Dr Philip Cross who reputedly poisoned his wife Laura in 1887. The postal directory for Dripsey in 1893 notes a Miss Henrietta Cross had possession of Shandy Hall and Robert Ford was the Land Steward of the premises. Around the year 1901, Patrick Murphy bought Shandy Hall. His wife was Miss Carroll. With an association with the quarrying of stone the 'Quarry' Murphys came from Templemartin, County Cork. At one time, the Murphys had a place on Nettleville estate on the Killinardrish side on the northern bank of Carrigadrohid village on the River Lee. The Murphy family have been in Shandy Hall for over 100 years and it has been a working farm for cattle and horses during that period. The present residents of Shandy Hall are the McSwiney family. Patrick Murphy was the great grandfather of the present resident, Ursula McSwiney (*née* Murphy). Ursula's husband is Peter. His father was Edward McSwiney, who owned the famous Anglers Rest Pub and Riversdale House adjacent to Rooves Bridge in Coachford. The pub was submerged by the Lee Hydro-Electric Scheme through the creation of Inniscarra Reservoir in 1956. Edward is buried in Aghinagh graveyard.

Patrick Murphy of Shandy Hall, *c.*1900. (*Ursula McSwiney*)

The new generation at Shandy Hall, Dripsey. From left to right, Rory, Emer and Neil McSwiney.

Following the road, one crosses the Dripsey River over Dripsey Bridge from Kilgobnet townland into the former townland of Upper Dripsey. The area is more commonly referred to Agharinagh, from Achadh Raithneach or 'Field of the Ferns'. The 1810 Grand Jury map of Cork County shows a large house on the western side of the bridge (Coachford side). Local resident Sean Hurley asserts that it was built between around 1740 and 1760, and that it was used by the local militia at one time. The Ordnance Survey Map for 1836 shows a Royal Irish Constabulary barracks on the site. The RIC Barracks was burned down subsequent to it being vacated in 1922. Later during the Irish Civil War of 1922, opposing sides alternately held Dripsey and many incidents arose because of the contradictory regulations governing civilian traffic. It is not known when the first bridge was built. Just by observation it seems to have been built at the last, lowest, most accessible and narrowest crossing point at the mouth of the Dripsey Valley before it meets the Lee. The Lee Scheme extended part of Inniscarra Reservoir two miles upstream into the Dripsey River Valley.

Dripsey Bridge is shown on the 1811 Grand Jury Map of the area and was initially a small stone structure. Like many other Cork bridges, it was possibly enlarged upon by local landlords and magistrates (local Grand Jury) through Westminster funding in the early 1820s. It is reputed that the bridge was blown up in the early 1920s during the War of Independence and rebuilt. Exploring its architecture, one can see evidence for reconstruction and further enlarging. The current bridge has six semi-circular arches with three overflow arches at the eastern end. There are corbels on some of the piers to support the centring of arches during construction. The riverbed is paved beneath the bridge. An upright stone with a benchmark is embedded in the parapet.

A library may be the source of much knowledge but every now and again, I meet a person during my fieldwork who fills in many of the gaps in the line of memory. Anna Ryan from Dripsey was born on 3 August 1905 and her memory is more than good, it is very impressive.

Armed with photocopies of a postal directory of Dripsey from 100 years ago, I had just had a list of names of residents in a small village in rural Ireland. However, Anna reminded me that history is about humanity – real people and real events. We talked at length but only scratched the surface of time. Our excavation of Dripsey's past became an effort to put flesh on people whose names were in a black and white decaying postal directory. However, as every researcher discovers and every explorer encounters, there is often a lot more to a place than first meets the eye. A crossroads of buildings and people can become a story really worth telling, and not just because Anna is 102. Anna's story is a human one of ordinary people, their place in the world, how they made Dripsey their home. In our time, however, they seem extraordinary. What follows is part of Anna's real-life story (well 102 years is a long time!):

Anna Ryan, Dripsey, August 2007.

The Ryans came from Tipperary. They bought 100 acres and farmed the 'The Acres'. We have been farming for decades. My nephew John Ryan and his family live there now. The Acres were connected to the men who owned the paper mills. I was born in 1905. There were ten of us there, eight girls and two boys. They are all dead now except myself. My mother was Catherine Ryan who became blind when I was quite young. I stayed home to mind her.

My earliest memory is working on the farm, cutting the hay, slying the hay – the neighbours would be of help saving the hay into our big sheds. We had ten fields and there was a name on every field, like Stoney Field – Mass was said there at one time. It is said that druids are buried there. From there you could see all around for miles, Donoughmore, Macroom and Ovens, all over the place. There was also Watery Meadow; we drained it at one time and there was a spring well above it. There was Middle Field, Cottage Field, William's Field, Longfield, Small Field, Field Behind the House, Field behind the Stall, the Road Field, Pier Field, Big Danny's and Small Danny's Field. The Dannys own what is now Patsy Regan's place.

I went to Dripsey National School in the 1910s. Hannah Allen taught us. She was from Rylane and married local man Tim Leahy. I can remember the big windows and the Irish classes and Hannah's words, 'Abair é sin arís!' The other teacher was Bartholomew Murphy. His father was a teacher at Dripsey National School at the turn of the century. We called him Michael Batty. He was from somewhere in Macroom. Anne Delaney was the other teacher in his time and she married Michael.

My secondary school days were spent on the Muskerry Tram – to give it a grand name. You know there are days when I sit down here and dream of the train. I went to St Aloysius School in Cork; a crowd of us went in on the train every day. All our relations went to schools in the city, the boys to Presentation Brothers and Christians. The girls went to St Aloysius College. I got up at 6a.m. every morning to catch the first train at 7a.m. at Dripsey Station. The school opened at 9a.m. We waited in the evening after school and got the 5p.m. train home. We had a monthly ticket, which cost one pence and tuppence.

The journey was ten miles and it took an hour, including stops. It travelled on the road as far as Leemount. The first stop was Carrigrohane. My grandfather was 'big' Tom Ryan from nearby Temple Hill. He smoked a pipe and wore a top hat. He was like the mayor of the area. He did not get off his seat until the train stopped. He lit his pipe and the train did not dare move until he got off. He was a farmer and a county councillor. The councillor tradition is in the bloodline, with my grandfather, my uncle and my nephew Tomás. Uncle Bill became a councilor when my grandfather died. They were important people at one time.

The train continued on to Healy's Bridge and to Coachford Junction. Here was the connection to the Donoughmore. We stayed on the train for Coachford while other passengers disembarked. The train continued onto Cloghroe and then to Gurteen. Gurteen had a shop but no stationmaster. The next stop was Dripsey in Dromgownagh, which had a station of its own. When we were young, we used to climb the signals and also hung around the blessed holy well. We were late for dinner on occasion and spoilt our appetite by eating laurel berries.

Local farmers brought their oats to Dripsey Station. All the local people went to Cork to do their shopping. Jer Long was the stationmaster. He used to bring me home in the evenings because he got milk from our family. Jer was from Coachford originally and was stationmaster for many years until the line closed in the 1930s. Jer smoked Tuppeny Woodbines. They were the favourite cigarettes at the time. He had two girls and eventually died in Westmeath.

There was a shop near Dripsey Station. A Protestant family called Williams had it. There were terribly nice people. We went there as children to get sweets. Bill Williams was a beautiful Irish speaker. I don't know where he learnt it. Mrs Williams had a Catholic working for them, which was a big thing at that time. When she died, they brought a Catholic priest into the house to say Mass. Bill's sisters were Lily, Janie and Rita (who later became a Catholic). There was a RIC Barracks in the locality that had three policemen and a sergeant, a Protestant. Sergeant Bateman's family went to our own school but they went outside the door when it came to Catechism time. His wife was a Catholic.

When I was growing up there was a post office in Dripsey village. There was a little old man who used to puff his pipe at farmers that stopped by. His name was Mortimer Kelleher. Michael Griffin built what is now the Weigh Inn. I did not know the man but knew his son Denis Griffin (who died last year). Denis's daughter Margaret owns the Garden Centre. The pub was known as Griffin's and then passed to Richard Sisk and then to Julia Sisk who was a nurse. There were others; shopkeepers Mrs M. Corkery, Upper Dripsey, Johannah Murphy and vintners, Mrs Murphy and Mrs Eliza Spence. Eliza was the grandmother of John Twomey who was secretary of the Woollen Mills.

In the 1930s, Kathleen Ford had a post office at Dripsey Cross in the bungalow where the Murphy family now lives. Kathleen lived in the two-storey house next door, which is now occupied by another Murphy family. The post office then moved to an area behind the public letterbox in Dripsey Cross where it was housed in a pre-fabricated building. This property belonged to the Sisk Family and Julia Sisk was the postmistress there until well into her nineties. That building is gone and the land in all that area belongs to the Feeney Family.

17. A WAY OF LIFE

As I made my way down the Lee Valley, I encountered a lot of interesting places and met a lot of people who had intriguing and different stories to tell. Another aspect of the Lee Valley that intrigues me is the community structures. I have attempted in each parish of the valley to give an account of the way of life, past and present.

The fabric of a settlement such as churches, graveyards, shops and old farmhouses all provide what I call searchlights for exploring people and places. They do, I feel, greatly help in getting at the heart or essence of a place, and unravelling the story of an area. The frightening aspect about studying the Lee Valley is that there is so much more out there to be researched, recorded and more importantly be made available to the public in local and in wider communities.

Passing through Dripsey on the way home from fieldwork on a Sunday evening, the lights and sounds of the Weigh Inn attracted me. Pubs are like churches. There is at least one in the centre of nearly every rural settlement. They must be the greatest places to attain stories of times past. I have no doubt that by visiting the older pubs of Ireland, you could create the most interesting publications. The older residents sit at the bar drinking, talking and more importantly reminiscing. My visit was met by the owner of the Weigh Inn, Kevin Feeney, who was amidst the Sunday night crowd.

The Feeneys have been there since 1969. However, the pub was built by the Griffins at the turn of the twentieth century and named after the family. Somewhere in time, there was a name change to the Weigh Inn. The name reflects fishing competitions in the River Lee, where the 'weigh in' determined the winner. Through the twentieth century, the pub passed to the Sisks, then to the Riordans and then to the Feeneys.

Kevin's father was Charlie Feeney from Kanturk. His mother Breda (*née* Monaghan) was from Galway. They met in England, then moved to Cork and bought the Weigh Inn pub from the Riordans in 1969. In 1988, Charlie and Breda's son Kevin took it over and continues to promote a good community-based pub. Kevin shared with me two highlights of his time in Dripsey. The first is that of the horse-drawn caravans which were hired out by Joe Reilly's travel agency in 1972/1973 to tourist who travelled around Cork and Kerry. There was a space for the caravans to park behind the Weigh Inn. The second highlight is the enjoyment associated with the St Patrick's Day Parade, which is organised by the Dripsey Community Association on an annual basis. It claims to be the shortest parade in the world by just crossing over the road from one pub to another.

Above left: Helen and Kevin Feeney, The Weigh Inn, August 2007.

Above right: Tess Begley, August 2007.

The Begley family, Dripsey, *c.*1938. Pictured are Mary, Brigie, Josie, Julie, Mary Ellen, Hannah, John, and Tess in the centre. (*Tess Begley*)

John Begley shoeing a horse outside the Begley forge, in the early 1930s. (*Tess Begley*)

Kevin's wife Helen owns the nearby successful guesthouse Sycamore Lodge. She informed me that amongst her recent guests were rowers from Galway, who won the 2007 Irish National Championship title on Inniscarra Reservoir at the National Rowing Centre in Farren Woods. Helen is a great friend with Dripsey woman Tess Begley who lives nearby in the village. Tess worked in the kitchen in Feeney's pub making dinners for most of her working life. In fact Kevin's mother Breda was great friends with Tess.

Tess was born in 1926. Her father was John Begley who for many years was a blacksmith in Dripsey. Tess's mother hailed from Ballyduff, County Waterford. In his younger years, John was a traveling blacksmith and met Mary through his work. John developed a forge adjacent to the family house in Dripsey for making shoes for horses. The building now stands as an ivy-clad ruin. Tess's mother is buried in St John's Cemetery, Coachford, and her father is buried in Knockavilla. Tess was one of the last to go to the old school in Lower Dripsey, which is now in ruins. At one time, the Begleys had a house, a forge and a tea house. A Mr Hudson from Cork City employed the services of Mary Begley in the tea house. Mr Hudson had a touring company based in Cork City, which hired out bicycles for tourists to travel around Cork and Kerry. The Begleys were on the tourist trail.

The interesting aspect about the tourist trail is that it dated back at least 100 years before the Begleys came into the area. From 3 June 1861, a four-wheeled coach car was despatched Monday to Saturday from the coach office of the Imperial Hotel on the South Mall, Cork at 9a.m. The coach travelled the course of the River Lee upstream. It passed by Carrigrohane Castle, Inniscarra, Dripsey, Carrigadrohid, Lough Allua of Inchigeela, Gougane Barra, the celebrated Pass of Keimaneigh, Carriganass Castle, winding round the head of Bantry Bay, and arriving at the Royal Hotel, Glengariff, at 6p.m. every evening. Another coach car departed Glengariff every morning for Killarney at 11a.m. and arrived in Killarney at 5.30p.m. Return cars from Killarney to Cork operated by the same route daily. Tickets for Cork to Killarney and vice versa cost one guinea each. Half an hour was allowed at Inchigeela and Kenmare for going and returning. There still are hundreds of tour buses that come through the Cork region every year. However, they operate mainly on our national roads and not on regional roads such as Dripsey to Cork.

18. SITTING ON A DRIPSEY STONE

Through fieldwork and talking to people, you can see that a community such as that in Dripsey or any other village in the country evolved from individuals and families. People brought their own ideas and talents in forging a family space, which is then set in the wider community. Every person has a story to tell and every person has an important contribution to make in society. The personal stories of those people are a very important part of the cultural heritage of the Lee Valley. One aspect that struck me is how much the heritage of the parishes such as Aghabullogue and Inniscarra runs in people's blood. It's amazing what has been passed down directly or indirectly. Twentieth-centuries histories are as important as the nineteenth-century ones, even though the more modern histories are not recorded and thus are hidden.

With that in mind, on a stone wall as you pass through Dripsey, there is a plaque which celebrates the shortest St Patrick's parade in the world. Plaques are powerful tools for keeping a memory alive but also make a public statement of what is important to a community. We have already seen the meanings involved with Seamus Murphy's Dripsey Ambush Memorial. Leo O'Sullivan, of Lower Dripsey, told the story of the shortest parade to me. Dripsey Community Association was active for many years but it declined in the 1990s. In the late nineties, informal discussions were held amongst interested people in the local community in Dripsey National School with a view to a party in the year 2000. Leo was in the 'thick of planning'. He notes that there were thirty at the first meeting. Through planning, the party did materialise in the year 2000. The overall result was the revitalisation of the community association. Following that event, Donal O'Riordan proposed a St Patrick's Day parade, the world's shortest in length for the book of *Guinness World Records*, from the Lee Valley pub (now closed) to the Feeney's Weigh Inn. Gardaí measured the route and sent away the data to the records people.

The parade has been held every year bar the year of the foot and mouth. Leo tells me that in more recent years people have come from the United States to see the parade. Leo O'Sullivan was chairman of the Community Association for a time. The present chairperson is Mary O'Mahony from Acres, Dripsey. A fun day is held every year in early September to include a barbeque and treasure hunt behind Feeney's Pub. The association is in the process of building a new community centre.

Dripsey Community Association are also concerned about the 300/400 houses to be built in Upper Dripsey. Seven districts are zoned residential under the Blarney electoral area 2005 local area plan in the Cork County Development Plan. An upgrade of the sewage system is needed to accommodate such developments. Water towers need to be built, as well a storm drains.

Representatives of Dripsey Community Association at Dripsey's Family Fun Day. Left to right: Donal O'Riordan, Ben Philpott, Paul Maher, Valerie O'Riordan, Rachel Deakin, Darren Hurley, Tomas Ryan, Mary O'Mahony and Leo O'Sullivan.

Dripsey Vintage Rally, 17 March 2008. Left to right: John Manley, Dave O'Callaghan, Pat Lehane, Jean O'Callaghan, Colman Cotter, Marie Cotter, and Paul Cotter with a 1979 John Deere.

It is interesting to see how history is repeating itself in terms of housing development in the Dripsey area. In 1899, Cork County Council came into being and encountered a housing crisis just like in the early years in Celtic Tiger Ireland. During the first decade of the twentieth century, many farm labourers needed housing. At the same time, it was claimed that the system of building a single cottage on land acquired from a farmer with the largest acreage in any given townland was inadequate to meet demand. It was further thought that erecting cottages in groups and each on an acre of land would do much to solve the housing shortage. In 1906, Cork County Council agreed to build four such groups named model villages at Bishopstown, Clogheen, Dripsey and Tower. Dr Barter of St Anne's Hydro was prepared to give an acre for each house built in Tower. The three others were restricted to a quarter acre.

The scheme for Dripsey began in 1910 and comprised sixteen cottages. Cork County Council acquired the land from Maurice Ring of Lismahane. The scheme was officially named Dripsey Model Village. In 1911, fourteen of the houses were allocated to farm labourers and two cottages to non-farm labourers. In the late 1950s, the French firm involved in the construction of Inniscarra Reservoir, on completion of their contract, offered their spacious and comfortable mass hut to the people of the Model Village. They sold it for £200. Dripsey Muintir na Tíre had the money and willingness to purchase the hut. A landowner in the village gave land for its reconstruction. But the project did not materialise. In 1960, however, Mill Rovers Dramatic Society took up the generous offer of the landowner when a grotto to Our Lady was blessed by the parish priests on 15 August 1960.

Eileen O'Connell (*née* O'Callaghan) was born in 1914 and grew up in one of the original Model Village houses in Dripsey. Her mother was Ellen Clohessy and her grandfather on her mother's side was Pat Clohessy who was a carder at Dripsey Woollen Mills. Pat's family originally came from the Midleton area in East Cork. There were eleven in his family, all girls.

Eileen O'Connell's father was Dan O'Callaghan who was a journeyman harness maker from Clondrohid, north west of Macroom, who met Eileen's mother on his travels. Eileen's grandfather on her father's side was Mick O'Callaghan who was a dairy farmer from Iniskeane.

Model Village Houses, Dripsey, *c.*1911. (*Cork City Library*)

O'Connell marriage photo, 1940. Left to right: Elizabeth O'Connell, Pat McElroy (father of Helen Feeney of The Weigh Inn), Jimmy O'Connell (best man), Denis O'Connell (groom), Eileen O'Connell (bride, in hat) and Lily Farrelly (Eileen's sister). (*O'Connell family*)

In 1911, Eileen O'Connell's parents Ellen and Dan moved into one of the Model Village houses in Dripsey. There is no library record of who lived in the original sixteen cottages. Each cottage had three bedrooms, a kitchen and half an acre of land. Many of the applicants previous to the Model Village resided in and around Dripsey Woollen Mills in a line of workmen's houses or cabins. Eileen, now ninety-three years of age, is in great health and possesses a great memory. She provides the majority of the names of the 1911 residents and tells of her time growing up and her life in Dripsey. Eileen notes of her earliest memories:

We were a large family. I had five brothers and two sisters: Bridie, Michael, Patrick, John, Lily, Ted and Joe. My younger brother John is still alive, aged eighty-three. When I was fifteen I went to work in Dripsey Woollen Mills as a darner. A girl came over from England to help us with invisible mending. I spent ten years in the mills and enjoyed working there. We started at 8.30a.m. and finished at 6p.m. when the hooter sounded. Lunchtime was between one and two. I worked as a darner but also did a lot of 'birling' or taking knots out of the cloth. I remember working with Eileen Brennan, Catherine Long, Hannah Noonan and Nora Gillman. They made beautiful blankets and serges for the men's suits. I got 15s a week when I started. I finished up at 25s a week.

Eileen O'Connell, September 2007
(picture: Kieran McCarthy)

I remember the men in the mill used to go for a pint and play cards in Dripsey. They enjoyed a few songs in the local pub. There was platform dancing nearby in Kilcolman and in Lower Dripsey. We also used to cycle to go dancing in the hall in Berrings. I used to dance with Steve McCarthy from Donoughmore. You know many a girl met her man sitting on a stone waiting to be asked to dance! I think my love of dancing was passed on to my daughter Helen and son-in law Jimmy, who have won many trophies for set dancing and ballroom dancing through the years. This summer, they went platform dancing in Laharn Cross in Lombardstown, six miles from Mallow. Dancing there has been organised every summer in recent years.

I got married to Denny O'Connell in 1940 who also worked in the mill. His family rented a dairy farm nearby from the Kellehers who were in Myshall [Meeshal on the OS map]. The O'Connells originally came from Ovens. I stopped working at the mill when I got married in 1940. Denny carried on at the mills until 1980. When we got married in 1940, Denny and I moved into one of the newer Model Village houses. Eight more houses had been built around 1930 on the Aghabullogue side. The road through the Model Village is the dividing line of Aghabullogue and Inniscarra parishes. Denny and I had two boys and two girls: James, Dan, Helen and Betty. Three of them married Millstreet people; Helen married Jimmy Kelleher and Betty and James married brother and sister Paddy and Noreen Golden. Dan went to Switzerland where he now lives.

Next door to my original family home (No.1) at the top of the village were Jerry, Hannah and Nora Noonan (No.2). Jerry was a carpenter by trade. The Noonans were good friends with Miss Lizzie Wheldon who was a dressmaker from Sunday's Well. Next door at No.3 to the Noonans were Jack and Julia Murphy (*née* Mahony). Both worked in the mills. Above that lived Matt and May Galvin (*née* O'Brien). They had four in their family. Neilus and Brigid O'Callaghan (*née* Delaney) lived at No.5 where they ran the local shop. They had two children, Denis and Ina. Next, at No.6, were Jack and Nonie McCarthy who had three in their family – Annie, Mary and 'Téad'. After the McCarthys, at No.7 were Peter and Sarah Coughlan who had three sons and one daughter. Peter senior was a ploughman by trade but his family all worked in the woollen mills. At No. 8 were John and Mary Burns and they had one daughter. My brother Ted and his wife Joan moved into the house after John and Mary passed away. Ted and Joan had two girls, Eileen and Marie.

Moving on to the second row of eight houses, affectionately known as 'the top road', at No.9 lived the Magniers who had one daughter called Nellie. Nellie married Bill Murray and they continue to live at No.9 with their family.

At No.10 were the Hallinans. Paddy Hallinan and his wife Joan (*née* Walsh) were from Grenagh and raised a family of seven. Next door at No.11 lived John Michael O'Brien and his wife Cathy (*née* Brennan) who had three in their family, Tommy, Dan Joe and Mary. At No.12 lived John Michael's sister Madge and her husband Dick Leonard who had two boys, Freddie and Tommy. May Galvin from No.4 was a sister to John Michael

Above left: Model Village, 2007.

Above right: Timothy O'Shea, Model Village Dripsey, September 2007.

Above left: Dripsey Pipe Band, 1936. Back row, left to right: Jim Long, Michael O'Brien, J. Tonge, Bill Murray, Bill Galvin, Dan McCarthy, Brian O'Connor, Paddy O'Callanan, Dan T. Murphy, Paddy O' Shean and Jim Noonan. Front row, left to right: Matty Galvin, Dan Collins, Timmy O'Shea, Dick Leonard, Willie Murphy and Jack Manley. (*Weigh Inn Pub, Dripsey*)

Above right: Dripsey Woollen Mills hurling team, *c.*1950. (*Timothy O'Shea*)

and Madge. Jim Noonan lived at No. 13. Pat and Kit O'Shea (*née* O'Mahony) lived at No. 14. Beside them at No. 15 lived Kit's sister Bina and her husband Willie Murphy, and they had two in their family. The final house, No. 16, was the home of Johnny and Julia O'Mahony (*née* O'Shea). Johnny was a brother to Kit in No. 14 and Bina in No. 15. Johnny's wife Julia was a sister to Paddy O'Shea in No. 14. Their brother Timmy still lives in the village today.

Timothy O'Shea was born in 1919 and went to Dripsey National School. He was raised in the Model Village at No. 16. His father was Pat O'Shea from Aghabullogue and his mother was Mary O'Mahony from Passage. He worked in the mills from the age of fourteen right until 1974. Down through the years, he worked in the carding and spinning department. Timothy notes:

In the mill, I reported to the foreman Jack Manley. He was the head carder and spinner. He lived nearby in mill house in Dysert. All the staff were like one big family. I remember working with Dan Horgan, Bill Murray and Paddy Callaghan. They were all band men. It was a very happy place to work.

A number of employees at the mills, Barry Galvin and Timmy Murphy, set up a band. They met at the big beech tree outside the mills during the summertime. The Band Room was nearby in a disused garage. I remember we had an oil lamp as a light. I joined the band at the age of fifteen and a half. I learned to play the drums initially.

Jim Long, the Pipe Major, came out every Sunday from Church Street in the City. I later learnt to play the chanter, a form of bagpipes, from the Pipe Major. We had several route marches on the road every month. On a fine frosty morning, the people in the countryside would come out to listen to the music. On New Year's Eve, we played out the old year and welcomed in the new. Every March, we would parade to Dripsey Ambush Memorial for the remembrance ceremonies.

I spent five years with them until 1939. They were five good years travelling to sports days around County Cork. In North Cork we played in places such as Donoughmore, Bweeng, Nead, Banteer, Castlemagner, Kilbrin and at Kanturk Show. In West Cork, we went to Rosscarbery and Kilmichael. Sports days were a major part of community life during the war years.

In 1939, I moved into hurling for Inniscarra. I was part of the team that won the Cork Championships in 1942, 1945 and 1947. We played some great matches. I also hurled with the mill team, which was an inter-firm team. We won the cup the first time we entered around 1947. We didn't enter anymore! I remember we played Thompsons in the final. Some of the lads on my team were Jackie Connell, Dan Maher, Micheal Sheehan, Mick Noonan, Tommy O'Brien and Dan Jo O'Brien.

I joined the FCA during the war years in the early 1940s. At that stage they were called the LDF. We trained in a tin shed in Upper Dripsey. We went to places such as Kilworth, Kinsale and Youghal for target practice. Captain (Gar) Aherne from the city was the training officer. Apart from family pictures, the two important pictures I have on the walls in the house are of my 47th Battalion. I'm in the centre in the front row. The battalion covered the north side of the city and also mid-Cork. The southside and surrounding region was the 48th Battalion. We were runners up in an all-army FCA shooting championships in 1957. Most of the lads involved were from the city and travelled out for training. In the second picture is Kevin Boland the then Minister for Defence and me. I won the individual category for shooting in the same 1957 championships.

In terms of Tim's story, there are history lessons to be learned. We learn that Dripsey Woollen Mills were very much at the heart of people's memories in Dripsey and in the wider region. We learn about the band and its travels and the importance of the sports days during the Second World War. We learn about the FCA and the hurling. However, we also learn how certain aspects become engrained in people's memories. Tim touches upon ideas of pride and identity. He talks about the idea of inheritance and memories and talents being passed down.

19. A JIMMY NOONAN PRODUCTION

Jimmy Noonan wrote into my column and added to the historical profile of social life in the Model Village Dripsey:

My first memory was the evening of my mother's removal. It was Christmas Eve 1939 and I was six. But at the height of the grief, I wanted to go to Cork to see Santa in Murray's. I remember my aunt Rose who was over from London on holiday. She attended the funeral in scarlet because she didn't have black with her and didn't expect a funeral.

My grandparents were originally from the Ballyvourney area. My grandmother was a domestic economy teacher in St Marie's of the Isle, Cork. My grandfather was a coachbuilder for Johnson and Perrotts. They met in Cork and came out first to live in Berrings and then came to the Model Village when the new houses were built in the 1910s. Our house was No.2. It was the card-playing house. As a child, I remember watching them playing cards at home. If they were short a player I was put in. I still play cards at least four times a week in Togher, Bishopstown, Coachford and Clondrohid.

Our house and Carrolls at No.1 were used as storehouses while the rest of the Model Village houses were being built. There was a well in the backyard between the cottages. I also remember the pump on the Kilmurray Road that had pure crystal water. There was a barrel under the downpipe that provided water for washing.

My father Jerry 'Darb' Noonan was in the Old IRA. He served in the Irish Army during the Emergency years. He was in Tralee when my mother died in 1939. My grandfather died in the same year. I had two aunts; Hannah who was darner in Dripsey Woollen Mill and Nora who worked on the looms. They were also in Cumann na mBan. They collected foods from the local farmers for fellows that were on the run.

At fourteen, I got a carpentry apprenticeship with Danny Sweeney. Danny was from Aghabullogue and we paid him £30 for the seven-year apprenticeship. In the apprenticeship deed, you could not smoke, drink, roll a dice or be abusive. I called him 'Sir'. I did five and a half years and then left. At that time, my father was working with Jimmy and John Breen, builders in Whitechurch. I got a job with them and it was my first paid job. I got £8 10s per week. It was eight to six every day with a half day every Saturday. The job took me around Whitechurch, Bweeng, Carrignavar and Templemichael. I spent seven to eight years working with Breens.

I paid £3 for digs in Carrignavar. I came home on a Saturday evening. I cycled from Carrignavar to Cork and paid a shilling to put my bicycle on top of the roof of the bus to Dripsey. The bike was second hand and I got it from Jack Healy's on MacCurtain

Street. My aunt paid £3 and 10s for the bike. I eventually progressed to a motorbike and came home every night. My next job was with Mr Hurley who was building houses in the 1940s in the city. In the mid-fifties, I worked on Inniscarra dam for two years. I worked on putting up timber shutters, types of moulds for the mass concrete poured into them. It was fast-setting cement. The foreman was from Bandon and he was secretary of the union there. I gave him my subscription. I remember working on the coffer dam, the wall to keep the River Lee out of the building site. During the quieter days, we spent a few hours playing cards in the out of reach places in the dam!

I worked with Patsy Shea on the extension of the North Cathedral. I then worked with P.J. Hegartys on the Cork Milling Co. and the Malting House in Ballincollig. I worked with Hornibrooks for nearly fourteen years. I remember doing repair works on Hayfield Manor by UCC. Mrs White Musgrave had repairs done to the house every year. Mr White gave a tip to everyone who worked on the house. The family was great friends with Liam MacLiomoir. The Whites published his work in London.

Since the age of seven, I have had a love of theatre. I remember being brought to *Little Red Riding Hood* in Cork Opera House. Ignatius Comerford was the Dame. That show has stayed in my mind all my life. It gave me a yearning for showbusiness.

I eventually did eighteen seasons, May to September, with the New Irish Players in the town hall in Killarney. I also went on to do a lot of pantos in Cork at the Fr Mathew Hall, Sunday nights at the Opera House, plays at Catholic Young Men's Society and St Francis Hall. I also worked with Duffy's Circus from 1982 to 1999.

At home, fit-up theatres used to perform in the field next to No. 3 the Model Village. They put on plays, variety concerts and talent competitions. There were Sunny Mirts, Purcells and Cullens. Sullivans came to Dripsey Bridge and the McFaddens to Peake. They all had a different play and variety show every night. They were wonderful people the way they kept the shows going.

There was a dramatic society in Dripsey when I was a child but it folded after three to four shows. I started Mill Rover Dramatic Society in the fifties. Most people in the society worked in the mills. We used to meet in my kitchen. We eventually got a shed from Maggie and Mary Ford of Dripsey Cross to rehearse. The FCA also used to train in that shed. The shed later became a grain store for a piggery. There was a big group of us involved in Mill Rovers: Josie Flynn, Synod Galvin, Maire Galvin, Mary Murray (O'Sullivan), Denis Noonan, Michael Sheehan, Ned Sexton, Denis Murphy, Hannie Murphy, Peter Buckley, Ann Buckley, Dinny Buckley, Tadgh Buckley, Billy Welsh, Olan O'Sullivan (who did the door), Mary Desmond, Mary O'Brien, Sean Noonan, Peter Coughlan, Jack Murphy, Maudie Barrett, Loretto Barrett, Michael Kitin, and John McSweeney. We were successful in attracting the local people. It was great having their support.

Left: Jimmy Noonan, September 2007.

Below: Members of the local community at the opening of the Model Village grotto, 1960. (*Tess Begley*)

We set ourselves the task of raising funds for the church and for Fr Dan Hallissey. We aimed to raise money for repairs to the church in Inniscarra and repairs to Berrings church. The original plan was also to try and raise money for a grotto in the Model Village as part of the Marian Year in 1954. At that time, the local canon disagreed believing that all the grottos going up would soon be ruins across the Irish landscape. In 1960, it was given the go-ahead. Jim Cooney, who had a forge in Ballyshonin, did the railings and Neffs on Fr Mathew Street, Cork (then Queen Street) did the statue.

20. ONE DAY AT A TIME

Margaret Baker has been actively researching the history of the Dripsey area and her family over several years. The Murphys on her mother's side and the Brennans on her father's side have been part of Dripsey for a long time. In 1912, just east of Dripsey village on the north side of the Cork road, Jerry Murphy purchased two acres of land. Jerry and his wife Mary were a self-supporting family, growing all kinds of fruits and vegetables that fed the family and generated income when sold in local villages and towns. Chickens and eggs were sold to add to the small family business. A horse and cart was kept to deliver the goods.

A small income was also derived from the sale of rock from the rock/slate face circling the property on the north side. Locals used the material from the site to build and roof local houses. At one time a road ran along by the rock and was probably used as access to the quarry. The old rock is still there today providing an interesting background for flowers. This rock is covered with wild bushes, providing shade to the many nesting birds and animals living there.

The Murphy family lived in an old stone dwelling called Quarry Cottage at the side of the road. Mary and Jerry Murphy had three children. They were named Jerry, Mick and Helena. Jerry emigrated to England where he married and raised a family. When Jerry Murphy senior passed away the property was left to his son Mick with provision in the will to ensure his wife Mary could live out her life in the house. Grandchildren, great-grandchildren and great-great-grandchildren of Mary and Jerry Murphy now occupy four houses on the Quarry estate. In recent years Quarry Cottage has been dismantled to make way for a new house. The stones were shared between various family members and neighbours. Mick Murphy, one of the brothers, stayed on at the old homestead but never married. He was the local postman for many years. For twenty-three years he delivered the mail, riding a high bicycle across the countryside in all kinds of weather. For those twenty-three years, he never missed a day's work.

Helena Murphy married Michael Brennan. Helena is Margaret Baker's mother. Margaret informs me that the Brennans go back centuries. A Michael Brennan worked in the paper mill in the 1700s. In a 1914 *Cork Examiner* photograph of staff at Dripsey Woollen Mills, there are Madge, Julia and Danny Brennan. Danny was Margaret's uncle; Julia and Madge were her aunts. Her grandfather Daniel Brennan senior was a shoemaker. Daniel went to America several times but always came back to live and work in Ireland. The original Brennan homestead is now a ruin, near the heart of Dripsey

Helena Murphy,
Dripsey, *c.* 1950.
(*Margaret Baker family
collection*)

Margaret started in Dripsey National School in 1944 with Master Twohig and
Mrs McCarthy. She notes:

> My school years were a very happy time – I loved Irish and attended the local Gaelic
> League, which was organised by Michael Ó Murchú. He provided extra tuition in Irish
> one evening a week. I remember when we were ten to fourteen years of age, we put on
> a play and won a cup in Coachford called the Coir Cois Laoi.

When Margaret left Dripsey school she attended the Cork School of Commerce
for some time but dropped out to go to work. She got a job at Dripsey Woollen
Mills and recalls:

The mills were close by and we cycled to work each morning, returned home for lunch and then went back to finish the afternoon shift. The loud mill hooter echoed down the valley at 8.30a.m., 1.00p.m., 2.00p.m. and 5.30p.m. It was a signal to start, go for lunch, return to work after lunch and go home. Most people in the area out of primary school at that time went to work in the mill if not going on to secondary school.

There was a great sense of community there. I had many friends. There was Maudie Barrett, Joan Shea, Eileen Crowley, Peg Shea and Joe McCarthy to name a few. I remember winding bobbins for the looms. We were nearly all local people from Dripsey, the Model Village, Aghabullogue, Coachford and Magoola. Staff could purchase blankets and material, which you could then bring to dressmakers and knitters in the region. I remember the tailors Mr McCarthy and Denny Carroll, Lizzie Weldon, a dressmaker who lived in Sunday's Well in the city, and the Sheehans in Macroom. We could get material for clothing and pay so much a week from our pay cheque. That was a great help and many people bought blankets this way as well. And they were beautiful warm blankets. I remember having a jacket and skirt made with a grey and white check patterned material.

My friend and I were waiting for a bus at Dripsey Cross on a Saturday and one of the mill designers came by and admired our outfits. Both of us had new suits made of mill tweed. My friend had a different pattern to mine. 'You are modelling our products and they look great', he said. Some people made small bags from waste material in the mill to hold lunch boxes and a vacuum flask.

I made a lot of friends there. There was great camaraderie; we went to dances and hurling matches. There was a Dripsey Mills Hurling Team. Apart from a small few, all of them worked at the mill. Hurling practice and games took place in the big field just north of Dripsey Bridge at the east end of the river. It was known and is known as 'the Inch'. This field belonged and still belongs to the Ryan Family, Agharinagh House. Hurlers changed under the arch of the bridge as did Inniscarra Hurling Team and swimmers in the summer.

BEYOND DRIPSEY

21. EXPLORATIONS IN AGHARINAGH

One aspect I love dabbling in is the archaeology of the Lee Valley; the human artefacts of a past age now long gone and all very much part of forgotten histories and memories. Only for the monuments' existence, insights into the society that constructed them would disappear forever. I feel we now live though in an era where the stature of the monument is important but we know very little about its reason for construction and its associated cultural meanings.

Many of the local residents I have met in my travels in the valley had limited knowledge of what era their local archaeological monuments were from and their general function in society. Many of the sites are kept because they have been there so long. Many of the sites I encountered are deemed mysterious entities that local people do not want to mess with or engage with. I have heard a myriad of bad luck stories that have been passed down through generations.

Patsy Regan introduced me to the earliest of Inniscarra parish's monuments, a stone row in Agharinagh townland, Dripsey. The row comprised five stones measuring a metre and a half on average in height, possibly dating to Bronze Age Ireland, around 5,000 years ago. Two of the stones have collapsed whilst three remain upright in three slots in the ground packed by smaller stones at the base. The stone is of limestone composition, which is not a common stone in this sandstone region. It has a north–south alignment and is located on a western facing hill, 130 feet over sea level. Standing stones and stone rows are part of the ritual tradition, identity and power structures of Bronze Age societies. It is known generally Bronze Age people lived in thatch-like cabins cooking over fulachtí fia.

Patsy, originally from Mawmore between Bandon and Iniskeen, dabbles in researching the past. He is a farmer with a deep and particular interest in the land, its geology, its shapes and form. His farmhouse overlooked the Dripsey River as it made its final journey towards Inniscarra Reservoir. We walked the land and could see how glaciation as well as the elements had eroded into the underlining sandstone rock. In terms of human monuments, the stone row he brought me to is not marked on the current Ordnance Survey map. Many of them are but this was an exception to the rule. From the map and the county archaeological inventory for mid-Cork, stone rows are not as common in this region as standing stones and fulacht fiadh sites, which are abundantly marked on the map.

Archaeological monuments are what are deemed material culture. They are tangible elements of the past plus they are the only aspects left of a constructed ritual. The fact that stone rows like that in Agharinagh have persisted for 5,000 years

Patsy Regan at Agharinagh Stone Row, Dripsey, Autumn 2007.

speaks volumes on how society passes its heritage from one generation to another.
Some of these monuments could also have been re-used in other times.

Human monuments from any era are a form of expression. They are signs, signposts and symbols. Through the passing of time all that is left is a by-product of a
long-forgotten culture. The only link is that they are people still living and farming
in the area – as they have been doing for 5,000 years. One is dealing with vast tracts
of time. Archaeologists have allotted a time to the Bronze Age based on excavation
work and the introduction and use of Bronze through to the introduction of iron,
which spans 2,00 years, from *c*.2500 BC to *c*.500 BC.

Knowledge distribution, human and cultural evolution, diversity, culture and
nature, and the importance of the individual and even the group are all key threads
to think about when studying a place, whether in AD 2010 or in 2500 BC.

With regard to the stone row at Agharinagh – when and why was it was built?
What is its cultural meaning? How valued was this site by the local community of
its time? Was there a sizeable local population in Bronze Age times? What was the

extent of farming? How much of the forested landscape was cut down? What were the grazing patterns and 'fieldscapes'? How do these monuments fit into the every-day routine of life? How did people negotiate the basics of life and death? What were the power or family structures?

We know that through creating monuments like Agharinagh stone row they, like us, had a huge interest in the power of myth and even nostalgia. Memories are bound up in archaeological monuments. Societies of the past preserved their histories in stone. I have no doubt that people would have chatted about life whilst constructing such monuments.

The creation of a cultural monument is also dependent on the depth of human emotion and self-belief structures. The community that built such monuments must have already been living in the area. One may decide to build the monument in a few minutes but monuments such as Agharinagh stone row needed some type of mental planning. Cultural and communal considerations had to be taken into account. The chosen landscape must have meant something to the community before construction took place. There was a pre-existing bond with nature. To decide to erect a monument, one must have an image of the landscape and a desire to attempt to reshape it.

22. ALWAYS BE PREPARED … AND YOUR TIME WILL COME

Further east along the road from Dripsey to Inniscarra is Griffin's Garden Centre. I'm always of the opinion that everyplace has a past, and even a recent past is important in the forging of an area's future. The great aspect about a garden centre is that there are usually multiple landscapes on display. The myriad of paths, flowers, statues and water features create a maze and provide a sense of exploration and adventure.

The owner of Griffin's Garden Centre is Margaret Griffin. Her journey in creating the business reveals a lot about the heritage of Dripsey and the legacy and input of the Griffin family. In Richard Griffith's land valuation of Agharinagh townland in the early 1850s, Michael Griffin is recorded as owning a house and garden. The area comprised thirty-seven perches. The land was valued at 5s and the building at 15s. The total value was £1. Micheal Griffin was a first cousin of Margaret's grandfather Denis. A total of 139 occupiers of other houses are also noted in the area in the 1850s. The high population in one townland was connected to Dripsey Paper Mills and many of the houses were probably part of Blackpool, an area that developed as a result of the mills but has now long since disappeared. At the turn of the twentieth century the family also established Griffin's Public House in Upper Dripsey. It later became known as the Weigh Inn.

Above left: Margaret Griffin, September 2007.

Above right: Griffin family photo, *c.*1925. Front row, left to right: Denis Griffin (senior), Hannie Griffin, Denis Griffin (junior), Josie Griffin and Margaret Griffin. (*Griffin family collection*)

Margaret's grandfather Denis Griffin (senior) was born an only child in Lower Dripsey near the former West County Bar. Margaret's grandmother was also Margaret Griffin (*née* O'Mahony) who was a midwife in Dripsey for years and was from Dromgownagh, a townland on the banks of Inniscarra Reservoir. Her father Denis was born in January 1916. He worked on the Lee Scheme for a while, then in insurance and then in the building trade. He was very involved with Inniscarra GAA. Margaret remembers her father after work walking from home to the pitch in Ballyanley and back again after training, a distance of a couple of miles. Denis trained the Inniscarra Hurling Team in 1965, the year they won the cup. A local man from Berrings wrote a song to commemorate the victory. Denis was also involved in the Gaelic League. He travelled around with friends in an open-backed truck and put on 'shows' for the general public especially in West Cork. Denis was MC. He retired early and worked on creating a mini garden centre at home.

Margaret grew up in Dripsey. She got a scholarship from the Kellogg foundation after her Leaving Cert to study horticulture at Termonfeckin Horticultural College in County Louth. She went on to work in Slough in England for six months. Being a home bird she returned home to Dripsey and looked to start up her own business. She trained as a florist under Pauline O'Callaghan (Ballincollig) by working at The Flower Shop on Oliver Plunkett Street. She cycled into the city to work every day.

Griffin's Pub, Upper Dripsey, *c.* 1920. (*The Weigh Inn, Dripsey*)

Griffin's Garden Centre, Dripsey.

Margaret bought land from the Cotters nearby her home in Dripsey for the purpose of setting up a mini garden centre. She notes:

> The land was on the site of the garden of Dripsey House. The gate to the land was near three little cottages. I became good friends with Mollie Lynch who lived across the way. Mollie knew a lot about the area and we had long chats about who lived there. That is why we have snippets of history on the walls of the garden centre. The history does add to a place. Mollie remembered the beautiful gardens of Dripsey House and the students who attended the agricultural college set up by Peggy Bowen-Colthurst. Mollie remembered the trainee agricultural students from English colleges in long dresses and aprons working in the gardens of Dripsey House. The big house is now gone but the outhouses are part of the Galvin's Cork Powerboat and Ski Club in Lower Dripsey.
>
> I remember passing the site of the garden centre on the way to national school. I remember the rabbits. It's an image that has stayed in my mind. I liked the place. I bought five acres initially with possibilities for a further extension of five acres. I worked on the planning in the early 1980s and we opened in 1986. The three cottages we converted into a mini shop. We opened in an economic recession and amidst massive emigration. Dripsey Woollen Mills closed its doors in 1988.

In the beginning Griffin's Garden Centre was a tough venture. The design for the gardens was based on Dripsey House and its outhouses. The current arches in the built structure reflect that. The overall design was based on my own ideas with support from English and New Zealand consultants. We created an orbital route that was not impersonal but a bit cosy in its approach. People need atmosphere if they come to shop especially if gardening is a recreational hobby. Starting off, the weekends were the busiest times. It was quiet during the weekdays. Today there is even trade despite the growth in the shopping-mall culture. Our clientele are from the general outer city area. During the Christmas period, the bulk of the people come from Kinsale and Carrigaline. That being said we also get a lot of people coming from Kerry.

It is a nice drive out. It is a very relaxing place with water, colour and flowers. It has a nice ambience. The stone and timber create that ambience. People like the place for its natural features. The water fountains attract adults but especially kids. The designs are based on having fun. We do monitor people's reactions to the various displays in the garden centre and change aspects around regularly.

People travel on average nineteen miles to get here. People meet at the centre's Spinning Wheel Restaurant instead of town. For children, we have a slug club twice a month for five to eleven year olds. Local nature is very important to us. The Bat Society gives public talks as well as other societies that promote wildlife such as owls, falcons and foxes. We recently had a talk on the wildlife value of our trees. I am also very proud of the fact that Griffin's Garden Centre has been the winner of the Garden Centre of Ireland three times, in 1997, 1999 and 2000. I do wish to thank my staff for their continuing hard work and support. The support of local people is very important to me.

23. COUNTRYMEN AND EDUCATI
DRIPSEY NATIONAL SCHOOL

Moving from Upper to Lower Dripsey towards Cork, ne
Centre, is Dripsey National School. Schools are great places ιο expiore an area's
past, especially because they collect records, photos of students and roll books. At
this juncture in particular I wish to point to the work of the Schools' Folklore
Collection, compiled in 1938.

In 1937/38, with the help of the Department of Education, a collection of folklore
was initiated throughout the national schools of the twenty-six counties. Teachers
and children alike were asked to approach their traditions as if 'it is the first time
and perhaps the last time they will be recorded'. Children were encouraged to
speak to the oldest living members of their family and their community. The work
was supervised by teachers, written up in copybooks and submitted to the Folklore
Commission. In the end 4,574 official notebooks were returned to the commission.
This fascinating archive is now in the custody of the Department of Irish Folklore
at UCD, and a microfilm copy of the County Cork material has been available
for consultation at the Reference Department in Cork County Library for several
years. The collection is known as the Schools' Manuscripts Folklore Collection.

Dripsey National School class, c.1950. (*Margaret Baker*)

Nancy O'Donovan, Vice-principal, Sheila Desmond, teacher and Gerry Dineen, Principal, Dripsey National School.

Ruins of late-nineteenth-century school, Magoola townland, Dripsey.

A number of themes can be viewed in the Dripsey National School copybook. Local folklore, humorous stories, riddles, signs of bad weather, and past ways of life such as local farming practices are all discussed. In particular, early education in the Dripsey area is explored. Mary O'Callaghan from Agharinagh interviewed Patrick Hanlon, Model Village, Dripsey. She writes that in olden times near Kilmurray (north), there was a kind of schoolhouse. It comprised of a close hedge of whitethorn about eight feet high, roofed with branches and sods. In the schools, there was only one teacher, a man called Mr Herlihy from Berrings. In the depth of winter when it was too cold for outdoor school it was carried on in the farmers' houses and the teacher lodged in the house that he was teaching in. The teacher's pay was only his food and a penny a day. The subjects taught were English, Irish, history and arithmetic. The pupils had no books, pens or pencils. The only way they had of writing was on slates. They used to sit on súgán chairs in front of a blackboard.

Junior and senior infants 2007/08. Back row, left to right: Aoife O'Gorman, Julia McDonald, Eoin Brennan, Sarah Healy, Kirstin Hickey, Rory O'Sullivan, Mark O'Connell, Shann Burke, Liah Dineen. Middle row, left to right: Darragh Sheehan, David Hogan, Kayla Noonan, Ellie O'Connell, Kellie O'Donovan, Jack Galvin, Tom Griffin, Caroline Barrett and Lucy Maher. Front row, left to right: Adam Lynch, Aaron Cotter, Jessica Cotter, Ayla O'Sullivan, Nicola Forde and Christopher Fehilly.

Noah Sisk, who was thirteen, interviewed the local postmaster, Mortimer Kelleher, who noted a school from the 1800s in the area. It was situated halfway between Upper and Lower Dripsey in the field near a Mrs Morrissey. The school became a ruin eventually amongst other houses located in Blackpool. It is said that in the school in Blackpool there was a teacher by the name of Mr O'Reilly, known by the nickname of 'German'. The children he taught used to write with pencils. The teacher also used to visit houses outside school hours to give private tuition. Mr O'Reilly was paid every three months and his salary was three or four shillings. He lived in his own house. A second teacher called Mr Cronin is also noted in Noah Sisk's notes.

In the 1880s a two-teacher school was built in Magoola near Lower Dripsey close to the Cork Road. The ruins of this school can still be seen. Michael Murphy and his wife Ann (*née* Delaney) taught there. They lived at Dripsey Cross, until the teachers' residence was built in Magoola. Michael Murphy retired in 1919. He was succeeded by his son Batt, who taught there until 1935. When the truce was signed in June 1921, the school in Magoola was overcrowded. When the troops vacated the military barracks which were situated across from the West County Inn, it was intended to move some of the scholars there. However, the barracks were burned down some days before the proposed move.

To relieve the overcrowding the infant classes were taught by Mrs Murphy in the teachers' residence. Mr James Ring remembers being taught there when he started school. Mr John Twohig was appointed as Principal to the school at Magoola early in 1936 and taught there until 1957. On 3 December 1939, the new school was opened and blessed by Bishop James Roche. When the building was begun it was to accommodate two teachers. Before it was completed pupil numbers had risen and the area intended for two teachers was divided into three classrooms. The builder was Jackie O'Leary from Donoughmore. The cost was £3,400. The site was bought from James Ring for £70. Pupil numbers dropped once more to require two teachers in the 1940s and '50s. Mr Twohig retired in the late 1950s and was succeeded by Mr Desmond.

Numbers rose gradually until it became a six-teacher school in 1983. There were two prefabs at that time and one teacher in a cloakroom. The extension was opened in September 1985. In 1993 Mr Desmond retired and went on to be ordained a priest. He is now a curate in Carriganima near Macroom. Mr Gerry Dineen succeeded Mr Desmond as Principal. In the meantime, some staff have changed and more added to deal with the changing face of education. Alongside its six teachers it now has three special needs assistants and a secretary. The school also benefits from the expertise of a visiting speech and drama teacher, and a music teacher. The school looks forward to continuing to educate and enrich the lives of the children of the Dripsey area for many years to come.

24. INNOCENT DAYS

This is the story of innocent days in the life of a small community, in the days before affluence and television, a community who worked hard, made their own entertainment and generally accepted the hardships of life.

Cork Independent, 'Our City, Our Town', 22 November 2007.

Lower Dripsey was and still is a small community, but it does have its own distinct identity. In fact that identity is established and reflected in the signs just past Inniscarra Waterworks on the Cork–Dripsey road. The local place names in Lower Dripsey on the north bank of the River Lee or Inniscarra Reservoir are pre-Norman or pre-Old-English colonisation. Dripsey, An Druibseach, 'the muddy river', is still evident when the river is in flood. There is Agharinagh or Achadh Rianach, which means 'Rianach's field'. Magoola is named after the Maighe Ghuaile clan who inhabited the area. Innislinga means 'Ling's Inch', an inch being a flat field by a river and the townland of Faha comes from 'flat field'.

At one time, Lower Dripsey had an RIC barracks, the Williams's Shop, Barry's Public House (later Murphy's and known as the 'long house') and the creamery. The Murphy family of Douglas Woollen Mills opened the first creamery in Lower Dripsey in 1934. Denis O'Leary from Lackaneen, Clondrohid, was manager until 1962. Denis qualified in 1926 and completed his training in Killowen Creamery, Bandon. He subsequently worked at various creameries in the Macroom area. He was affectionately known as 'the Manager'. As a result of his position in the community, he had a great knowledge of events in the wider world of County Cork. People came to him for advice and on many an occasion Denis assisted the local community in their endeavours. Mick Roche was the manager until the creamery closed in 1972.

The creamery was steam powered. Ned Ring, who had his own steam engine and thresher, was the boiler man. Jack Healy of Berrings took over that position in 1952 (until 1972 when the creamery closed). A Blackstone engine was also used. It was restored by John Carroll and exhibited at local steam rallies. The creamery yard was a colourful place every morning, with the horses and carts of fifty suppliers as well as tractors and trailers of the 1950s style. At the time milk was bought by the creamery at 1s 4d per gallon (the cost was nine cent in 2007). Today, approximately ten suppliers have survived in the wider catchment area. Tankers operated by Dairygold now collect the milk.

Left: 'The Manager', Denis O'Leary, Margaret O'Leary and John O' Leary. (*Joe McCarthy*)

Below: Swimming by the Lee. Back row: Charles O'Leary, Senan McCarthy, Jerry Cremin, Tadhg McCarthy, Jack Buckley. Front row: Pat Gilmore, Billy O'Cornell, Jerome O'Leary. (*Laurence Buckley*)

The five-hundredweight van was the most versatile mode of transport of the 1950s, taking churns to the creamery, families to Mass on Sunday and bonhams and young calves to Coachford fair. One local van used so often for maternity purposes became known as the 'ambulance'.

In 1941, the creamery was taken over by the Newmarket Dairies. The O'Leary family opened their shop selling groceries and hardware in 1938 and closed in 1991. Butter cost 2s 8d (17c in 2007) and ration was 1s 10d (€1.60 in 2007). Socialising changed with the seasons. In winter, Miss Murphy's shop behind the creamery was a popular haunt for games of rings and cards. Many an amusing incident took place when locals gathered in Thade Joe Burn's house. Summer saw open-air dancing at the platform next to the creamery. Bowls were played on the Magoola road. Tim Murphy of Magoola was the expert bowler and many from other counties working at the Lee Scheme joined in enthusiastically. In the creamery yard, games such as handball and pitch and toss were played. Swimming in the Lee near Fitzgibbon Bridge was a popular pastime on summer evenings.

Hurling was the popular sport. Playing with Inniscarra overshadowed everything else. Training took place in Ryan's Inch at Dripsey Bridge. Lower Dripsey produced fine hurlers such as Fr Timmy and Danny Murphy, two of the most skillful to play with Inniscarra. Both were on the 1947 team that won the Mid-Cork Championship. Danny later played with Ballincollig senior team and finished a long career playing with Éire Óg. He won an All-Ireland cross-country with Kildinan in 1943. Tadhg and Billy O'Connell of Magoola are also remembered, especially Bill's long puckouts and fine clearances.

The Twohig brothers Padraig, Chris and Seán were fine hurlers. Seán went on to play minor hurling with Cork. Patsy O'Connell won an All-Ireland minor medal with Cork. Henry O'Sullivan was an All-Ireland under-21 and county senior with University College Cork. Two other great men from Faha, Con O'Sullivan and Tim O'Mahony could always be depended upon to give sterling performances when the going got tough. Con O'Sullivan had a distinguished career on the rugby field, winning eight senior cup medals with Cork Con. Jerome O'Leary, running in the Blarney colours, had many successes, capped by a personal best when representing Ireland at White City, London in 1967.

Irish classes began in the local school in the early forties. Micheal Ó Riabhaigh, father of the well-known piper, was the first teacher, followed later by Micheal Ó Murchú. His pen name was 'An Gabha Gaelach' ('the Irish Blacksmith'). Dripsey Gaelic Players, a dramatic society, was formed and presented plays in many halls during lent. *Knocknagow*, *Arrah na Pogue* and *Autumn Fire* were among the outstanding plays, presented with full period costume hired from Burke's of Dublin.

Coachford Fete Ship, 1951. Back row: Paddy O'Mahony, Faha; Dick Morrissey; Tommy O'Brien; Jerome Coughlan; Fr Tim Murphy; Dick Carroll; Tim O'Mahony; Dinny O'Mahony; Eoin O'Sullivan; Nellie O'Mahony; Mary O'Callaghan; Paddy O'Mahony; Finbarr Barry-Murphy. Front row: Dan Brennan; Peggy Murphy; Joe McCarthy; Joan O'Mahony; Catherine O'Mahony; Con O'Mahony; Myra Galvin; Kitty O'Mahony; Peter Coughlan; Dan McCarthy; Pat Carroll; Miah Noonan. Tractor: Noel O'Mahony and unknown. In front are Dan O'Mahony and George Hall. (*Lower Dripsey families*).

The expertise of the stage was put to good use in 1950 when Dripsey entered the fancy dress at Coachford Fete, organised to raise funds for the new vocational school. A 'Circus Wedding' based on a wedding photograph of a member of the famous Duffy family on the *Cork Examiner* provided the inspiration. An open-air carriage, borrowed from Fordes Undertakers, Barrack Street, drawn by four grey horses and accompanied by many riders on horseback paraded through Coachford. Clowns joined in, led by Jimmy Murphy of Model Village, doing spectacular cartwheels to the amazement of the large crowd. In 1951 the inspiration came from another photograph in the *Cork Examiner*, this time of the SS *America*, then the fastest liner crossing the Atlantic. A tractor trailer fitted out by Dick Carroll in O'Mahony's farmyard at Faha resulted in a most convincing liner and it too was paraded through Coachford, towed by Noel O' Mahony driving his span-new Fordson Major tractor. Puck Fair was the theme in 1952.

25. IN SEARCH OF BILL WILLIAMS

The journey to penning this section began by investigating two unused and ruined petrol pumps at the side of the road in Lower Dripsey. They are reminders of a past enterprise but also in a sense, reminded me of archaeological monuments but of the modern kind.

Chatting with local residents, the name Bill Williams came to the forefront. Those I spoke to initially were able to paint a partial picture of the enterprise. The pumps were part of a garage and a shop was across the road. They also made suggestions and referrals to other people. After about half a dozen referrals the picture became clearer and I was more intrigued by the life and times of this man, who the local people held in such high esteem. Born in the 1890s, Bill Williams seemed to bring a twentieth-century freshness to the area.

Bill died in the 1960s, but I eventually caught up with his eighty-nine-year-old niece Oonagh, who has connections in Inniscarra and College Road. She was able to help me compose a clearer portrait of her uncle Bill Williams, and not only the petrol station and his shop but also his family roots. Oonagh was born in 1918 in Cork City. She went to primary and secondary school in Rochelle. She lived in Eudion, Castle Road, Blackrock. It is reputed that Quaker William Penn, founder of Pennsylvania, stayed in the then existing dwelling house while awaiting passage to America in the late seventeenth century. Oonagh's parents were Jack Williams, born in Dripsey and Ellen, *née* Cholorton Fitzgibbon, born in Kinsale. Jack was a brother to Bill. Jack had one of the oldest stockbroker–accountancy firms in the city on the South Mall. He had his office open at 8a.m. every morning. Oonagh married Francis O'Mahony from the city centre. He was an engineer. Oonagh inherited

Ruins of Williams petrol pumps, Lower Dripsey, 2007.

'the Studio' (now AIB) opposite UCC. The artist Harry Houchen designed and built it. When he died, his widow married an uncle on Oonagh's mother's side.

Oonagh's paternal grandmother Mary McDonald came from Galway, and Oonagh remembers her as an old lady who talked about being born just after the Famine. Oonagh's grandfather was John Williams, a Protestant from Dripsey. The story goes that generations back, way before the Famine, two men with surnames Williams and Burke quarrelled over ownership of land in Dripsey. The Williams family won. At one time they were involved in three houses in Dripsey. It is known that other branches of the family also had shops in County Cork, at Canon's Cross, Inniscarra, the Castle Hotel in Macroom (living in Coolcower) and at the Mills Inn in Ballyvourney.

Oonagh's grandfather John Williams had a shop in the Dripsey area. He also enjoyed fishing on the Lee. He died quite young from pneumonia. Subsequently, his wife was a widow for thirty years. John and Mary had twelve children; six boys and six girls. Oonagh could remember the vast majority of their names Sarah (the eldest), Jane, Francis (Fanny), Evalena (Eva), Rita, Lilian, John, James and Bill. Oonagh's father was christened John but was affectionately known as Jack.

The house in Dripsey became too small and so the family decided to build a larger house and to uproot the small shop, which was attached to Lower Dripsey. The new dwelling was a large structure with each member of the household having their own bedroom. It was deemed essential to have some other income besides the farm. Hence, the new house also had a shop attached at one side.

Above left: John Williams and Mary Williams (*née* McDonald), Lower Dripsey, *c.*1900. (*Oonagh O'Mahony*)

Above right: Ellen Williams, Ellen's friend and Oonagh Williams (married name O'Mahony), *c.*1935. (*Oonagh O'Mahony*)

Above left: Eva and Rita Williams, *c.*1915. (*Oonagh O'Mahony*)

Above right: The Williams family *c.*1915. Standing, Bill Williams. Middle row, left to right: Jane, Granny McDonald(?), Rita, Mary (mother). Front row, Eva and Lillian. (*Oonagh O'Mahony*)

On Oonagh's mother's side, her grandmother was Mary Fitzgibbon from Kinsale. When her husband died, she bought Dereen, a house a half-mile west of Coachford. She had seven children. Ellen was the youngest and became Oonagh's mother. Of the seven Fitzgibbon children, Bob and Neillie were the only two who stayed in Ireland. Bob eventually went off to war but never returned.

Oonagh had two options for entertainment in her youth; visit her relations in Dereen or visit those in Lower Dripsey. In the beginning Oonagh travelled out regularly by bus. She also used the Muskerry tram on occasion (before its closure in 1934). Occasionally her uncle Bill Williams might come in and collect her by car. He had one of the first cars in Dripsey. Oonagh remembers Bill to be a good-humoured man who told funny stories about local goings on. She recalls that one day, Bill brought a man, a water diviner, onto the land to search for a new well. The twigs started jumping and Bill subsequently created a pump near the kitchen of the house.

Bill nurtured in Oonagh a love for the land. He brought her to point-to-point races. They went shooting snipe. He taught her how to clean the rifle and how to aim by shooting at tins. Indeed, he had several rifles, so when visitors came they could join the shooting party. He brought Oonagh and other relatives to the seaside. All the family had an interest in art and the love of art is still enjoyed by Oonagh today.

In time, Bill inherited the local shop in Lower Dripsey from his father. Bill also ran a small farm and had about six cows. Bill had a man who worked full-time on the farm. His sister Lily had poultry. At one time, Bill tried pigs but they did not work out. Bill got on well with the local community to the extent that he was not interfered with during the Irish War of Independence.

The more I researched Bill's past the more I could see that his story is on the borders of remembering and forgetting. I seemed to encounter the very point where memory begins to fail and history sets in. So the following is a reconstruction based on a number of interviews with local people in Lower Dripsey. There are those who actually remember and met the man. There are also those who don't remember Bill but who have an interest in recovering their local heritage and who before my arrival gleaned their own information of Bill, which they kindly shared with me.

The Williams's shop was another icon in Lower Dripsey. The shop had two very large windows in front with a double wooden door between them. It was a long room with a mahogany counters running the full length of the room, one on the left and one on the right. At the back of the shop, there was a wrought-iron spiral staircase up to Bill Williams's office. Bill's sister Fanny helped out regularly in the shop. His other sister Lily Williams was much older than Bill and looked after the domestic products within the shop (such as pots and pans, and rolls of material). Lily often went to nearby Staigue Fort near Waterville, County Kerry for a break. She booked seats in the postal van for their transport and stayed in a small hotel.

Local woman Margaret Baker recalls of the Williams's shop:

I remember going down to Williams's Shop in Lower Dripsey as a young child. They sold everything: shoe leather, wool, sewing material, groceries, oil, petrol, meat and fish. If they hadn't an item in stock it would be ordered from Cork City. The haberdashery was on the right side of the shop with a copper measuring tape running at the inner edge of the counter for measuring cloth and ribbons. This is where they kept ladies' nylons, socks, handkerchiefs and all kinds of knick-knacks. And they had a small wood stove in the centre by the wall. On the other counter at the back end they had a large meat slicer that was always spotlessly clean and shining and well serviced. Bill was the only one allowed to use or clean it for safety reasons. In the centre of that counter they had a huge metal scoop for weighing flour. The flour was put into the scoop and the appropriate heavy metal weights were put on the platform to weigh it.

Further on there was a shining scale for weighing tea and sugar and sweets. The weight was displayed at both sides for staff and customer to see. Next to the scales stood tall shining glass jars holding bulls' eyes, lozenges, glassy mints, fruit drops and liquorice allsorts. They had a back room where a large cupboard was kept to store meat and perishable products. It had a screen covering each end to protect the food. There was no electricity at that time.

At Christmas time the shop was decorated and one of the big windows in front had a real pig's head decorated with an apple in its mouth. At night wooden shutters were put on both windows. Inside the other window Bill very often sat on a high stool behind a partition doing the 'books' and from time to time peered out over his glasses to provide help or information. My brothers and I all served our time there learning to order, weigh and label food and other merchandise and of course serving customers. We did this on Saturdays and summer holidays.

I remember tourists coming into the shop and it was in the heart of the country-side. But they were met by a family who were able to hold a conversation on any topic worldwide. They had an excellent command of the English language and were knowledgeable, eloquent and articulate. They were dignified, a little bit reserved, hard-working and honest, but also had a great sense of humour.

Bill lived all his life in Lower Dripsey, initially with his mother Mary and his sister Lily. He never got married. After, his mother's death, Bill lived on at the main house with Lily, and his sister Fanny joined them and took over the main housekeeping duties. There was just one maid at that time. Another sister, Eva Williams, came home from England to help out but eventually went back to live her own life. In later years, Bill installed petrol pumps across the road outside a cottage. The cottage was Williams's property and was rented out. Lily died before Bill. Fanny broke her hip in her late '70s and died soon afterwards. In those days, they did not operate on broken hips.

Bill sold the shop in the 1960s and lived in the rented cottage across the road. He died in his seventies. When he was a boy, he contacted pleurisy and that left him with a weakness. The main house and shop was eventually converted into the Four Seasons Hotel in the 1970s, under the ownership of Dan Donovan. After a short time, it was then converted to the West County Bar owned by Denis Dilworth. There was a South County Bar owned by the Dilworth family in Douglas. Today the house is still the property of the Dilworth family. As for the garage, all that remains are the petrol pumps, monuments of modernity.

The Williams Garage, mid-twentieth century, character on right unknown. (*George Williams and Kevin O'Mahony*)

26. DAZZLING HISTORIES

We have already met Dripsey woman Anna Ryan on our journey. Anna talked about a number of aspects of the area's heritage and in particular Dripsey Station. Up to that point exploring and researching Dripsey, I had forgotten about the impact of the Cork–Muskerry Tram on people and place. Whatever happened to the small station that Anna had remembered so vividly? I looked up an old Ordnance Survey map and compared it to a present-day map. I spotted the site and went searching for the building but I didn't know what I would encounter. Near the site in Lower Dripsey, I met local man Dermot O'Sullivan who was building a rubble wall in his driveway. That is how I discovered the site of the old station. Dermot brought me next door to the Carroll family, who now live in the revamped ticket house of Dripsey Station.

Pat Carroll is a knowledgeable man who is clearly proud of not only the area's cultural heritage but also his family's story. I spent an evening and an afternoon with Pat. He offered more insights into how the area within Inniscarra parish came to be. Firstly, his father Denis was the local tailor and, like the manager of the Lower Dripsey creamery, he met a lot of people in his travels and knew the comings and goings of the region. Secondly, Denis transformed the ticket house of Dripsey Station into living accommodation when the Cork–Muskerry Tram closed in 1934. Thirdly, it transpired that Pat had a keen interest in hunting, a sport he learned as a young man. The interesting aspect about a hunter is that they know the land intimately. They are the local geographers. They are the guides who know the names of the fields and the 'rhythms of nature' that we do not often see in the heart of a buzzing city.

To begin at the beginning, Pat's father Denis Caroll was born in Cummeen, Donoughmore on 4 July 1904. He was an apprentice tailor to a Mr Cremin in Srelane. In 1934, he married Kate and they had seven children, three girls and four boys. Kate was from Donoughmore. Her mother died from a stroke when Kate was eleven. Her father died three or four years later from throat cancer. The neighbours raised the rest of the family bar three of the girls who moved to Philadelphia. Kate never saw her sisters again. A decade ago Pat Carroll (the son), whilst in Philadelphia, went to his aunts' house and his cousins were still living there.

In 1935, the Carroll family came to Dripsey Bridge and lived on the Murphys' land at Shandy Hall near Upper Dripsey. Denis began tailoring and built up a decent reputation for himself. He made all the clothes for the community's communions and confirmations. He made suits for Cork Bishop Con Lucey. When Denis got busy, his brother Paddy helped him out. Denis was fond of his grand piano, which served as a work bench. He loved music and was able to play the fiddle and accordion.

Above left: Pat and Mary Carroll, Lower Dripsey, outside their revamped Dripsey station ticket house.

Above right: Denis Carroll, tailor, Lower Dripsey. (*Carroll family collection*)

When Marshes, the auctioneers, were selling off the houses and sheds of the Muskerry Railway in 1938, Denis bought the ticket house for £50. He bought two railway bridges with the ground originally but in later years swapped the ground with a local farmer for an acre of a pond that was going between the two bridges. He revamped the ticket house into living accommodation and worked from there.

When I was talking to Pat, he was passionate about his upbringing, what he learned and what was passed on to him. It was a way of life that he inherited. Pat notes that:

'Growing up my job was the open fire and to maintain wood for it. Water was got from a well down the railway line. You brought two buckets instead of one to keep a balance. We also used to snare and dazzle rabbits. I remember going out at 5 or 6p.m. in the winter months when it was getting dark. We would attach a car light to a six-volt battery and shine it into the rabbit's eyes. The greyhound by your side would do the catching. My brother Tim was also big into the sport. I still hunt today and shoot game with three gun clubs, that of Coachford, Macroom and Rylane. We do eat the bounty, that of the duck and pheasant.

Pat went on to live in a house near Bealnamorive in western Aghabullogue. In 1981, his father died and left Pat the house to look after. Pat's wife Mary originally lived in Farren, not far from what is now Quaid's photographic studio on the Cork–Macroom main road. She spent thirty years in London before she came home to her brother in Coachford. It was at this juncture that she met Pat.

As both Pat and Mary were brought up in a cottage environment, they put a lot of thought into the modernisation of the old ticket house. They were conscious of the heritage of the building but wanted to create a warm, homely and peaceful feeling. They made a number of changes but in general kept the essence of the ticket house. The exterior facing walls were completed in cedar wood and so they re-cladded the walls with cedar wood. They rearranged the house to make sense in the modern world. For example they changed the location of the front door. They wanted to create a space that would give room for cupboards and furniture. They fixed the galvanised roof, which was in poor repair. They put in new timber roof beams where appropriate. The ceiling boards needed replacing. They also discovered in their renovations one inch of horsehair inside the galvanised roof that had been used as insulation. It was rolled on. Heat wise they say that there is great dryness within the building. The same heat is retained through the wood in summer as in winter.

27. AT THE BORDERS OF MEMORY

There is a holy well situated not far from my house in Timothy Kelleher's field at the junction of three townlands, Magoola, Agharinagh and Dromgownagh. Formerly it was a place of great interest to the old people but, nowadays, like everything else, veneration for it is dying out. It is neglected now; its sides are falling in, but still it is loved by a few old people.

Timothy Murphy, a student from Magoola,

Dripsey, for the School Folklore Collection, 1938.

It was 6.30a.m. at Cork Airport. Sitting by the gate waiting for the plane didn't require effort. The fact the flight was early in the morning meant my senses were not fully awake. Everyone seemed to move slowly at that time. Looking out on the runway, the darkness before sunset meant that somehow beyond the glass was a black void of the unknown. But as the minutes rolled on, the blackness turned to purple and eventually half-light. The void in minutes became full of shapes and new colours, planes and staff on the runway. Time was called to board as my own senses began to waken, as did those of my fellow passengers.

I always feel that remembering and forgetting is like that hazy world of consciousness I felt at the airport. All of us choose to remember certain things that happen to us. Over time, these stories become fragmented as we remember the key points and when we pass on the story to a willing listener, the listener can dilute the story if it is passed on. One can also choose to forget entirely a life narrative. Hence, as the years pass on, the researcher has nothing to study.

There have been times in my journey down the Lee where I would love to find out more about a certain person or a place. However, there has been many an occasion where there has been a limit to discovering the historical data. Data could be lost or in many cases was never researched or compiled. Oral histories are great to fill in some of the line of memory. A memory can be forgotten about as time marches on but the event becomes history if it is written down.

With all this in mind, on the current Ordnance Survey map, two holy wells are marked on the northern valleyside of the Inniscarra Reservoir, half a mile from the main road. When looking for archaeological monuments off the main road it's better to have a guide. It cuts down on searching through briars, even though climbing ditches still has to be done, as well as avoiding electric fences. With a guide, one can negotiate these obstacles. In addition, you get to chat to your guide about the monument and its relevance in their lives; how it has informed their cultural beliefs and their education of the world. We have already met Pat Carroll of Lower Dripsey. With the help of Pat and another local resident called Martin McCarthy, I explored the local holy well of Sunday's Well.

Crossing a number of fields that had seen their autumnal cut, we headed into a narrow stream valley. In the midst of the overgrowth, there was the well, but it did not have a 2007 feel to it. In fact, the artefacts it held were of the 1940s and 1950s. The holy well had remained intact and untouched for over fifty years. It was like being in a time warp. I felt that hazy consciousness, as if I was at the border between the real world and the world of the well.

Timothy Kelleher remembers from a 1938 interview with his father, Edmond, that many cures were said to have taken place at the well, 'Cripples came to be cured and went away leaving their crutches after them for they needed them no longer.' The construction date for Sunday's Well is unknown. P.J. Harnett, in the *Journal of the Cork Historical and Archaeological Society* of 1947, notes that there were two wells at one time, the former in the townland of Agharinagh and the latter, twenty yards to the east, in

Explorations at Sunday's Well, Agharinagh, Lower Dripsey.

Pat Carroll and Martin
McCarthy at Sunday's Well.

the townland of Magoola. P.J. visited both. A horizontal flagstone covers Sunday's Well. Above this, supported by two stones on edge, is a second slab, and the intervening space contains the customary religious objects found near holy wells. P.J. noted that Lady's Well was also almost sealed by a large flagstone. He noted only a few faded flowers and ferns placed on top of the covering stone. Rounds were made at both wells and were paid on three successive Sundays. The Rosary was recited first at Sunday's Well, with a circuit of the well made after each decade. The formula was repeated at Lady's Well. Lady's Well no longer exists and is probably overgrown with topsoil.

Like the stone row, after their construction the holy wells would have grown in stature in the mindsets of the local residents. Particular places become very important landmarks, linking the movements of individuals and communities. Myths also seem to enable a community to establish a sense of belonging within a landscape. Through such media, people create a sense of place and identity. A place becomes a home. That transformation is as important in today's world as it was when Agharinagh holy well was constructed.

28. THE WAYFARER

Watch her carefully, every movement, every gesture, every little peculiarity: keep the camera whirring; for this is a film you'll run over and over again.

Gar Private, *Philadelphia Here I Come.*

The above line from *Philadelphia Here I Come* has come to my mind a lot over the last couple of months with the several people I have interviewed and written about. Of course, I have been affected emotionally from the life stories I have listened to, but I have thoroughly enjoyed my adventures to date. I like being an explorer of my own doorstep.

There is great scope in the use of oral history in exploring the human heart of any area. I am indebted to the countless strangers I have met who were willing to impart their story over the hundreds of Kimberlys and Mikados I have eaten. That being said, I try not to over analyse what the participants have said; I try to let the stories do the talking.

John Manning, January 2008.

In my interview with John Manning, Inishleena, Inniscarra, County Cork, he imparted a vast amount of information about his life experiences. His account was full of nostalgia. He talked a lot about tradition and past ways of life, ways he cherished and which now linger in his mind as memories. He talked much about changes in his life, 'when I was a child', 'in my twenties', 'when we got married', 'on my ninetieth birthday', and so on. That way of narrating the story revealed the layers of his life. He was not born, married and aged over one day. As I read recently, time just flows on but the undercurrents can change. I think sometimes we rarely reflect on the time (temporal) dimension in history.

At ninety-one John is in good health but partially deaf. However, both John and I negotiated our way through our conversation. It is generally agreed that oral history should be recorded in an interview setting, using a structured and well-researched interview outline, with a witness to or a participant in a historical event. I have found recording people difficult and some see it as intimidating. So much of what I record is in the form of handwritten notes, and using photographs to provide some sense of the person to the reader.

Oral history is as old as civilisation itself. In pre-literate societies, everything had to be remembered: crafts and skills, times and seasons, the sky, territory, law and speeches, transactions and bargains. In modern times, oral history has developed as a sub-discipline of history, but through the oral narrative, historians have been brought into contact with other fieldwork disciplines such as sociology, anthropology or dialect or folklore research.

In my own opinion, the live experience creates understanding and makes the most telling and thought-provoking local history. At a basic level, interviewing can bring together people from different social classes and age groups who would otherwise rarely meet, let alone get to know each other closely. Reminiscing is an important way in which people, especially older individuals, keep their sense of self in a changing world. Oral history is a way of helping the past to speak to the present in a conversational way, and in doing so it provides a public forum for people who might have been otherwise historically invisible.

John Manning lives at Inishleena, Inniscarra, adjacent to the recreational amenity. Like many other stories, his biography is part of the identity of the Lee Valley and the valley is part of who he is. John talked about many aspects of his life on my visit. The following is based on his diaries and notes he has taken through the years. There is so much to be gleaned from his story:

I was born at home in Tír na Spideoga, Inchigeela in the early hours of Saturday morning, 9 December 1916, and I was baptised in the same afternoon. The christening wouldn't have been a problem because my godmother who was my mam's first cousin was in the house a day or two before the 'event' and my godfather, who was my Dad's nephew, lived only half a mile away. I was christened in the Parochial House, which was in the same townland, by the then parish priest, Fr James O'Leary. I never got a chance to see him, for he was transferred soon after to the parish of Dunmanway, to fill the vacancy created by the death of Canon Magner who was shot by the Black and Tans in 1921. I was three and a half years of age when the Black and Tans came over in the latter months of 1919. A number of them were stationed in the Lake Hotel in Inchigeela. I never saw them for my parents never took me with them when going out. There was always someone at home, to mind the child – a granny or an auntie or even a next-door neighbour. My father John was from Inchigeela and my mother was Mary McCarthy from Cappabui on the Bantry side of the Pass of Keimaneigh.

John Manning in FCA.
(*John Manning*)

Maggie, Paddy, Kit and John at Inishleena in the 1970s, with O'Flynn's boats behind. (*John Manning*)

I went to school in Ballingeary in the spring of 1923. The Black and Tans had left and the Civil War was over. I made my First Communion in 1924 and I was confirmed in 1928 by the Bishop of Cork, Dr Cohalan (when I was around twelve years of age). I had two brothers and two sisters. Sadly one brother and two sisters have gone to their eternal reward. My interest in exploring began in my schooldays in Ballingeary, seventy-five years ago. A five-foot high by four-foot wide map of Ireland hung on the wall opposite my desk. Blessed with the keen vision of youth, I was able to see and read the names of all the cities, towns and villages, and it occurred to me, there and then, if the good Lord spared me, that I would visit all these places. In my innocence, I imagined that if I cycled up to Donegal I could come back down again on freewheel. The truth, as I was to discover later, was quite different. Cycling up to Donegal was, in fact, much easier, for the prevailing winds are always from the South West. On the return journey, the breeze was a handicap, no matter how gentle it might be.

In my youth, I suffered from asthma, and couldn't take part in strenuous games such as hurling or football. So there was nothing for it but to get on my bike, and take to the open air of the countryside. That suited my lungs and, over the years, I built up a great store of energy. However, I was in my forties before I fulfilled my boyhood dream of cycling the length and breadth of Ireland.

At the time, I lived in Inchigeela, and hadn't as yet met my future wife. I got myself a new Raleigh bicycle with the latest Sturmey-Archer three-speed gears and a few pounds of pocket money (not easy to come by in the 1940s).

And so on a beautiful Sunday afternoon in the month of July, John set off on his first trip, an eighty-three-mile cycle to Mount Mellery, the monastery on the slopes of the Knockmealdowns, in County Waterford:

> I caught my first glimpse of the monastery from The Cats, a public house on the road to Clogheen, and a welcome sight for the weary traveller.
>
> A visitor to Mellery was obliged to arrive before eight o'clock in the evening. When you arrived, you put back your watch because they went by 'old time' then. I stayed a few days and was thrilled by the chanting of the monks of the Salve Regina at Vespers. On the return journey, I went via the Vee – a valley of breathtaking beauty – and took in a wide circle of country before arriving home again.
>
> I then got my mind set on the idea of sleeping in all thirty-two counties. As it transpired, I managed to sleep in twenty-nine counties, missing out only on Sligo, Fermanagh and Armagh. Though I travelled these three counties extensively, I had left all three before bedtime.
>
> I was fascinated by the outline of Ben Bulben, and hadn't realised that County Leitrim had such a short coastline of half-a-mile or less. On my travels, I looked for accommodation in a place called Summerhill in County Kilkenny. The lady regarded me suspiciously, and mentioned something about the IRA. Was I shocked and dismayed? She certainly 'brought me down a peg'. It took the wind out of my sails. I turned my trusty Raleigh out onto the road again and, helped along by my Sturmey-Archer three-speed, ate up the miles and eventually got accommodation in Castledermot, County Kildare. But I was to later get an opportunity to sleep in County Kilkenny, and add it to the growing list of places where I laid my head.
>
> I followed a threshing set for one season in the Suir Valley. The owner of the machine lived in Kilmeaden, County Waterford, but most of his harvesting work was in and around Kilmacow, in neighbouring County Kilkenny. We had to cross the bridge at Fidown, where you had to pay a 1d toll. So as to make things easier, my boss secured accommodation for me at Mrs Walsh's in Kilmacow, while the threshing season lasted. The combine harvester was making its appearance just then, and was an early harbinger of the monumental changes that were to come to rural life and harvest time. Unfortunately, I got an attack of asthma and had to spend six days in Ardkeen Hospital (since upgraded to Waterford Regional Hospital).
>
> My next set-back – a minor one – was in County Cavan. Having visited all the towns and villages in east Cavan, I intended 'putting-up' in west Cavan. But, when I got there, it was nine o'clock at night, and all the B&B accommodation and guest houses were occupied by members of the Garda Síochána. One Garda offered to share his room with me. It was a kind gesture, but it didn't appeal to me, and so I struck off south-west towards the nearest town, Ballinamore, in County Leitrim.

Ballinamore was all of seventeen miles away, and I know car owners who'd grumble at having to drive that distance at the end of a long day. But I pumped the pedals of my trusty Raleigh. A mile or two from Swanlinbar, I crossed a bridge under which flowed the infant River Shannon on its way to Lough Allen.

I stopped for tea in a café somewhere in County Clare, and was given watered down milk for my tea. However, I didn't make any great fuss about it, and left County Clare on the same good terms as I entered it. I slept in twenty-nine counties, but not all of my slumbers were enjoyed in beds. I encountered 'house full' signs, and had to sleep on an armchair or a couch on more than one occasion.

My asthma continued to give intermittent trouble. I spent a week in Bantry Hospital. In between cycling expeditions, there was work to be done. I was a painter and decorator, and twice I found myself in the orthopaedic ward following mishaps with a ladder. I fractured the bone you stand on, on my left foot, and again, the bone at the back of the heel of my right foot. In hospital, I studied the medical chart as closely as I'd studied the wall map of Ireland at school, and noted that both bones resemble the back of a soup spoon on the medical chart.

Back on my travels again, I found himself working on the chassis of caravans and mobile homes for the owner of a fleet of them in Ballylickey in West Cork. A tedious task, for I spent most of the time underneath them, on my back. And then at the end of a day, I had to sleep in one. I also slept under canvas on many occasions.

I was in the FCA and served in numerous Camps and Barracks around the country, from Templemore (now a Garda Training College), to Lahinch in West Clare. Once, in Ballincollig, I got a taste of what jail must be like. I had reached the rank of NCO. It was quite a big summer camp, with chaps from all over the Southern Command so the payroll had to be a big one. £4,000 was a colossal sum in the 1950s. Camp usually broke up on a Friday. Many long-distance personnel would leave early to catch buses and trains. The payroll was withdrawn from the bank, but little did I know that, as night came, I'd have to sleep with it!

The army payroll was a very substantial sum; you could probably have bought a sizeable house with it and had a fleet of brand new motor cars to park in the driveway. When the army payroll arrived at camp, it was taken to the basement of Block D. The Commanding Officer and Quartermaster asked me 'if I'd mind' bringing along my bed and sleeping in the basement that night. Whether I 'minded' or not, I could hardly refuse. My door was closed and secured with two strong locks, and I can assure you that it wasn't a pleasant experience. However, it was summertime. I slept soundly and wasn't a bit the worse for my ordeal. On thinking it over later, I thought that such a precaution was ridiculous, given that there was, ever and always, an NCO and three men on sentry duties, on a two-hours-on and four-hours-off roster. However, it was one of the 160 different places in which I slept.

Most, if not all, of the B&Bs and guest houses had registers, and you signed your name. Some had little booklets specifically designed for 'comments'. The charges for B&B varied from 12s 6d, 14s, 15s, up to £1. However, 17s 6d was the most common charge I paid on my travels. The cuisine, too, was far different then, far less complicated than what one might expect today. We seemed to have far warmer summers, and I never had a fry for breakfast, for thirst would overcome me before too long. So I was satisfied with scrambled egg and toast.

Each of the thirty-two counties has their own individual features and characteristics. Most people, I imagine, would go for 'The Kingdom', with its Ring of Kerry and Lakes of Killarney. I had a bit of sympathy for County Carlow, squeezed in between its four big neighbours. But I spent a night in Glendalough and thought County Wicklow was best. I was no Sean Kelly or Stephen Roche. I just careered along at a reasonable pace and took in the marvels and scenery of the countryside.

Some of my trips were so long – ninety or one hundred miles – that I wouldn't and couldn't have a meal during the day. Instead, I'd purchase a supply of Kimberley biscuits (which you could buy loose or in packets, in the shops, back then) and eat them as I rode along.

29. IN LOVING MEMORY: KILBLAFFER GRAVEYARD

The inscription on the gravestone nearest to the gate says 'kneel and pray'. Only wind chimes and the occasional passing car broke the oasis of silence. I stumbled upon the church and graveyard complex in Kilblaffer, or more locally known as North Kilmurray, by accident as I was exploring the area just east of the Model Village, Dripsey towards Berrings. Like many graveyards, it is a quiet and peaceful space for reflection. In North Kilmurray, my visit was met with a silence that called for respect for the dead but also to see what the living had created for their deceased loved ones.

I have grown more and more interested in graveyards in my travels in the Lee Valley. To me graveyards are silent but very important markers of civilisation. The art and architecture of gravestones tell the story of the ordinary person – the everyday people whose life stories are lost in the 'sands of time'. In a sense people are inscribed in stone and not in history.

Detail of a window on the eastern end of the ruined church, North Kilmurray.

In loving memory. A view of the older section of North Kilmurray graveyard, Kilblaffer near Berrings, County Cork.

North Kilmurray church is in ruins and lies in the north-west quadrant of the graveyard. It consists of an ivy-clad ruin of a rectangular-gabled church in an east–west orientation. Much of the western wall stands. It was formerly a chapel of ease for Inniscarra parish and according to the archaeological inventory of mid-Cork, the surviving architectural details suggest a structure of late medieval date (AD 1000-1600).

Within the interior of the church, there is evidence of a gallery. There is a central window in the altar gable and there is a second ruined window in the eastern end of the south wall. There are many headstones within the church from various times. It was sometime in the nineteenth century that the church went out of use and they were placed inside. Not all are readable, but the ones I could read I am recording here to give a sense of the families buried in North Kilmurray. Those of a nineteenth century date comprise William Drumney, Daniel McCarthy (died 1884) and Louise Shinwin O'Mahony (1825-1896). Louise's gravestone notes that she was the wife of Jeremiah Gurteen, Bandon, and mother of Ellie, Jerry, Joe, Tim, Willie, Julia, Lizzie, Mary and Anne. The gravestone was erected by her great-great-granddaughter Mary Karen O'Neill, Chagrin Falls, Ohio, USA.

The twentieth-century gravestones mark the burial places of the Ruby family, Denis and Margaret O'Brien, and Mary Mahony (of Fergus, died 1904). In 1907

Ellen Walsh erected a gravestone in memory of her mother and father, Ellen and Michael. The Buckley family of Ballyshonin, Berrings, are also present, as are Timothy Buckley (died 5 May 1987) and his wife Mary (died 26 January 1997).

Most modern cultures mark the location of the body with a headstone. This reputedly serves two purposes. Firstly, the grave will not accidentally be exhumed. Second, headstones contain information or tributes to the deceased. This is a form of remembrance for loved ones; it can also be viewed as a form of immortality. Many gravestones carry an epitaph, an inscription in memory of the dead. Sometimes the epitaph offers a warning to the young. Some express resignation in the face of death.

Some designs of gravestones are more common than others in accordance with the fashion of gravestones at the time. Social functions and the level of investment are important factors. Lettering is also interesting. The line length even provides insights into the inscriber. The iconography and symbolism can differ in accordance with tastes and fashions, changing technologies, standards of education, creativity and ingenuity of the stonemason, and even the evidence of human error is interesting.

There are mainly late-eighteenth-century and nineteenth-century plots. The earliest grave is that of Maurice Haly, who died in 1784, and his family. There are no signs telling you where the oldest graves are located. One must explore the full extent of the graveyard. The earliest grave noted by the mid-Cork Archaeological Inventory was from 1766, but I was unable to find it. Other late-eighteenth-century graves include those of Daniel Mullane, who died on 26 March 1784 aged twenty-two, Cornelius Mullane of Newcastle, Blarney, who died on 4 August 1977, John Riordan who died in 1790, and Daniel Kelleher who died in 1793 aged sixty-six.

There is a Hennessy family plot with a date range from 1795 (John Hennessy) to 1980 (John Vincent). The Hennesseys still live in the local area. Edmond Coffey, died on 27 March 1792 aged forty-two. Daniel Coffey from Dromatimore, near Aghabullogue, died on 15 November 1914, aged seventy-six. His daughter Hanna is also mentioned on the gravestone. Daniel Blake died on 9 April 1806 aged twenty-four. Francis, the son of William Blake of Dromgownagh, died on 21 December 1903, aged twenty-three. There are four coffin tombs, three of which are unreadable. One is that of the McCarthy family of Kilclough. Denis McCarthy died on 18 January 1968. Stephen McCarthy, died 12 May 1908, aged eighteen years, a pupil of the Christian Brothers. His sister Hannah died on 4 March 1892.

For the sake of record the following modern plots were noted: Ball, Byrne, Crowley, Cunningham, Dilworth, Donovans, Fitzgeralds, Harrington, Healy, Herlihy, McCarthy, Murphy, Murray, Noonan, Parker and Sheehan. The latest additions to the graveyard on my visit were Patrick Walsh, Berrings, who died in August 2001, and Paddy Barrett of Lisladeen, Berrings, who died in December 2001.

30. FOLKLORE AND MEMORY, EVERYTHING AND NOTHING

In this graveyard [North Kilmurray] is buried a priest named Fr Dilworth who it appears was a native of the parish of Inniscarra. While living it is said he cured many people of some ailments and after his death and burial in Kilmurray graveyard, people continued to visit his grave and paid rounds there in the hope of being cured of whatever ailment they suffered from. Some rounds are still being paid especially on Palm Sunday, Good Friday and Easter Sunday and it is said that many have benefited by the rounds.

The round consists of walking slowly round the grave of Fr Dilworth a number of times and saying custom prayers. Across the road, in a little field, is what is looked upon as a holy well, and in order to gain full benefit of the round, a visit must be paid to the well to drink some of the water.

Berrings School File, Schools' Folklore Commission, 1938.

In my own travels in the Lee Valley, many people have said to me, 'it is said'. The names of the original tellers have been lost but the essence of the story of human endeavour has survived the test of time. To some people, these stories may be just data but this passed-down knowledge says much of how we inherit traits of the past and select what to pass on.

I have developed an interest in folklore in my travels and have learned that it can colour the land with the human story. Below is a flavour of stories that appear in the 150 pages of folklore collected by students of Berrings National School as part of their work for the Irish Folklore Commission in 1938. Riddles, signs of bad weather, death, marriage customs, songs, poems, religious customs, the process of growing potatoes, and methods of house construction are among the things discussed in Berrings. Berrings comes from the Irish Boirinn, meaning 'Place of Rocks' or 'Stoney district'. In particular the name Boireann means 'Rocking Stone'.

ON THE ROCKING STONE:

Adjacent to Berrings National School in a farm owned by Donal O'Relly, Berrings South, is what is known commonly as the Rocking Stone. It is a large irregular-shaped slab and is supported underneath by, or rather rests on, a smaller stone, which acts as a kind of pivot on which it used to rock. Many of the local boys sat on it and rocked it when they were attending Berrings School.

Ballyshoneen Mass Rock.

ON SIGNS OF FROST:

When the stars shine brightly and when it is possible to hear vehicles on far-away roads, or to hear the sound of the river plainer than on any other night. When the fire gives out a red light and when the wind blows from the porch.

ON DEATH:

When the person dies, the clocks are stopped and the mirrors are covered. The corpse should not be left alone in the room … when the corpse is taken out, the feet should be faced out. The bed clothes should be turned over as the corpse is taken out … When the corpse reaches the graveyard, the corpse is taken all round it, before it is put into the grave. It is believed that if a person fell in a graveyard while attending a funeral that he would be the next person to be buried there. The relatives of the dead person wear black clothes as a sign of mourning.

ON THE PRIEST'S FACE:

In the townland of Ballyshonin, Berrings, and adjoining the road from Cork to Kanturk is a rock (amongst many rocks) known as Carraig an Aifrinn. It is said that Mass was celebrated here in the Penal Times. On the roadside quite near is a projection of rock, resembling a human head and believed locally to be the image of a priest's head.

Priest's Face, Ballyshoneen.

ON KILN STREET:

In the townland of Ballyanley, Berrings, County Cork is a lonely portion of the by-road called Kiln Street. It appears several families lived in several little houses many years ago and nearby was a lime kiln. A member of one of the families, who was considered to be rather witty, because of the many little houses and the kiln all adjacent to each other, called the place Kiln Street and it is known by that name to the present day.

ON MARRIAGE:

People generally get married in this district during Shrove time. Monday, Wednesday and Friday and the month of May, August and October are considered unlucky days and months for getting married.

ON LADY'S WELL:

There is a place in this parish called 'Lady's Well'. It is believed that one night, there was a great feast held in the 'Great House'. One of the guests that were at the feast went out for a walk in the middle of the night. As she was going along she fell into the well and got drowned. For some time afterwards it is said that she was seen walking from the 'Great House' to the well and went into it and disappeared. She was also seen walking along the bridges at about twelve o'clock.

31. TESTING YOUR SKILL WITH THE TWENTY-EIGHT

Jackie Lenihan is well known as the sacristan of Berrings church and in a sense is the first port of call for all church/community-related activities. However, Jackie also a great knowledge of the game of road bowls and in a sense grew up with the sport. Jackie talks about the game and the sense of fun, pride and identity, plus the interaction of the local and Cork community with the North Kilmurray road that he played on:

I remember the first big game, or as we call it the scór, being played as a young teenager around 1943. I remember it was played after the second Mass on the Sunday morning. It was played from Reen's Pub in Berrings to Mary Murphy's pub in North Kilmurray. That was the playing space for many many years. It was a distance of about two miles. I remember the road pure black with people. The road was one of the only roads in County Cork where bowling has been kept going from the 1930s to the present day.

I remember the lads coming out on Sundays from Togher and Fairhill and from Waterfall to play bowls. They also came from local places such as Donoughmore, Bealnamorrive and Macroom. I can recall James O'Mahony, or Jimmy as we called him, winning the All-Ireland bowling championship. I also remember the other great players such as Paddy Cotter of Cloghroe and Jack Dinan of Donoughmore.

The best players in Munster played in the championship, which was played from the church in Cloghroe to the 'yellow house' on the Cloghroe–Kanturk road. The Healy family in Cloghroe owned Blair's Inn and were always involved in bowling as committee members and by looking after players with food and free drink after the game. Mary Murphy of Murphy's Pub in North Kilmurray also looked after the players.

I got into bowls growing up, going to school in Berrings in the 1940s. We used to follow the bowlers along the road looking for the bowls in the ditches – that's how we got to know them. As young lads, hurling was the big game in this parish. When it was not being played, the lads played bowls. I remember going to a house in Ballyshoneen having the craic and around a dozen of us would go bowling until dark in the summertime. We soon found out how good we were. Two or three of us blossomed out of it. I was lucky I was one of them.

As the years went on we began to throw bowls ourselves as young men. Small bowls were made by McBrides on Merchant's Quay of sixteen, twenty, twenty-six and twenty-eight ounces and with our small hands we started with the sixteen ounce. We moved onto the heavier bowl at maturity. The late Dermot Murphy of the pub in North Kilmurray and I formed a club under the Ból Chumann na hÉireann rules. I remember in particular in the early days playing against Mick Murphy from Mallow, Jim 'the Gent" Driscoll from Cork City, Mike O'Cealleachair from Macroom and Dooley O'Mahony from Ballincollig. There have also been great players such as Con Desmond from Ballyanley in Berrings, Jackie O'Callaghan of Matehy and the Brennans of Dripsey.

I kept at the game and eventually began to throw down a couple of bob. But you had to be careful as the stakes were high. Back in the sixties, the competing sides played for £300 or £400. The player paid an entry fee of five to ten shillings. There was usually a silver cup if you won the tournament.

There was a great interest in bowls around the 1980s. Committee members such as Johnny Connors, Christy Naughton, Peter Buckley and I kept it ticking over. The bowls took place on the Cloghroe–Kanturk road. There is a pub on that road called Regan's Bar. All-Irelands were played on that road. Lads from West Cork, the city and all the way from Armagh used to play there, Sunday after Sunday during the summer. Mick Barry played many a scór there. He was one of the greatest players; one of the most consistent winners. He won a good few All-Irelands. In the past nine or ten years, Tim Sullivan has been successful at All-Ireland level, as well as John Walsh who won a novice All-Ireland up in Drogheda around 1997. Bowls stopped on the Cloghroe–Kanturk road when it was tarmacadamed. The bowlers were not happy playing on the big chips. The big chips never settle and the bowl could fly off the road.

Above left: Jackie Lenihan.

Above right: Jackie, North Cork Championship, 1963. (*Jackie Lenihan*)

Inniscarra hurling team, which won the mid-Cork junior championship in 1957. Jackie is the last player sitting on the front row on the left. (*Jackie Lenihan*)

We call the game the scór – the distance to be thrown is always about two miles. You can play singles or doubles, which we did. You create a starting line at the starting point. You make the line with a bit of paint. You make another line at the finish, two miles away.

Two fellows start and whoever reaches the finishing line in the least number of throws is the winner. If one fellow got seventeen and the other fellow got fourteen, in bowls terms, the winner would have won by 'three bowls of odds'. If beaten by one throw, the term is 'beaten in the last shot'. To cross the line is a fowl. If the bowl is 'called', the bowl would be re-thrown. In the old days before Ból Chumann [est. 1954], there were no rules, no referee and each player would call the shot. Intimidation was a big thing in the old days; generally the hard men won the day. The hard men would make noise to upset their components. Ból Cumann did away with all that.

You need to be a good judge of the road. Your followers will give you the best play, so you can get the best possible throw. You put a 'sap' of grass on the road and you'd aim for that. In fact, a lot of fellas don't like their own road because they know the points of failure and success of it! It is a very healthy pastime. Every muscle of your body is working, arms and legs, as you're throwing two pounds of weight the whole time. The speed of your hands is important. A fast bowler would get the acknowledgement of a good fast bowl. A slow bowler would get shouted at by the crowd to 'get the bowl annointed'. A total of seventeen out of twenty is a handy scór. There is also the skill of lofting the bends of the road. Seventy to eighty yards is a good loft. Mick Barry was known for lofting ninety yards.

32. LONG TIES

Pat Reen was born in 1953. He went to Berrings National School in 1958 (until 1966). His teachers were Pat Carroll, Mrs Herlihy and Madge Collins. It was a two-roomed building with boys taught on one side and girls on the other. His father died in 1965 and he was sent to boarding school first in Trabolgan in East Cork and then to Coláiste Íosagáin in Ballyvourney. He went on to study at Coláiste An Spioraid Naoimh in Bishopstown. He went to technical school in Coachford and for a time attended the Radio and Electronic Institute in Tivoli.

In the 1970s, he came back to the family post office and bar to tend to it with his mother. But in the 1980s, rural life was heavily affected by the economic downturn, which resulted in the pub being closed in 1985. The pub was reopened and refurbished in 1994. It closed shortly afterwards and Pat remains its owner. He has long family ties with the pub:

We're here in Berrings for four generations. My great-grandfather was Pat Ring from Codrum and Tierbeg near Macroom. They also had property in Manchester and Liverpool. The name changed from Ring to Reen through a family dispute. Pat became secretary to Richard Barter at the world-renowned Turkish Baths at St Ann's Hill in Blarney. He became a merchant after that and had the Byrne's Mills in Blarney where he manufactured meal and flour. He was known as a general merchant and served the farming community.

In the year of the Famine, things went against him and he was evicted. His wife Margaret though had property in Berrings, where the O'Mahony family owned 400 acres on the Berrings estate. The Reens moved to Berrings. Pat Ring ran the pub, the post office and was the land agent. Local people paid him the rent, which was sent to Dublin Castle. The pub/store catered for the local farming community. We sold products such as bottles of stout, coal, oil, tobacco and cigarettes. All kind of dealers would call in *en route* to Coachford Fair and Dripsey Woollen Mills. I remember the Youngs of Young's Mills in Clonmoyle who also had premises in Crosses Green in the city calling in for a drink *en route* or travelling home from the city.

People would send potatoes, turnips, and agricultural produce to the city via Reen's. The horse and cart was the king of transport. Pigs were sold in the Farmers' Union in Ballincollig. To help with the sales, weighing scales were on the premises. One could get the paper, which would have information such as births and deaths.

The post office was the focus of attention. Old-age pensions could be got and dog and bull licences could be bought. The post office had a phone and switchboard that served the community. The post office provided a day and night service if people wanted a doctor or vet, whatever the case might be. Telegrams were a big part of the post office. There were two postmen. Mail would come at 6a.m. and be delivered by pushbike after it was sorted. Mail for sending would go to Cork every evening.

Electricity came to Berrings in the early 1950s. It was one of the first areas in the county to get it. Lighting for the most part prior to that was by gaslight. There were also 'tilly' lamps on the counter. You would fill it with oil and pump it with a small pump and the mantle would light up. We also had oil lamps with a globe. We sold paraffin oil. We had a Primus to boil a kettle. We got them from Wickham's in Cork on Merchant's Quay. They supplied rural people with household items such as kettles and lamps.

Pat Reen.

Reen's Pub, 1940.
(*Pat Reen*)

John Daly's on Kyrls Quay supplied us with porter, bottled beer. Murphy's Brewery supplied us with kegs for years. We did a lot of business as well with Ormond's Distillery in Bandon and John Reardon's on Washington Street. Reardon's supplied us with tea, coffee and sugar. They brought out chests of tea. We got cigarettes from T.J. O'Leary on Washington Street. Woodford and Bourne were, I suppose, the cash and carry of their day for publicans. They were based on Sheare Street but had their main shop for general customers on Daunt's Square at the top of St Patrick's Street.

There were seven children in my grandfather's family. Due to the social and economic conditions over 100 years ago all of them emigrated. The five boys went to the United States. William went to Chicago and became an architect and sculptor. Johnny went to New Hampshire and was in the property business. Jim went to New York and had a liquor store. My grandfather Patsy had a pub business in Jersey City but returned to Berrings Pub on his father's death. He married Kate Forrest from the nearby townland of Gurteen. Of the two girls, Julia had a hotel business in India with her husband O'Hurley from Kilmurray, Berrings, who served in the British Army in India, and Mini married into the Hawkes family from Bandon and went to New York, where her family was involved in the liquor store trade.

My father was Jeremiah Reen. He was married to Hannah Herlihy from Coolea. They had two children, Catherine and me. My father was the stationmaster at Peake on the 'Hook and Eye Line' [Cork–Muskerry Tram] for many years. He was able to organise goods to be sent for the pub on the train to Gurteen or the Peake stops. He worked in the railways for thirty-five to forty years.

As a teenager he worked at Eustice's Timber and Slate Merchants on Leitrim Street opposite Murphy's Brewery for a year [building there until the early 1960s]. At the age of sixteen he got a job as stationmaster at the Cork–Muskerry terminus, now Jury's Hotel on Western Road. He lived in a lodge in nearby Wood Street. He got up at 5a.m. each morning and opened the gates. He had a narrow escape during the Troubles. He was arrested and thought to be a man on the run from the British authorities who worked on the train. My father was lucky as the man on the run had his wages awaiting collection. Security was tight as ammunition was being transported illegally on the rail lines in County Cork providing arms to the Irish Republican Army. After the closure of the Cork–Muskerry Tram, my dad Jeremiah worked in Wexford for a time but eventually came back to Berrings to run the pub/store and post office.

33. MEMORIES AT BERRINGS CROSSROADS

Berrings Cross is a crossroads of contrasts. At Berrings Cross, Reen's Bar, the local church, the school and modern housing are signposts of the past, present and future. On the southern side of the cross, the modern housing is brand new and stands out, untarnished by time. It seems to await the impact of memories.

Across the road, Berrings Hall stands as the contrast to the new – a tin, ruined structure, but with a rich past. Berrings Hall was a parochial dwelling. It belonged to the people of the parish. It was known far and wide. Dances were held weekly in decades gone by, some in preparation for the annual Farmer's Union Ball in the Arcadia in Cork. In the 1950s, Master Driscoll, the local national school teacher, held drama classes and public-speaking competitions there. It was a tremendous meeting place. Buses came out from the city. Reen's Bar became popular as a consequence.

At Berrings Cross in the 1860s there was a forge, and that site is called the Forge yard. The smith who worked there was named Collins. When he died, his family left the district and little is known of them. It would appear that the old forge was a meeting place for the local boys, where many a prank was played and story told. The forge in the twentieth century was reopened by Timmy Lane. Timmy Lane's aunt Margaret Mary Lane worked in Leicester's Chemist for many years (now Quill's, on St Patrick Street). Local people got their horses shod at Berrings Cross forge. Travelling shows stopped at the site and tended to the shoes of their horses. The forge, Pat Reen remembers, was a hive of activity. Cooking utensils were made there, such as tin dishes for baking. Gates were created for the farming community. There was a second forge owned by the Cooneys in Ballyshonin, a mile east of Berrings, next to a creamery.

On the northern side of the cross are the ruins of the second Berrings National

Berrings sign.

Old Berrings
National School,
2008.

School with a plaque on the wall stating '1846-1979'. Inside the building, the only memories left are a map of the world dated to 1961. Looking at it, it shows how much the countries of the world have been re-jigged in more recent years. One can explore education in Berrings back 300 years with the help of the Irish Folklore Commission of 1938.

In the local townland of Gortatrea, in the 1730s, there was a low thatched building. The old teacher who taught there was remarkable for his beautiful style of writing. His name was Looney. Many of his pupils came from places five miles distant. There were no desks or benches but the pupils, some grown men, sat on large stones and on their knees placed large copies or sheets. The ordinary subjects, writing, composition, grammar, geography and mathematics were apparently taught there. It was passed down that both languages, English and Irish, were taught. As far as was known, the school continued for many years and continued working during summer and winter months. Each pupil paid a certain sum per quarter to the teacher.

At Berrings Cross was another old ruin, part of which was at one time used as a school. It was conducted on the same lines as the old school at Gortatrea but of an earlier date. The teacher who taught in the school was named Pat Herlihy and when a new school was built at Berrings in 1846, he was appointed Principal. A school was held at the home now occupied by John Hennessy of Kilblaffer, Berrings. This school, which was in the house or barn, was more or less for the Hennessy family and the immediate neighbours, and was held during the winter months only. The modern school is a late-twentieth-century structure.

The church of Berrings was built c.1808 on or near the site of the church that did duty before that time. That older church was a long, low building with a slate roof. Fr

Lane, a native of Inniscarra parish was involved in building the present church. Local man Eugene Lane, in the 1938 Folklore study of the Berrings area, narrated a great story about the priest. When he was a young student, Lane walked to Cork City from Cloghroe – a distance of seven miles. As he was going to the city one morning along the Lee Road or the Asylum Road (before the present Carrigrohane Straight Road), he saw before him in the road a poor man travelling barefooted while his boots hung from his shoulders. As the road was bad and wet the poor man was keeping to the dried portion of it.

Suddenly a horseman appeared, coming from the city direction; he too was keeping to the dry portion of the road and would not leave it with the result that he drove his horse right against the poor man and knocked him to the ground and rode on as if nothing had occurred. Young Lane, who saw what had happened, prepared to meet the bully of a horseman as he approached, apparently intent in treating him as he treated the poor barefoot man. The horseman held the road, as did young Lane, but just as he was almost directly on him, Lane side stepped and with one blow of his walking stick he brought the horseman flat on the ground where he gave him a few further severe blows. Young Lane then jumped the fence, went across the fields as fast as he could and did not enter the city that day as he was aware that the horseman he had knocked down was a 'gentleman of impor-tance'. The next day yeomen were scouring the countryside in search of the young man who had knocked down the High Sheriff of Cork. Young Lane disappeared to France and returned after some years as Fr Lane!

Above left: Modern Berrings church.

Above right: Front garden memories. Daniel Horgan with an old mangle for 'wringing-out' wet clothes at Berrings Cross.

34. THE O'MAHONY LEGACY

I'm a firm believer that people make places. In a sense, we are all the spokes of the wider wheel of life. This section is about an important spoke in the wheel of life in County Cork, the O'Mahony family who lived in Berrings, County Cork. The research started off more or less as a blank canvas with the story of a motor company to begin with but soon the search blossomed into a search for an entire family. The tools and colours to paint the full picture are based on a number of interviews with relatives, friends of the family, Mass cards, family photos, family objects, street directories, census documents, property valuations, and insurance maps.

The O'Mahony name belongs almost exclusively to West Munster, the great majority of Mahony and O'Mahony births being registered in County Cork. In 1852 in Richard Griffith's Valuation of land for the Berrings area in County Cork, James and Richard Mahony owned approx 350 acres of land between them. The land seems to have been divided up over the latter half of the nineteenth century, because in a County Directory of Cork for the Berrings area in 1886, the principal landowners are listed as Denis Mahony, James P. Mahony and Jeremiah John Mahony. I have not been able to ascertain the relationship between the persons in 1852 and 1886.

We do know that in the late 1800s, Patrick O'Mahony, a farmer in Berrings, married a Miss Margaret Scanlon. The census of 1911 notes that their family comprised nine children: Richard (born 1887); Peter (born 1889); Paddy (born 1891); John Patrick (J.P.) or Jack (born in 1893); James (born 1895); Mary Ellen (born 1896); Leena (born 1899); David (born 1901), and Joseph (born 1907).

A sister-in-law through marriage of Patrick O'Mahony was Julia O'Herlihy (née Reen). Julia and her husband Timothy O'Herlihy from Kilmurray amassed an extensive fortune in India through the hotel business in the late 1800s. They owned a number of hotels, one of which was in Darjeeling. They also built up a range of business contacts. The wealth amassed by Julia Herlihy found its way back to Cork. In 1914 she formed the Universal Motor Company and bought the huge site of 40-42 North Main Street (or the old St Peter's Market site), which backed on to Cornmarket Street. The business had associated sites for showrooms on the Grand Parade (now the site of the tourist office). There were also storage sites in Rochestown and Carrigtwohill. Julia's mother was an O'Mahony and when Julia died in 1917 she bequeathed the business to her nephew John Patrick (J.P.) O'Mahony. John Patrick carried it on as a mercantile business and was also involved in the coach-building trade.

The business became the first Ford garage in Cork, when Ford came to the county in 1917. The Ford car was known as the 'universal car', hence the name of

Berrings Crossroads, *c.*1954, with Bishop Scanlon (brother of Mrs Margaret O'Mahony *née* Scanlon) in the centre of the picture. Bishop Scanlon was Bishop of Honolulu in Hawaii at one time. (*Sheila Healy*)

the business, 'Universal Motor Company'. The company advertised samples of the cars in the *Cork Examiner* in 1922, when a chassis cost £105, a runabout £120, a touring car £128, a delivery van £130, a ton chassis £145, a ton truck £170, a ton van £175, a coupe £215 and a sedan £240. The company also shipped the famous Ajax tyres in all sizes from New York directly to Cork.

It is said that Julia also bequeathed her house Dromdeiah in Killeagh in East Cork to John Patrick in 1917. Its present-day ruins are of an impressive two-storey house over a basement. Roger Green Davis completed the dwelling in 1833. The view on the front or the south-east reveals five bays. There is a pedimented portico on the northern east wing and there was and still is cut limestone Neo-classical detail throughout. When John Patrick acquired it, it was in poor condition and he accordingly revamped it.

In 1925, John Patrick decided to make the Universal Motor Company a limited company. The National Archive in Dublin holds the company formation documents. The certificate of incorporation of the Universal Motor Company Limited is dated 2 September 1925. The company was formed with compliance to the requirements of the Companies (Consolidation) Act 1908. The first directors were John Patrick O'Mahony, David O'Mahony (a brother), both registered at 40 North Main Street, Joseph O'Mahony (a brother) of Knock, Rochestown, and Charles P. McCarthy, an incorporated accountant of 50 South Mall. The chairman was John Patrick O'Mahony. The nominal capital of the company was £10,000 divided into 10,000 shares of £1 each.

The money was borrowed in late September 1925 from the Munster and Leinster Bank Limited on 66 South Mall Cork. However, in February 1926, the company ran into financial problems and the bank appointed Mr Alexander Joseph Magennis as a receiver and manager of the property of the company. By 1927, the receiver had sold off the Cornmarket Street premises and the garage on North Main Street was replaced by the Lee Hosiery and Clothing Factory (now Maher's Sports). The Universal Motor Company Limited was eventually dissolved in July 1945.

In East Cork *c.*1934, John Patrick O'Mahony diversified into the hurley-making business in Killeagh. His brothers Joe and Paddy were also involved in the business. They brought ash in from forests in Clare and Longford for manufacture. The hurley manufacturing continued until the 1970s. Hurling was a competitive sport in East Cork. Dungourney Hurling Club were All-Ireland champions in 1902 and Munster Champions in 1907 and also in that decade were winners of the Roche Cup, Cork Athletic Grounds Cup and the Dr Mangan Cup. So there was a great heritage of hurling in the area before the O'Mahony brothers set up their business.

On the walls of O'Mahony's Pub in Killeagh is a picture of the Killeagh Hurling Team with Paddy O'Mahony as part of the team, highlighting also that the O'Mahony family participated in the sport. The pub in Killeagh also proudly displays a hurley signed by Christy Ring. The hurleys were sent far afield to New Zealand and Australia to Irish clubs. During his time as Taoiseach, Jack Lynch presented a gift of a hurley to the son of the Ambassador of Copenhagen.

The brothers also had a farm, which they worked on. Paddy eventually moved into the saw-milling industry. Another brother, James, who was better known as Jimmy, lived in the home place in Berrings and was married to Bridie. He joined the Volunteers in the Berrings area in 1919. His brother Richard became a commandant in the Old IRA. Jimmy joined the Fianna Fáil party on its foundation and was a staunch Republican who for many years delivered the oration speech at the Dripsey Ambush Memorial. He also played road bowling and has the honour of being the first 'official' Cork road-bowling champion, following the formation of the Ból Chumann na hÉireann in 1954. At the end of his bowling days, he became involved at administration level with Ból Chumann and was its President at the time of his death in 1983.

Above left: Jimmy and Bridie O'Mahony. (*Sheila Healy*)

Above right: Mary Ellen O'Mahony. (*Eamonn O'Mahony*)

35. THE RHYTHMS OF LIFE

The road south from Berrings Cross takes one through Ballyanley near the site of Inniscarra Community Centre. The scenery southwards into the townlands of Magoola, Faha and Gurteen is picturesque. The land rolls up and down as it meets Inniscarra Reservoir and reminds me of the rolling southern suburbs of Cork City such as Ballyphehane and Turners Cross, but without the houses. Ballyanley or Baile Uí Áinle means 'Hanley's Habitation'. Magoola or Magh Guala means 'Plain of the Shoulder', whilst Faha means 'lawn' or 'green'.

Travelling further east is the townland of Gurteen, or Goirtín, which means 'Little Field'. At one time, Gurteen was famous for being a stop on the Cork–Muskerry rail line. The station house is gone but the memories of the building are still enshrined in the mind of local resident Margaret Harrington, who lives in a bungalow on the site. Margaret's mother was Nellie O'Brien from Annemount, Friar's Walk. She married Jack Field in 1942. Jack was from Freemount originally but his family moved into the Gurteen station house in 1935, a year after the rail line closed. Nellie, on marrying Jack, moved in. They had two daughters, Margaret and Mary. Jack worked for John A. Woods and was a very keen gardener. Neighbours asked him to grow cabbage plants for them. The family lived in the house until 1962. They then moved into the nearby cottage of Pat Larimore who died in the same year. The Harrington family built a new house on the site of the station house in 1984.

The hinges of the gate that stopped traffic to allow the train across the Gurteen road can still be seen in the old stone wall. The stones of the station house have been built into the garden wall and driveway wall of the adjacent house of the Olden family.

Further south from the site of the old station house is Fairy House Cross. It is the intersection of three country roads, but a mini oasis has been created in the centre. I encountered the site by chance. Local man Brian Flynn explained that the site was originally a rubbish dump and a dangerous intersection for drivers who could not see traffic coming around the corner. The small community of twenty-five houses of Gurteen, Ballyanley and Faha aspired to change its appearance. The site was chosen to create an oasis. Some of the community members were keen gardeners and landscaped the overgrown roundabout area. The community got help from the County Council who provided the community with materials. The site was named Gurteen Cross but the community renamed the site Fairy House Cross to give it a special, even mythical feel.

The sign by the waterworks on the Dripsey–Cork road says 'The beautiful Lee

Above left: Margaret Harrington, April 2008, with her hand on the part of the gate that opened to let the Cork–Muskerry Tram across the Gurteen road.

Above right: Gurteen station house, late 1950s, with the Field family, Nellie (left), Mary (behind) and Margaret (right). (*Field/Harrington family collection*)

Valley'. It invites people to partake in its beauty and the scenery and to be inspired. At this point in the townland of Faha (from Faithche meaning 'Green' or 'Lawn') the viewer can stop and appreciate Inniscarra Reservoir. Many times I have stopped at the sign and admired and photographed the sunsets on the way home from fieldwork. I feel this is an important site in the Lee Valley for the explorer; from a geographical point of view, you get to see the bigger picture of the Lee Valley.

From our viewing point, it is easy to admire the Lee, to be drawn in by the water. Looking at Inniscarra Reservoir from a distance is easy on the eye. The countryside rolls back towards the Millstreet area. On closer inspection, one can see the effects of the Lee Hydro-Electric Scheme. In particular, one can view the field systems on the south bank of Inniscarra Reservoir in Walshestown and Castleinch and see the edges of fields disappearing. It is like the area's geography and history are being eroded over time by the lapping waters, just like the memories of the place and the tide of time.

At this part of the valley, the explorer is quite open to Ireland's dynamic weather systems. I have always been intrigued by the changing atmosphere of the place. During the spring months, I have encountered the cold fogs descending on the reservoir and shrouding the water in mystery. On sunny summer days when blue skies are present, the water flows at a slow and hypnotic pace. The autumn has brought me shorter days and a chance to see those marvellous sunsets. The winter has brought me the openness of the valley, its darkness and rough textures, as the wind attacked my bike and forced me to completely concentrate on the road and not admire the passing view. The natural heritage here is very much alive and has a dynamic and vibrant pulse. At all these various times, I have had different feelings for this place. Well, being blown off the road by a wind down the valley is bad, but contrasting are those sunsets, which as a 'town mouse' I rarely get to see because of the city's dense canvas of buildings.

This viewing platform also provides a bird's eye view of Faha House, the home of the Burke family, which nestles alongside the reservoir. John Burke warmly invited me to his house to hear his family history and even more of the cultural heritage of the area. John has two sisters, Elaine and Sr Teresa, and one brother Colm, who for many years was Cork City Councillor and is a former MEP for Ireland South. In terms of a site biography for Faha House, John informs me that it is said that Hugh O'Neill, Earl of Tyrone crossed the river at a green-field site on his way to Kinsale in the early seventeenth century. The site was a lowest crossing point over the Lee. Arising out of that, a coach house and bar were developed on the site. It is also said that Daniel O'Connell stayed here in the early nineteenth century. Revamping the nineteenth-century house in 1999, John also unearthed the underlining dilapidated flooring tiles that came from the old Dripsey Paper Mills. John notes that his father Timothy (from Carrignavar) married into Faha House in the 1950s. His father John was from Béal na mBláth. John's mother Kitty Healy was an only child. Prior to that, the Healys have been rooted in the area for many centuries.

Seamus Healy from across the reservoir in Walshestown has completed extensive work on the Healy family in the region. The Healy name is one of the most common in Ireland, having been at one time forty-seventh place in the list of most common surnames. At one time, the Healys in Donoughmore parish were the owners of around 22,000 acres across 40 townlands, and possessed the land for 1,000 years until the time of Oliver Cromwell and the dispossession of land, when the Healys were dispersed in Ireland and abroad.

Seamus Healy has traced back the Faha House Healys to Andrew Healy, who was born in 1785 and who died in 1864. John was married to Mary Downey and they lived in Walshestown. John had four brothers, Denis, James, William and John, and one sister, whose name is unknown. The parents are also unknown. In fact in Griffith's Valuation of property in County Cork in 1852, Andrew, John and sons have a collective land bank of ninety-two acres in Walshestown, which was leased from Lady Carbery. Denis went on to attain lands in the adjacent townland of Castleinch. It was a son of Denis, by the name of John, that went to live in Faha House, where the Burkes now live. Interestingly, in 1852 Richard Griffith records another family relative also called Denis Healy who had a cottage with relatively no land in Faha.

Above left: Fairy House Cross, 2008.

Above right: The stopping point, Inniscarra Reservoir, summer 2007.

Left: John Burke, right, with his two sons Timothy and Shane, and Faha bullán stone, April 2008.

On my visit, John Burke told me that his grandfather was Denis Healy. He died in 1959 in his seventies, so he was born in the 1880s. Denis, apart from being a farmer, went fishing a lot for salmon in the Lee. He also at one time won a trophy for best horse at Coachford show. He was married to Ellen McCarthy from Clashanaifrinn, Ovens. She was sister to Edward McCarthy, who was founder of the Mayooth mission to China. The accompanying and evocative pictures tell more of the story of the Healys and reveal more of the human and natural pulse of this very interesting area of the Lee Valley. And as Mr Healy in his book *The Healy Story* notes, 'the heritage of the past is the seed that brings forth the harvest of the future'.

INNISCARRA DAM RETROSPECT

36. GENERATIONS: SNAPSHOTS AND TALENTS

I went along to the launch of the Elysian Tower, Cork and Ireland's tallest build-ing. Over the years of its construction, I have photographed its 'putting together'. I, probably like everyone, had mixed emotions about it. I was excited about seeing all the different pieces added but also fearful of the change; this building dominates Cork's skyline and is so different to most other Cork buildings. But the entire work grew on me as I watched them add all the new parts. There seemed to be always a buzz, a rhythm and a pulse to the construction.

The Elysian took shape, etching itself well into the emptier parts of Cork's sky-line. The building now seems to bookend the city in the east, whilst County Hall bookends the city in the west. The launch was good. The speeches commented on how iconic the building was and the risks of launching apartments on our recessive economic scene. Ideas of leadership, public realm ownership, inspiration and com-parisons with Shandon were put forward but overall I though the whole concept was undersold to me in terms of the Elysian as a leader in Irish architecture.

The speeches ended and I joined the tour of the show apartments. I marvelled at the views down on the city, especially the docklands and I imagined the changes that hopefully will take place in the next twenty years. The tour carried on to the top penthouse balcony. And there it was a view 'to die for' – Cork City in all its glory. This was a view of my city I had not seen before.

The tour came down and we entered the Japanese-style garden, another impressive piece of work. I came away from the launch very impressed. The Elysian is changing place and identity once again in Cork. As a place the Elysian evokes feelings of pride, stirring something deep and emotional in me that connected me to my experiences on that evening and in my photographing of the Elysian since it initiation.

It was only when I think about the Elysian that I begin to understand what life might have been like during the construction of the Lee dams, and all that went with it. The ever-growing need to provide an improved level of electricity service for existing customers, as well as the new demands created by an ambitious programme for rural electrification, set in motion the process for the building of the Lee stations and the damming of the valley, forty kilometres in length and over twenty-two kilometres wide. This was a colossal task, and necessitated years of minute planning, geographical surveys and preservation orders on, for example, the Gearagh region, and land purchase, with the final contracts for the works in place towards the end of 1952. Detailed land acquisi-tion records and newspaper documentation afford a fascinating glimpse into what must have been an enormous upheaval for the 200 families involved, who were relocated as the valley was flooded and their homes were submerged.

The success of the enterprise depended on the effective deployment of manpower (650 personnel, many of them highly trained or skilled), both from home and abroad. The sheer scale of the project required a sophisticated infrastructure of housing, lodging, catering and entertainment, as workers were drafted in from not only the Cork region but from all over Europe.

The Lee Hydro-Electric Scheme transformed the Lee Valley by opening up new tourism opportunities for fishing, waterskiing, sailing and rowing, and by securing the future supply of clean and economical electricity and water throughout the Cork area and beyond. The impact of the Lee scheme has been positive and lasting.

The Lee Hydro-Electric Scheme is still very much at the heart of people's memories in mid-Cork and in the wider region. This section is based on a series of interviews conducted with former and present-day workers. There are lessons to be learned from the Lee Hydro-Electric scheme. All of the workers interviewed, past and present, touched upon ideas of pride and identity. Many were young adults when they arrived to the building works.

The Lee scheme is also about the power of creativity and imagination, and the evolution of ideas. It was and still is about taking risks and pushing out the comfortable boundaries of life. For each person written about in snapshot many more are represented through their life experiences. The Lee scheme should encourage us all to ponder on the power of the individual and their contribution to society, whether at a local or international level.

Inniscarra dam site, 24 March 1957. (*ESB Archive, Dublin*)

37. HIGH NOON: MAURICE SWEENEY

It's difficult not to be impressed by the Lee Scheme; the transformation, the real-life stories, the infrastructure, the effort, the commitment, and the emotion put into the project by all involved. It always adds to the quality of research when one gets to chat to those who were physically involved.

It's important to tap into as many memories as possible before the event fades into the unknown. In the context of the Lee Scheme, the initiative has been well recorded by the ESB archive and contemporary newspapers. But one aspect that perhaps fell by the wayside was the more human side of the work. I was delighted when I heard the memories of the construction manager of the Lee Scheme, Maurice G. Sweeney, which came to me through his son Maurice.

Maurice G. Sweeney was born in 1917 in Oughterard, County Galway. He was known to his family and close friends as 'Dev'. The name arose because he was born on the day De Valera was returned to power for County Clare. He married Bridget ('Dilly') Pettit from Ballygar, County Galway, who was a sister of Ted Pettit who founded the very successful Cork engineering firm E.G. Pettit.

Above left: Maurice G. Sweeney, *c.*1942, at around twenty-five years of age. (*Sweeney family collection*)

Above right: The Sweeney family at their dwelling on Coolcower House estate, Macroom, during the Lee Scheme in the mid-1950s. Pictured are Maurice Senior, his wife Bridget, and their sons, Maurice, Terence and Gary. (*Sweeney family collection*)

French soirée celebrating the Lee Scheme, pre-1955, and before Maurice G. Sweeney took over. (*Sweeney family collection*)

After graduating as a civil engineer from UCG in 1942, Maurice worked with his father in Sweeney & Sheahan Engineers, and then with Jennings Builders in Dublin as a chief engineer on the building of the sea wall in Dún Laoghaire. He took up a position as an engineer with Société de Construction des Batignolles, the French company that had been given the contract to construct the dams for the Lee Scheme. After about a year, following some general difficulties with the progress of the dams, Maurice was put in overall charge. He was a tall man with a passing resemblance to Gary Cooper and was known as 'High Noon'. He was also a determined man who never suffered fools gladly, and he got the whole project back on track.

Maurice Sweeney junior notes that his dad was great at managing people and putting jobs together. Maurice has fleeting memories of the dam. He was eight years old at the time:

> I remember the blasting and taking shelter, but mostly lots of parties and everyone learning French. I remember the prefabs as a child, with the Christmas parties and the showing of movies. There was a great social aspect to the scheme, it was a big thing compared to other things some of the older men worked on. I remember Jim Irwin who played Santa Claus. He lived on Magazine Road in Cork City. My father was a great angler/fly-fisherman. He fished on Lough Corrib and fished on the Lee when he came to the Lee Scheme. I frequently went with him on the Lee outings. I remember going out on Sunday outings and ending up in the dam and my mother being annoyed.

Maurice Sweeney, son of
Maurice G. Sweeney, July 2008.

For the Lee Scheme, the Sweeney family rented a house in Coolcower, near Macroom. Maurice junior remembers the owners of the Big House were the Williamses, the family of Sam Williams. The family moved to Orchard Road in Cork towards the end of the scheme. Maurice went to school in the convent in Macroom and later went to Cobh when his dad began working on Whitegate oil refinery.

Maurice Sweeney was the chief engineer on the construction of the oil refinery at Whitegate. After that he spent some years in Iran, where he oversaw the construction of a major bridge in a town called Khorramshahr in the south of the country (the bridge was to become the site of one of the most ferocious battles in the Iran–Iraq war) and the building of a railway station in the holy city of Mashad in the north.

After returning to Ireland he joined Irish Engineering and Harbour Construction (IrishEnco), of which he soon became managing director. This company specialised in marine works and was responsible for many major projects in this country. The biggest project was the building of the oil terminal jetty at Bantry in the late 1960s, a job that Maurice oversaw directly. After leaving IrishEnco in the early 1970s, he worked as a consultant engineer until his death in 1983. He was predeceased by his wife by ten months and was buried in Galway.

38. ADVENTURES OF PURE THOUGHT: FERDIE O'HALLORAN

Talking about the green-field site of Inniscarra dam takes me back to day one. The people at senior level on the senior civil-engineering team in the ESB were Frank Clynch and Brendan Brennan, a man who was a superb engineer with very high standards. I was one of the junior civil engineers.

I was born in 1929 and I'm originally from the Commons Road, Blackpool. The River Bride ran at the foot of the garden. Today, the motorway and the shopping centre are on the site. My father Joe worked for Eagle Printing Works for a time. My mother Brigid (*née* O'Riordan) was from Ardfert and was more affectionately known as 'Babe'. In later years, my mother and father ran a shop on the Commons Road.

I went to the North Mon[astery] and through my mathematical interest attained a scholarship of £50 per annum to attend school. Interestingly, at that time I was also offered a job as a trainee clerk in the post office at £1 a week. Before going to college, I spent a short space of time with the Met Service in Dublin Airport. Meteorology was great in developing my interest in hydrology. My two brothers, Louis and Brendan, and I went to University College Cork. The eldest of the family was Michael. All four of us went into engineering. Job opportunities were great in engineering. We were just beginning to build the country after the war. Electrical engineers and civil engineers could get jobs. Rural electrification was up and running.

My degree in engineering took three years. We learned our basic tools for learning and applying knowledge. I had already some basic philosophical knowledge for maths, logic and geometry. I loved the mental gymnastics of maths. I describe it as having adventures in pure thought. Geometry is essential to all structures for strength and layout. The formula is important. My lecturer Professor Paddy Coffey was a fabulous teacher.

As well as attending my undergrad courses in civil engineering, I also attended night courses, two nights a week for three years. Canon Bastible gave a course on the social teachings of the Catholic Church. Alfred O'Rahilly, who was also president of UCC at the time [1945-1954], gave a course on religion and science. I also attended courses on theology and social science by Professor and Fr James E. O'Mahony of the Philsophy Department, UCC. He had a way of putting ideas in your head that you thought of them even a week afterwards. I was also a member of the Loft Shakespearean Company, through which I had a number of parts in different plays. I was also inspired by our director Fr O'Flynn and his approaches to education, especially his critique of the government's approach to education. He wanted to give students what was lacking.

Most of us in UCC were inspired to make Ireland a better place to live. We weren't altruistic; survival was important financially. I graduated in 1950 from UCC and I was sad to leave college. I was offered a post in UCC in the engineering department but left to become an assistant lecturer in civil engineering in Queen's University, Belfast. There I was still young enough to attend the undergrad dances and dinner at the staff table. I gave two lectures a week on geometrical aspects – surveying and how to set out on projects. I also assisted drawing offices to lay plans out and relieved senior staff within offices on occasion.

I spent two and half years working and also completing a Masters in Foundational Engineering (the interaction between the soil and structure). I also met my future wife, Claire (*née* Loughery) who was Belfast born but lived in Belleek and Omagh in her younger years. I was offered more academic work but opted for practical civil-engineering work.

Posts for junior engineers were advertised for the Lee Hydro Scheme. Forty to fifty civil engineers were interviewed. Many of the younger guys taken in were sent to work on the steam-powered Marina site [Cork]. I was delighted to be offered the post, especially as I loved Cork and was thankful to come home. Indeed from the age of twelve, I had a bike and used to swim in Hellhole at Inniscarra and by the ruined Inniscarra Church of Ireland church and graveyard. The Lee was one of my early loves and working on the Lee Scheme was a thrilling thought.

I worked on the initial stages of the dam. Jerry Mahony in the Marina [Cork] housed and looked after the young staff. Frank Clynch looked after the construction team. Seamus Ertin and I were in charge of setting out the dam works. I remember we came out in a baby Ford. We had to know the valley and the history of the water flow to carefully select the sites of the dams. The completed surveys of the valley were important to the design of the stations. Sir William Halcro and partners, a huge international organisation, had their head man visit Joe MacDonald on occasion. Joe was one of the men at senior level, making decisions regarding form and layout of roads and bridges.

I started my work on the Lee Scheme by devising the geometry of the site and looking at the shape of the dam and the valley complex. I took accurate surveys on the ground and created drawings. In a sense, I created the basis to marry the ground and the foundations of the dam and questioned how deep should we dig. I was briefed from the top on a day-to-day basis. Donal O'Leary was the section engineer at Inniscarra and he had great experience of maintenance at Ardnacrusha on the Shannon Scheme. Donal made a great contribution to us, the junior civil engineers. Meticulous detail, resulting in maintenance-free results, was important. He let me get on with the job and I was there for three years, between 1953 and 1956. I was there from the beginning and was there for the cutting of the first sod. I became a very good and efficient construction engineer. I married Claire whilst working on the Lee Scheme and began a family during those years.

Above left: The O'Halloran family, Leicester, England, 1959. Pictured are Ferdie and Clare with Richard, Tony, Nicholas and Jacinta. (*O'Halloran Family Collection*)

Above right: Ferdie O'Halloran, July 2008.

In 1956, I opted to leave the Lee Scheme and sent off CVs to a couple of design offices in Dublin. I had worked in the academic and practical side and wanted to get work on the design side. I got a job with British Reinforced Concrete (BRC) Co. Ltd, Stafford, who had a Dublin office. They were highly specialised masters of the production of steel – cut, bent, fixed – and drawings for reinforced concrete construction. I subsequently went to England and joined the nuclear power section of English Electric Co. Ltd at Whetstone, Leicester. I came back to Cork on the *Innisfallen* in September 1960 and taught in UCC in the Department of Engineering for thirty-five years till my retirement.

39. CAITNE: DONAL O'HALLORAN

I was born in Kileens, near Blarney in 1932. In my youth, my family moved a couple of times across the city and ended up in Turners Cross and eventually in Bishopstown. I went to the North Mon. I saw a guy wiring a lamp in a house once, developed an interest, and wound up in a job in electricity. I went to the Crawford Municipal Technical College and studied in the electrical section. Tommy Glavin, known as 'Juice', was in charge of the electrical section at the time. I put my name down for the ESB and got a job as an apprentice with them. I moved from job to job. I did a lot of the panel work in most of the power stations – setting up instruments. I was dead keen to be on the Lee Scheme and I became the first electrician to work on it. The civil work's inspector Mr Healy needed a shed with a light bulb, so in a sense I became the first electrician on the site.

I was also the one who started the flooding of the Lee. Guys came down from the Hydro-Electric department in Dublin to start the flooding; Carrigadrohid was flooded first. On the day, two of the spillway gates were closed and one was left open. The start button didn't work to close the third gate – so I was brought in to fix the trip overload, which I did, and the motor started. The guy from Dublin informed me to leave it running. Within an hour, the headrace trench began to fill.

A lot of design work went into the Lee Station. Tens of miles of cables were installed and there was also the cable between Inniscarra and Carrigadrohid – which was an early form of multiplexing. I worked very hard on the site. I didn't see a holiday for three years. When work was finished in 1958, Jack Higgins asked the boss of the station, Dermot O'Shea, for a week off. The time off was dependent on the weather; poor weather meant rain and money for the ESB. However, I got my holiday. On day one, I sat down, lit the fire at home and had a lovely lunch, and then a knock came on the door. It was Jimmy Sweeny from the dam. I was called to Carrigadrohid to attend to technical problems. I sat in Jimmy's open van wrapped up in coats. Something was wrong with the remote control in Carrigadrohid, it was the worst combination of system failure – generator increasing in load, brakes on, lifted, brakes burned. The generator ran into overload and tripped on over-speed. Three spillway gates got signals to open wide, hence spilling water.

I remember coming through Carrigadrohid village. There was three or four feet of water. People were taking furniture and carpets out of houses, and a man raised his fist at us. We were there till three o'clock in the morning sorting out the problems and we eventually shut down the whole system. The following morning we were back out and had to call the Germans [the Voith firm] over for a couple of weeks to replace parts and brake pads.

Above left: Donal O'Halloran, aged fifteen/sixteen. (*O'Halloran family collection*)

Above centre: Donal O'Halloran, Bishopstown, July 2008.

Above right: Donal, mother Josephine and sister Pauline, Cork Summer Show 1951. (*O'Halloran family collection*)

I remember the acceptance tests. We had problems with the 4MW generator. The 4MW turbine in Inniscarra was designed to keep the river flowing in normal conditions. Short circuiting was an issue and we had to isolate the problem. We were also aware of the huge currents flowing. Those problems were solved but the station had to be shut down for a couple of days.

My supervisor was Jack Higgins from St Luke's, Cork. He was a boxer in his younger days. Dermot O'Shea, the station manager was a hurler at one time. He was from the west of Ireland, a nice, gentle type of character. In 1959, I moved to the refinery in Whitegate. I was offered a bungalow out there but stayed in the city. I went to the refinery as supervisor but moved to engineering and resigned as senior project engineer with the refinery.

In later years, I took up another interest, that of geology. My wife Peggy comes from Ard na Caithne, north of Dingle Bay in County Kerry. The name Ard refers to height. Caitne can mean 'Arbutus' but also can refer to a reaction with the sand after a storm, where a type of spray is sent across the land (just like electricity). During Cork Geology Week in 1989, hosted by the Geology Department in UCC, I met lecturer Betty Higgs who invited my wife and me on a ten-week course. We attended and then signed up for more; eventually we took on the Diploma in Geology, which took two years to complete. We discovered afterwards that some of the oldest rocks in the geological world can be found in the Dingle region. In 1992, a group of us founded the Cork Geological Association.

40. STAND ME ON MY FEET: JACK SHEEHAN

I was born in 1919 on Dunbar Street, Cork, but my family moved shortly afterwards to Blackrock Road and was there for a good many years. I went to school in the South Monastery. I served my time with the ESB in Albert Road, where the old Tramway Company was located. I started there in 1939 in the installations or contracts department. We specialised in installing electric motors and wiring houses. The other departments included operations, which dealt with overhead wiring and public lighting, and the meter department, which installed the meters.

My department was run by J.J. Ryan from Northern Ireland. The supervisor was Maurice Desmond, who lived in Castle View Terrace on the Lower Road. Where I lived on Blackrock Road, there was also Hubert Launders, who was one time chief of the Cork Tramways Company. He had come over to Cork from England to start the company. He was a top engineer in his day. The ESB had taken over the Tramway Company in the 1920s. The ESB then appointed their own engineer, William Roe, a well-built Kilkenny man, who wore thick glasses and had a bubbly personality. In Cork, he lived in Ardfoyle Avenue, Beaumont. He became known as a 'District Engineer'. In later years, he was chosen by the ESB to head up the rural electrification scheme of Ireland. Mr Hannah replaced him as district engineer in Cork and was there at the beginning of my time.

I became an apprentice in 1939. I remember the other apprentices in my department, Gus Connolly, Finbar Cronin and Con Donovan. There were two other apprentices as well, Tom Mason and Hubert Hughes, who were in the cable jointers section. During our time as apprentices, we were sent to Dublin for three a year months for four years to Kevin Street Technical School and we were put up in digs. I remember seeing radios at the time that said, 'Stand me on my feet.' William Roe used to say that to us when we came up to Dublin. We had never been outside of Cork, never mind coming to live in Dublin.

At the end of four years, the ESB told us that they wouldn't keep us on – they informed us they would take us back if we got three years experience. I got a job with Tom Millard on Oliver Plunkett Street, Cork. Tom had worked in the Cork Tramway Company as an engineer. The silent partner was Fred Bolster. We did maintenance work for firms such as Sunbeam Wholsey and Beamish and Crawford. I remember wiring Matehy Church in Inniscarra. We also wired pubs; I remember working on the Olympia on the Lower Road, which was being wired for the first time.

I spent ten years with Tom Millard and then went back to work for the ESB. At that time, the ESB were changing from direct current to alternating current. They carried it out for free but it meant that every motor in every factory had to be changed as well as rewiring some houses. The section the ESB set up for the changeover employed a

Staff group shot, during acceptance tests for turbines and generators at Inniscarra, 1958. Back row, left to right: Flor Deasy (welder), Gerry Power (fitter, Waterford), 'Corny' O'Callaghan (helper, local), Unknown, Mr O'Connell(?). Third row: Dermot O'Shea (station superintendent), Jack Higgins (supervisor, St Luke's Cork), Donal O'Halloran (electrician, Cork), John Shine (local), John Reidy (helper, Cork), John O'Leary (worker, looked after turbines and their lubrication), Denis/'Dinny' O'Mahony (worker, Blarney), Unknown, Tim Deane ('The Chauffeur', brought out the office staff in the morning). Second row: John Murray and Jack Sheehan (electrician, Cork). Front row: Willie Walsh (Midleton), Terry Deasy (helper), Unknown, Unknown, Unknown, Unknown, Tom Clifford (electrician, Cork), Unknown. Joe Carr and Cyril Foley were also part of this group. (*ESB Archives*).

lot of outside electricians. The direct-current generators in the powerhouse in Cork depended on the transport of raw materials. Coal-fire boilers created steam to drive generators. This was a very expensive business. The place was lined regularly with horses and carts of coal, drawn from ships at Albert Quay. This was a messy process; even to dispose of the ashes was costly. Alternating current was generated free from the River Shannon at Ardnacrusha. Siemens from Germany did the turbine work at Adnacrusha. There was a high cost involved in buying coal from England. Rural electrification had started as well. Meters had to be installed in houses.

For the Lee Scheme, my first job was to put up lights along the wall at the top. I remember the turbine room, the alternator over that and the control room over that. Rooms had to be lit; drilling through concrete was done using diamond-tipped drills. Joe Carr was the supervisor on Albert Quay. Originally from Cobh, he was in charge of

Jack Sheehan, Togher, Cork,
July 2008.

the installation of lighting and the control cables to transformers by the compound. He
built two bungalows by the tailrace. Jack Higgins lived in one. I remember Herr Leitil,
the head electrical engineer from Voiths. I also remember Dermot O'Shea, who was
the station manager. He lived just past the Canon's Cross in Inniscarra. From his house,
you could see the Inniscarra station upstream.

At the end of the time on the Lee Scheme, Dermot O'Shea told me there was a job
in Kilbarry, Cork. At the same time, whilst calling into St Francis church, I met Eddie
Murray, who was working on the Whitegate Oil Refinery for Lumas, who were the
principal contractors. Eddie said I should look into getting a job down there. I did and I
got a job. I remained in Whitegate after its construction and retired from there in 1984.

I remember the foreman electrician on the Lee Scheme, John Looney from
Coachford, who also moved to Whitegate. He moved down with his actual timber hut
to Rostellan and had it done up with a plaster finish. It's still there near Cloyne Cross
and overlooking Rostellan Lake.

41. NETWORK OF IDEAS: JOHN O'DONOVAN

The more I chatted to those who worked on the dam, the more I could see what I call the network of ideas – the technical thinking and science that were brought to bear on the development of the Lee Hydro-Electric Scheme Dam. John O'Donovan was another retired engineer I luckily came across in my fieldwork. He worked as a junior civil engineer and was involved in the concrete mix design for the diamond-headed buttress-type dam at Inniscarra, the concrete gravity structure at Carrigadrohid, and the associated new roads and bridges (creating a grand total of 250,000 yards^3 of concrete mix).

John O'Donovan was born and bred on Model Farm Road. In the 1940s, he went to Christian Brothers College, Wellington Road. During those years, he developed a huge interest in athletics and was an Irish champion sprinter. He got a scholarship to go to University College Cork (UCC) to study engineering, where he was influenced by the work of Professor Harry Walsh.

Harry Walsh, a Corkman and a pupil of the 'North Mon', graduated with a degree in Civil Engineering from UCC in the 1910s. He subsequently graduated with a diploma from Imperial College London. He returned home and became an assistant to the contemporary Professor of Civil Engineering, Connel Alexander. Also in those years, Harry played his part in the Irish War of Independence by transporting gold coins for Michael Collins between Cork and Dublin. When the professor in UCC died, Harry (in his twenties) assumed the role of Professor of Civil Engineering in 1921. Harry was professor for forty years. He was the first Cork graduate to serve as President of the Institution of Civil Engineers of Ireland, in 1940 and 1942 respectively.

UCC's Intervarsity squad, late 1940s. Left to right: Paddy Huber (swimming), John O'Donovan, John O'Jagoe (chairman of Cork City sports for many years), Gerald Murray, Billy O'Regan. The picture taken atop the now-demolished *Cork Examiner* offices, Academy Street, Cork. (*O'Donovan family collection*)

Throughout his career, Harry worked hard in his lab in UCC with an array of machinery, and pioneered the study of modern concrete mix. Compressing test tubes of cement aggregates led him to test crushing strength, the water cement ratio and tensile strength. Scholars in England further developed his pioneering research. Harry was a well-read man and subscribed to a number of journals, including French ones. He had a great respect for French engineers, who at that time, through the work of Le Corbusier, were critiquing and attempting to forge new debates on modern architecture. Harry developed a keen interest in photography and trout fishing and also was fascinated by rainfall and all its implications such as flooding and other aspects of the hydraulic discipline.

Professor Harry Walsh attempted to create a better understanding of concrete, mix design and construction techniques. Harry became a well-respected consultant and established his own firm of H.N. Walsh & Partners. Cork County Council asked him to design water and sewage schemes in County Cork. For example, he designed the old water tower in Cobh.

Harry was also a regular contributor to the *Journal of the Institute of Engineers*. In one of his most celebrated academic books, *How to Make Good Concrete* (1939) Harry noted it was easier to buy ready-mixed concrete – if the job was within reach of a ready-mixed concrete factory. However, most engineers, contractors, builders, and manufacturers cannot rely on these facilities. They have to decide which are the best of available aggregates, which may be used or must not be used, and, often, how to make the best possible use of aggregates that are known to be far from good but must be used.

Harry Walsh passed on his enthusiasm for his work to many of his students, including his son Malachy who set up his own engineering company in time (Malachy Walsh & Partners). Professor Walsh also influenced John O'Donovan. John qualified in the early 1950s and worked as a demonstrator in college under Professor Walsh for a year after qualifying. It was Professor Walsh who encouraged John to go for the job of junior civil engineer in Inniscarra Dam. He got it and was there for three years, living during the week in Innisluinge House with other civil engineers. John became the site laboratory engineer.

Influenced by Harry Walsh's advice, John built up the scientific analysis needed for the concrete mix necessary for the various blocks. All of John's meticulous research was published by the Institution of Civil Engineers of Ireland in 1957 and survives today. The rounded sandstone gravel pit at John A. Woods's was selected for aggregates. The site was already equipped with a modern washing and screening plant but required a number of changes to produce the required gradings of the aggregates needed to produce high-quality concrete. The development of an adequate mixing and placing technique for concrete at the early stages was greatly facilitated by John A. Woods.

John O'Donovan, Blackrock, Cork, August 2008.

The preliminary experimental grading and mixes were prepared in the civil engineering laboratory at University College Cork, and the results obtained from these were used successfully at the site laboratory at Inniscarra. In all eighty trial mixes were made at laboratories. The final arrangement adopted was to produce four sizes. John also arranged the pours and mixes. All concrete was kept damp until the subsequent pour was in place. The methods adopted by John were extensive and impressive.

After Inniscarra Dam, John went into O'Connell Harley, Consultant Engineers on the South Mall. They were designing churches and buildings across the country. He worked with Cyril Roche on the concrete design of Youghal Bridge. In 1961, John started his own practice, John O'Donovan & Associates (still in operation under his sons). His firm did the concrete design for some of the 1960s buildings you see on the South Mall. In the 1970s, John was involved in the concrete design work of such buildings such as the IDA buildings, Douglas Community School, the Convent of Mercy, the VEC School of Art, Cork Examiner Offices (recently demolished), Grange church, Irish Crown, Shield Insurance, Verolme Cork Dockyard, Tralee Fruit Company, Marathon Petroleum, Punch & Company, and Topps.

John also worked with architect Boyd Barrett on several churches; examples include Bishopstown's Descent of the Holy Ghost with Jim Barry, and St Patrick's church on the Rochestown Road. With the Department of Education, he completed a lot of concrete design for schools across the country. In the 1980s, John was involved in the concrete design of shopping centres such as Douglas and Wilton. John was one of the founders of Cork Civic Trust and was chairman for many years. John was very much part of the making of late-twentieth-century Cork.

42. LEGACY: DIARMUID O'SHEA

The River Lee Development Project will add a total of 27MW to the generating capacity of the Electricity Supply Board's system and will contribute a further sixty-five million units approximately to the annual output of the Hydro-Electric scheme … These stations are also intended to provide standby capacity for the important load venue at Cork.

Diarmuid O'Shea, 'River Lee Hydro-Electric Scheme', *Engineers' Journal*, 1954.

Diarmuid O'Shea was the first station manager of Inniscarra Dam. He was born and raised in Cahirciveen, County Kerry. His father Diarmuid was originally from Gerald Griffin Street near the North Cathedral in Cork. (His parents came into Cork from Inchigeela.) Diarmuid (senior) was a Volunteer, a Private (1915-1921) in the 1st Cork Brigade of which Tomás Mac Curtain was the Commandant. After the Treaty, he became a Garda, rising up through the ranks to that of Superintendent and was stationed in Cahirciveen for a time. In a sense both Diarmuid and his son forged a modern Ireland, one fighting for it and serving it, and the other building it. That sense of a legacy is an important one for the O'Shea family and for the making of modern Cork. His mother was from Westport in Mayo. As Diarmuid (junior) says, 'We had a mixed household on Munster final day!'

Diarmuid went to Christian Brothers School. He pursued mechanical and electrical engineering for four years at University College Dublin. He recalls:

Far left: Diarmuid O'Shea, August 2008, Douglas, Cork.

Left: Diarmuid O'Shea and Patricia Graham pictured in a Dublin dancehall in the late 40's. The couple married in 1952. (*O'Shea family collection*)

I always had an interest in the subject. In those days, you took what work was available or you took the boat to England. I qualified in Dublin and during that year of my graduation, 1947, I started with the ESB. After a short few years, I was sent to Ardnacrusha on the Shannon as a maintenance engineer. In January 1956, I came to Inniscarra. I remember arriving on New Year's Day and starting the following day. The site engineers were there in full strength. I was the only one of the long-term staff there.

I was appointed as station manager and that included the job as mechanical and electrical site engineer. When I arrived the roof was on the station building but there were no walls, and the dam was only three-quarters finished. It was a rough building site – a hive of industry, with a lot of work being done on the dam and the bridges and the new roads.

I liaised with civil works staff on things that would be needed after the construction was finished. It was very satisfying work. Every day we got one more step ahead. In no time, the turbines were installed and the indoor electrical equipment was built. New people started working continuously, and the staff were first class. The phase from installing the turbines to switch on was done on budget and on time, despite a national recession in the country. The quality of men and their quality of work was great. It was much the same people that built Carrigadrohid Dam.

Frank Clynch, site engineer, was from Dublin and lived in Cleave Hill while in Inniscarra. His wife and two sons stayed with him. He was a very meticulous man. He left in 1961 and went back to head office. His assistant was Brendan Brennan, a Dublin man. He went to work on the Clady dam in Gweedore in County Donegal. Donal Murphy from Cork, another site engineer, went to work for the Department of Fisheries.

I was also involved in the recruitment process of the long-term staff. I remember the lads we took on, like Joe Carr, Jack Higgins, John O'Leary (who we took on to operate the power station cranes). I recall other guys as well on the site: Jimmy Sweeney, a driver who was also on the Irish team that won a number of angling competitions; Seamus Madden, a well-known soccer player; Jim Driscoll a local man from Inniscarra; Philip Ryan, an electrician and control operator from Cashel in Tipperary. Philip had been in New York in the 1930s and had worked with electric public utilities. He came home and joined the Irish Army [31st Battalion] during the Emergency and rose to the rank of captain. He went on to work in Caroline Street ESB station, Cork, and the Marina in the early fifties. He was then assigned to Inniscarra and remained there till his retirement in the mid-seventies.

There was also Gerry Power, who came up from the Marina; he had a lot of experience. Then there was 'Corny' O'Callaghan from Inniscarra, Jack Higgins [who died shortly after the group picture in the turbine room was taken], and Joe Carr, who was the very first man I got. He was from Cobh and was involved in the lighting and heating contracts for Inniscarra and Carrigadrohid. Cyril Foley, a Cork City man, was an apprentice when he came to us. He later joined the generations staff in the Marina.

Diarmuid O'Shea receiving a present from Jack Higgins to mark Diarmuid's departure from Inniscarra dam in 1960. (*O'Shea family collection*)

Aileen Aeger was secretary. She looked after the paperwork with Paddy Murphy and Tom Atkinson. Aileen went on to work as the district manager's secretary in Wilton. Joe O'Keeffe, control operator, later went to Great Island power station.

I remember Herr Leitil who was the head electrical engineer at the dam [he took the group photo in the turbine room]. He was born in Vienna, Austria, and as a young man he served with the German navy. When he came to Inniscarra, he brought his wife and they lived in a bungalow near Cloghroe for a couple of years. He was very popular with local people. After the Lee Scheme, his next job was in Venezuela, South America. The last I heard, he was living out his retirement in Germany.

Many of the Inniscarra staff found jobs easily afterwards. The oil refinery at Whitegate and Cork Airport were being built. When the dam was finally finished, the site was reduced to a small number of staff. Inniscarra dam was commissioned in April 1957 and Carrigadrohid in the autumn of that year. I stayed on as station manager until 1960, when I went to the Marina to work as assistant manager. In 1965, I was appointed manager.

In 1969, I was appointed ESB Regional Manager and was based at the Marina. The region at that time comprised the Marina plant and other plants at Great Island, Tarbert and Cahirciveen. By the time I retired in 1991, Aghada and Moneypoint had been added. I was involved in the staff selection, organisation and training side at these plants. My work was on a much larger scale to Inniscarra. Indeed twenty-five years after Inniscarra Dam, the ESB were building 500MW stations, compared to 15MW at Inniscarra. That's huge progress.

43. THE COSMOPOLITAN LEE: AILEEN AEGER

Inniscarra dam was busy, noisy, full of activity, very much alive. By the time I left, all the temporary staff had gone and it became a very quiet place. That was in complete contrast to when I first arrived. The scheme was such a big deal and changed many people's lives.

Aileen Aeger, ESB Secretary, Inniscarra Dam, 1955-1959.

Aileen was brought up in Glanworth in North Cork, where she went to the local national school and later Mercy Sisters boarding school in Cahir, County Tipperary. She did a commercial course in Fermoy and worked for a solicitor for a year. After sitting typing exams for the ESB in 1955 she was appointed to Inniscarra dam at the age of twenty-one. She was to replace Marie Brady, a Roscommon lady, who was transferred to ESB headquarters in Dublin. Frank Clynch, one of the senior site engineers, was her boss, with Brendan Brennan as his assistant.

In 1959, Aileen was transferred out to the ESB district office on the Mallow Road, Cork. She was there was for a year. When the city and county district offices were amalgamated to be located on St Patrick's Street (now the Eason's site), she worked there from 1960 to 1984. When the ESB built a headquarters in Wilton, Aileen spent the remainder of her career there. Aileen kindly wrote to me of her experiences:

Aileen and Tom Atkinson, Boreenmanna Road, Cork. (*Aileen Aeger*)

Above left: Jim Phipps (who learned to speak French fluently from the French personnel), Margaret Murphy (secretary to the French company SCB) and Godfrey Dunlea (clerical). (*Aileen Aeger*)

Above right Staff party, mixture of staff, including Maurice Sweeney, Bill O'Regan and Frank Sorenson. (*Aileen Aeger*)

When the ESB decided in the early fifties to construct two dams and two power stations on the River Lee, the sites chosen were Inniscarra and Carrigadrohid. The contract to build them went to a French firm, Société de Construction des Batignolles whose head office was in Paris.

The Lee development would touch the lives of many. It would bring together the expertise of an amalgam of Irish, French, Germans and Austrians. It would be known as 'the Lee Scheme', and it would be my experience to be a minuscule part of it from 1955 to 1959.

I worked as secretary for Frank Clynch, the site engineer. He did a weekly report of the development of the dam, roads and bridges. I remember the first morning; I was to write a report about Culvert D and did not understand the terminology, but I mastered it in time. I lived in digs in Summerhill North and was collected by Tim Deane every morning in his ESB van, which he was always polishing. Tim later got a job with O'Connor's Funeral Home.

By 1955 the majority of French management personnel had returned to Paris, but the glory days of the French at Inniscarra had been committed to eternal memory. Their exuberance, their love of fine wines and their penchant for parties were legendary. Most of all, they were remembered for their Bastille Day celebrations. July 14 held all the eager anticipation of Christmas. The French revolutionary ideals of liberty, equality, and fraternity held enormous appeal for the Irish, and thus, powerfully motivated, they pitched in and helped the French celebrate. Massive hangovers ensued.

Similarly, the Irish could empathise with French tragedy. May 1954 saw them grieve with the French for the defeat of France in what is now Vietnam, and the huge loss of French lives at the battle of Dien Bien Phu. A Mass on site at Inniscarra commemorated the fallen dead. The French were devastated, and the Irish understood. Irish history is littered with defeat, despite, at times, the best efforts of the French.

The departure of the French from the Lee coincided with the arrival of the German company, J.M. Voith, to install turbines and generators in the new power stations. Max was the first German to arrive. He smiled a lot but had little English. 'Strudel!' he observed one day, pointing to custard at lunch in the workers' camp. 'Strudel', we echoed cautiously – our first German word. But Max was picking up English on site and soon our pathetic progress in his language paled next to his colourful fluency in ours. The older Germans were generally uncommunicative. Of an age to have seen active service in the Second World War, they seemed older than their years, and sometimes you looked at them and wondered. What memories were theirs, those taciturn men who never laughed, with set faces that never smiled?

Blonde and blue-eyed, Germany's Rolf was, at twenty-two, the youngest member of the group. His wartime childhood had scarred him with a deep hatred for Britain. Back from holiday in Edinburgh I blundered into revealing where I had been. 'Eethenbourg! Breetish! Bad!' he scowled, his accent thicker than ever.

Later there would be an Austrian engineer called Rudolf Lettl. He not only spoke English but wrote technical reports in English. These had to be typed and were sometimes difficult to decipher. 'For always I am writing like a doctor!' he'd apologise with melting charm. In time the Germans too returned home, but not before they had been given a traditional Irish send-off. Though still a party culture, the parties had become farewell gatherings. Inexorably, it was migration time. I remember many of the parties in Innisluinge House and the lady in charge, Mrs Cotter from Cloghroe. I remember the auction at the house, just before it was levelled. That was a sad day.

Fifty years have passed since then. Up-market houses with dream gardens have replaced the camp where Max taught us to say 'strudel'. Coincidentally, perhaps, it was in Paris in the early days of the French Revolution that poet William Wordsworth penned the lines, 'Bliss was it in that dawn to be alive/But to be young was very heaven'. He spoke for all of us. Impressed forever on a young memory, images from the Lee Scheme drift in and out of focus: dances, parties, sing-songs, laughing faces round a bonfire in the twilight of a June night, friends who were young when I was young.

The French have a saying, 'When someone goes away, there is a kind of death.' It is fitting that they too have given us the simple wisdom of '*C'est la vie*'.

44. SIGN OF THE TIMES: MARGARET MURPHY

The Lee Hydro-Electric Scheme is a fantastic project to research, especially as many of the young people who were involved in the scheme are still around to talk about it. There are positives and negatives to the project, which had a huge impact on the geography of the Lee Valley and its people, plus also the people employed to carry out this large-scale project and all it entailed.

With this in mind, we continue on our journey with Margaret Murphy who was a secretary to the contractor Maurice Sweeney, who replaced the French construction company, Société de Construction des Batignolles, halfway through the construction process. Born in Millstreet, Cork, Margaret was a farmer's daughter. She went to national school in Millstreet and had a choice of secretarial or nursing for her career path. She decided to go for secretarial and trained at Skerries College on the South Mall in Cork City.

After that, she worked for two years at the Royal Typewriters on Washington Street, Cork City, for John McCarthy. He had an office and shop across the road from St Augustine's Street. Two years later, in 1955, she answered an ad in the paper and went to Inniscarra at the age of twenty to work for the head contractor Maurice Sweeney. On her arrival, the French had more or less departed the scheme. She lived near Collins Barracks in a flat on Wellington Road, Cork City. Margaret notes:

> I travelled out with Stephen Kelleher from the city in his big station wagon to the office, which was on site. Maurice Sweeney was a lovely man to work for. There were a lot of figures to cope with. I remember the carbon paper and the making of five to six copies of everything. We did not even have a photocopier. My main job came every month when I had to type the measurements document or write up the figures used for different aspects of the job, especially the gravel mix consumed. I remember the six columns of figures.
>
> There was no automatic phone; one had to call Ballincollig exchange to get a number through. Killinardrish post office was the exchange for Carrigadrohid. There was a walkie-talkie system between Inniscarra and Carrigadrohid.
>
> I would not often go down to the site but in the summertime I would go down to the river. I remember seeing the salmon lying in the sun seemingly waiting for the fish pass to open, which it did at different times of the day. I remember going to the canteen daily. The man running it was from Northern Ireland. I remember Jim O'Brien, engineer, and Billy O'Regan. Billy went into the real-estate business afterwards in the city. Jim Irwin, from College Road, Cork, was in charge of purchases. Godfrey Dunlea

Above left: 'Sign of the times', *c.*1957. Maureen Foran (left) and Margaret Murphy (right) sitting at the entrance to the Inniscarra dam site. (*Margaret Murphy*).

Above right: Going away party (*c.*1956) for the last two French personnel at Rob Hotel, Cork City. Back row, left to right: Percy Swan, Godfrey Dunlea, Con Murphy, Mick Ruane, Dave Horgan, Paddy Cogan, Jim Irwin, Jim O'Brien, Jack Regan, Stephen Kelleher, Olaf Sorenson, Frank Sorenson, Unknown, John Young, Tom Cooney and Jim Phipps. Front row, left to right: John Looney, Unknown, Gene Fitzgerald, Margaret Murphy, Unidentified, Pierre Valleye Bertain, Maurice Sweeney, Unidentified, Paddy Hadon. (*Margaret Murphy*).

worked in the Timekeeper's Office. He looked after the time cards. Time had to be calculated, which was a lot of work. Maureen Foran was on the switchboard.

John Cotter was the gate man. Norman Jones was in charge of the cable bucket. He conducted a Dublin man whose accent I was always fascinated with. During my time, there was one draughtsman on site, Mickey Murphy. There were thirteen civil engineers: Donal O'Leary, Tim Nunan, Seamus Ayrelton, Jim Seery, Ferdie O'Halloran, Donal Murphy, Paddy McMeyler, Mick Jordan, Frank O'Connell, Tom Carey, Martin Quinn, Paddy Deane, and Douglas Dennehy. I remember Douglas Dennehy had an unusual DKW car, wore a scarf, a silk handkerchief in his top pocket and was involved in the clearance of the Gearagh. All those lads were in accommodation in Innisleena House. Mrs Cotter cooked dinner for them every evening.

During my last few weeks in Inniscarra dam in the summer of 1957, I wrote up the final measurement documents on a fourteen-inch typewriter in Blackrock. I went to Whitegate afterwards and was secretary again there to Maurice Sweeney. There was a different and bigger set up. I was working for American contractors. Director of Construction there was Edward Benas. I then went to New York for a few years. There I met my husband Jim McAllister who was from Sligo. We came back to Bantry to open the Bantry Inn in 1978 and ran that until our retirement in 1988.

45. ALL DAY, EVERY DAY

It is easy to take for granted that the water we use at home and at work will always be pure and will never run out. But in fact tap water is a sophisticated product, requiring a great deal of technology, skill and science to provide it.

The Cork Harbour and City Water Supply Scheme is located a half a kilometre upriver from the ESB's Hydro-Electric dam at Inniscarra. At the time of the scheme's construction, the facility was one of the largest public-works undertakings ever built in Ireland. The government approved £40 million in 1973. The total cost in 1982 was £48 million. The scheme was infrastructural in its nature and was expected to cater for the water supply needs of industry in the Cork area well into the twenty-first century. The scheme in 2008 serves 110,000 persons in Cork, all day every day.

In a wider context, preparations for the water supply scheme coincided with the optimistic economic climate that grew in Ireland during the middle and late 1960s. The country was rapidly emerging from the post-war depression of the late 1940s and 1950s. Emigration was in decline. Staple economic growth was becoming a reality. A regional study of Ireland was commissioned by the United Nations on behalf of the Irish Government of the day. It was compiled by Colin Buchanan & Partners and was presented in 1969. The Buchanan Report recommended the establishment of two government-sponsored industrial growth centres located at Cork and Limerick/Shannon Area respectively. The plan did not completely take off but the idea of Cork as a growth centre was pursued somewhat.

The decades of the 1960s and 1970s in County Cork were a time of rapid industrial growth and development in the harbour area. Cork had a considerable variety of industries, including Ireland's only steelworks, an oil refinery, a shipyard and a major vehicle assembly plant. In 1969, the first major water-using company, Pfizer, was established in Ringaskiddy with a water demand of two million gallons per day. In expectation of further developments it was decided that building new infrastructure would bring more business. That was acknowledged in the publication of a Cork Harbour Plan in 1972. Cork County Council's development plan of 1967 and the plan to promote the growth of satellite towns led to thinking about the need for an increased water supply.

In the early 1970s Cork County Council and Cork Corporation jointly commissioned a report on the provision of a water supply scheme that would cater for the future needs in the harbour and city area. In order to predict future water demand in the Cork area, considerable research was carried out in relation to the growth in demand in Cork City itself. Presented in 1970s, the report formed the basis for the design and construction of the Cork Harbour and City Water Supply Scheme.

Significant impetus was given to the development of the first stage of the scheme in the early 1970s when the Industrial Development Authority decided to establish two major industrial estates in the harbour area, namely Little Island and Ringaskiddy. Two sources of underground water were investigated – a carboniferous limestone syncline stretching from Youghal in the east, through Cork City, to Crookstown in the west and the gravel deposits of the Lee Valley west of the city. However, on examination, the limestone synclines did not have enough bulk quantities of water, and the gravel deposits created hard water. From further investigations it was decided to locate the intake site upstream of the present city and draw on the reservoir created by Inniscarra. The Ballincollig Regional Water Supply Scheme was already in place and abstracted water through a pipe built into the wall of Inniscarra dam (i.e. upstream of the dam).

It was decided by Cork County Council, Cork Corporation and the Department of Local Government that Inniscarra Lake, with the assistance of the ESB dam would provide the volume of water needed. Payment would be made to the ESB for the use of the water and compensation given as appropriate for the loss of generating capacity brought about by the water scheme. By 20 September 1973 the Minister for Local Government had approved the contract documents for the waterworks at Inniscarra. The works were completed between 1976 and 1982 under the executive authority of Cork County Council.

The overall plan and layout of the project was the brainchild of Michael C. O'Sullivan, who was the appointed engineer. He brought with him the necessary knowledge, experience and engineering vision. Michael was a senior engineer with Harry Walsh & Associates. When Harry's company stopped trading, Michael formed his own company, M.C. O'Sullivan & Co. Harry's son Malachy also formed his own company. Out of those companies emerged other fine engineers who eventually formed their own companies in order to generate work for themselves, such as Brendan Feehily and Derry Nestor.

As well as Michael O'Sullivan, his colleagues Brendan Feehily, Brendan O'Halloran, Jack Stanley, Kerry O'Sullivan and Jim Healy had significant inputs into the Water Supply Scheme. The senior site staff included John O'Sullivan, Liam Bohane and Peter Haughton. There was much expertise brought to this project, as is evident from the various contractors consulted to oversee and build their respective sections. The following Irish contractors built the scheme: HMC (Construction) Ltd/SIAC Ltd; Public Works Ltd; Irish Enco Ltd, and Bowen Construction in a joint venture with EMCC, France. The mechanical and electrical contractors included: Mahon & Phillips (Water Treatment) Ltd, Kilkenny; Maher & Platt Ltd, Manchester; M.F. Kent Ltd, Clonmel; Cosor Electronics Ltd, Harlow, Essex, and

O'Shea's Electrical Ltd, Cork. The plant operators through the years included Sean Crowley, Joe McGroarty and Michael Jones, and the plant managers included David McBratney, Fred Willis and currently Pat Murphy.

The overall workings of the site are impressive. In order to build the intake tower it was necessary to construct temporary works in the form of a cofferdam in the lake. The intake and pump house was built into sixteen metres of water at the edge of Inniscarra Reservoir and can withdraw water from the lake at varying levels – avoiding the intake of deoxygenated water. The water intake tower is connected to a large pump house on the valleyside by means of a reinforced concrete tunnel about forty metres long, which was blasted out of solid rock. The ESB is required by law to maintain a minimum flow in the Lee downstream at about thirty million gallons per day. The water taken from the lake is sent through a treatment process that includes settling tanks, filters and chemical treatment. Today, the Cork Harbour and City Water Scheme has a production capacity of over fifteen million gallons per day and makes a really important contribution to all those living within Cork Harbour and City area, serving 110,000 persons.

Above left: Pat Murphy, plant manager, November 2008.

Above right: Selection of staff at Cork Harbour and City Water Supply Scheme, November 2008. Back row, left to right: John Forde (general operator), Jason Forde (shift curator), James Mulqueen (gardener and safety rep.) and Pat Murphy (plant manager). Front row, left to right: Ken Hurley (instrument technician), John Cronin (water services supervisor), Gavin Kelly (engineer) and John Sexton (foreman and on staff since 1981).

INNISCARRA
NARRATIVES

46. SAMUEL LEWIS'S INNISCARRA

Travelling the Banteer–Blarney (R579) reveals a lot about the character of Inniscarra parish. The Shournagh River, a tributary of the River Lee, as well as sub-tributaries of the Shournagh, have created a rolling topography of small valleys – an undulating landscape. This is clearly seen from the height of Donoughmore parish (one of Inniscarra parish's westerly neighbours).

Inniscarra parish, like the other parishes around the River Lee, has its own important stories to tell about the rich architecture of life. So to begin my study, I open Samuel Lewis's *Topographical Dictionary of Ireland* to be briefed on the key features of Inniscarra's history in pre-Famine Ireland. The text was published in 1837 and is a very important record not only for historians but also for genealogists of the early nineteenth century. Samuel Lewis was the editor and publisher of topographical dictionaries and maps of the United Kingdom of Great Britain and Ireland; England (1833), Wales (1833) and Scotland (1846). The firm of Samuel Lewis & Co. was based in London.

The aim of the dictionaries was to give, in 'a condensed form', a faithful and impartial description of each place. It is an invaluable tool to the genealogist and a most interesting read for those who want to find out that bit more without having to delve into historical manuscripts. Some of the entries are but a few lines long and then others give us history, geography, anecdotes, superstitions, and the life of the people in an area. Samuel Lewis gives details about every parish, town and village in Ireland, including numbers of inhabitants, the economy, history, topography, religion and parish structures, administration and courts, schools, and much more. He also gives the names of the principal inhabitants (generally landlords, merchants and professionals).

A *Topographical Dictionary of Ireland* relied on information provided by local contributors and on the earlier works published such as Coote's *Statistical Survey* (1801), Taylor and Skinner's *Maps of the Road of Ireland* (1777), Pigot's *Trade Directory* (1824) and other sources. He also used the various parliamentary reports and in particular the census of 1831 and the education returns of the 1820s and early 1830s. Samuel Lewis despatched thirteen agents to Ireland to travel the country, parish by parish. They distributed their questions amongst the gentry and clergy. The content was collated and sent to London. The subsequent proof sheets were sent back to Ireland for correction. From Ireland there were 9,000 subscribers of whom 1,400 possessed County Cork addresses. Of Inniscarra Samuel Lewis writes:

> Inniscarra, a parish in the barony of Barretts, County of Cork, and province of Munster, 5
> miles (W. by S.) from Cork, to which place it has a penny post; containing 3,442 inhabit-

ants. This parish, which is situated on the River Lee, comprises 9,982 statute acres, valued at £8387. 10. per annum. The surface is varied; to the west of the bridge over the Lee is a fine expanse of meadow, which, with the old church, backed by a range of hills, and some rich woodland scenery, forms a pleasing landscape; and from the heights is obtained an extensive view of the course of the river from west to east through a richly diversified tract of country, abounding with objects of local interest. The farms are in general very small, and the lands are continued under tillage till they are quite exhausted; the system of agriculture, though improving, is still in a backward state; there is no bog.

A slate quarry is worked on a very limited scale. Ardrum, the seat of Sir N. Colthurst, Bart., is pleasantly situated in an extensive and well-wooded demesne; Cloghroe, the residence of J.C. Fitzgerald, Esq., is also in the parish; and the glebe-house, the residence of the Hon. and Revd W. Beresford, is delightfully situated on the River Lee, to the margin of which the lawn and shrubberies extend in beautiful contrast with the steep and rocky mountains on the opposite bank, which rise to a considerable elevation and are partially ornamented with plantations; the house commands a beautiful view of the vale formed by the ranges of hills on each side of the river.

Participants at Inniscarra Show, Autumn 2008. Those pictured include, from left to right: Cllr Dan Fleming, Daniel McCarthy, Jessica Braun, Shauna Kavanagh, Katelinn Looney, Sheila Walsh, Niamh Byrne and Erin Looney.

Celebrating fifty years of Inniscarra Macra na Feirme at Inniscarra Show. Back row, left to right: William Ambrose, Richard O'Callaghan, Claire Hurley, Noreen Healy and Donal Casey. Front row, left to right: Laura Duggan, Anne Marie Hurley, Emer O'Shea, Jennifer O'Shea.

At the western extremity of the parish are the Dripsey paper-mills, belonging to Messrs Magnay & Co. and situated in a deep and well-wooded glen; the buildings are of handsome appearance, and the works afford employment to a number of persons, varying from 70 to 100, in the manufacture of large quantities of paper for the English market. In another part of the parish is a small stream, which turns the Cloghroe boulting-mills, which are capable, when there is a sufficient supply of water, of producing 140 sacks of flour weekly. A new line of road has been formed to facilitate the communication of this parish and the neighbouring district with the parish of Macroom. A manorial court is held by the seneschal of the manor.

The living is a rectory and vicarage, in the diocese of Cloyne, united by act of council to the rectory and vicarage of Mattehy and the chapelry of Kilmurry, which together constitute the union, and the corps of the prebend of Inniscarra in the Cathedral of Cloyne, and in the patronage of the Bishop. The tithes amount to £635. 5. 9., and the value of the prebend, including tithe and glebe, is £1,076 per annum. The glebe-house was built by a gift of £100 and a loan of £1,500 from the late Board of First Fruits, in 1816: the glebe comprises 15 acres. The church, a neat structure on an elevated spot near the road, was built in 1818, by a grant of £1,000 from the same Board. In the R.C. divisions it is the head of a union or district, including the parishes of Inniscarra, Matehy, and Carrigrohane-beg, and has three chapels, two of which, at Cloghroe and Berrings, are in this parish. About 30 children are educated in the parochial school, which is aided by the rector, who, with the late Sir N.C. Colthurst, Bart., built a handsome school-house. There are two private schools, in which are about 200 children, a Sunday school, and a dispensary.

47. COONEY'S FORGE

Now we will journey back to the early years of the Irish Free State, to native local industry in Inniscarra parish. I was introduced to the work of James Cooney, blacksmith in the Model Village in Dripsey, who completed the railings for the grotto. Subsequently, I met his daughter Sheila Desmond (*née* Cooney), a teacher in Dripsey National School, who brought me out to the site of the forge in Ballyshonin.

Perhaps what is intriguing about the work of James Cooney and his father Jeremiah before him, is that the forge survives as a ruin and has remained untouched. In addition, the family have kept many of his tools and the day-to-day records of running the forge from the 1930s to the early 1960s. Those historical records, coupled with first-hand accounts from his surviving family, paint a vivid picture of life in the forge and its role in the community. Of course for the Cooneys those objects are very much part of their links to their past and keeping them is a large part in celebrating their own personal heritage.

The School Folklore Commission records in 1938 from Berrings National School, compiled by Principal Domhnall O'Drisceoil, reveal the earlier associations of the Cooneys with the work of blacksmith. Jeremiah was the first member of the family who took on the role of smith. Born in 1888, he subsequently went to America for several years and it was there he learned his trade.

Above left: James Cooney, *c.*1950. (*Cooney Family Collection*)

Above right: Marriage picture, 1951. Left to right: Dan Looney, Coachford, James (Groom) and Nora (Bride, *née* Coleman) Cooney and Leena Coleman. (*Cooney Family Collection*)

The original forge was about two miles from the present one, and was situated near a public house on the roadside and near a stream. The forge was closed down for some time owing to the fact that the smith took part in the Irish War of Independence and was interned in Ballykinlar in County Down. On his release from the camp, Jeremiah's next forge was built by local help at the present site, which was considered a better centre, because of its proximity to the local creamery, the roadside, the crossroads and an adjacent little river called 'The Sheep River'. The forge for several decades was a focal point in the community. It served as a meeting place where people shared news, yarns and jokes as they waited while their repairs were being carried out. It was very popular to congregate there on wet days when little work could be done in the fields. Because the forge was situated across from the creamery, it was also a very busy place in the mornings. The late Minnie O'Mahony had a little shop next to it. The only remaining shop and agri stores is Dan Donovan & Co. Ltd, now managed by Dan O'Callaghan.

The folklore collection goes on to describe that the walls of Cooney's forge were of concrete and the roof was in timber covered on the outside with felt. It was a small rectangular building with an ordinary door. There was one fireplace within on a raised bench or hob. The bellows were of the ordinary fire style – heart shaped – two sides of timber bound with leather.

In the yard of the forge there was provision made for a second fire, which was lit for the banding of cartwheels. The smith had the usual implements: an anvil, a rather heavy sledge, a lighter sledge, a shoeing hammer, a drill for boring holes in iron, large pinches, rasps, a soldering iron, a vice, a trough of water for cooling hot iron, horseshoe nails, chisels of various sizes. Jeremiah Cooney made shoes for horses, ponies and donkeys. Cattle were never shod in the district. He made field gates and small ornamental items, such as wicket gates, iron railings and very occasionally an iron harrow. He repaired all farm implements but did not make ploughs, spades, shovels, pikes or axes. Cartwheels were banded in the open on a circular concrete slab. Jeremiah also did some soldering, especially to carts belonging to the milk suppliers of the nearby creamery.

The forge was a centre for storytelling in 1938 (the year of the Folklore Commission) as it was in previous years. In the neighbourhood, there were three or four shops and a parochial hall, where the younger people of the district met during the winter nights to play cards and hear any news of the locality. It was in 1931 that Jeremiah's son James completed a course of instruction in farriery in Coachford. James (born 1911) worked with his father Jeremiah for a time but moved to Crossbarry to work as a blacksmith. In the mid-1940s, Jeremiah, now in his mid-sixties, asked James to take over the business. Jermiah died on 7 January 1948 aged sixty-eight and James took the business. James married Nora Coleman from Ballinhassig in 1951. Nora remembers that James bought his iron from Cork Iron and Hardware at Kyrls Quay, Cork City. Jim would travel in on the bus or take the van a couple of times a week depending on his work demands. At Kyrls Quay he conducted his business with John Scannell.

During the decades of the 1950s and 1960s, James branched out into electric and oxy-acetylene welding. He travelled to the Irish Oxygen Co. Ltd, Waterfall, near Cork, to purchase oxygen cylinders for his welding apparatus. The extant account books and price lists reflect this gradual move from shoeing horses to welding parts on tractors and ornamental ironwork. Much of the information on James's day-to-day work can be readily accessed thanks to the neatness of his sister Nellie O'Sullivan, who wrote up the account books.

James's daughter Sheila Cooney's earliest memories of her father are of him shoeing horses. She notes:

> Ballyshonin fifty years ago was bustling with activity. As we lived across the river in Gortatrea adjacent to the road, the first sound heard every morning was the horses and carts bringing churns of milk to the creamery, which also had a shop attached to it. The late Minnie O'Mahony had a little shop and we loved to call to her because she always gave us sweets.

The 'nostalgic currency' of Cooney's Forge, including Mass cards, forge keys, account book, farriery certificate, Emergency Years medal, and invoices.

Every evening, afternoon tea was brought to all those in the forge. This was a family occasion, which we looked forward to everyday. My mother, sisters and brother would carry an enamel jug filled with tea (no flasks in those days), fresh scones or currant bread, which my mother baked daily, and some enamel mugs. We loved to meet my da and explore the various machines and play with his tools. We loved to climb on the lengths of iron lying on the floor.

Banding wheels, as far as I can remember, was mainly done during the summer time. The operation was carried on at the side of the forge. Timber wheels had an outer ring of iron. When this got worn down from rough roads and potholes, it had to be replaced. The iron was heated to be able to bend it to fit the wooden wheel. A little stream trickled into a manmade tank and this was used to cool the iron. In the spring I often saw frogspawn in it, which later became tadpoles and finally frogs. It was common to find frogs jumping in the long grass in this area.

James Cooney died on 20 February 1963. The forge closed later that year. On spending time with Nora (James's wife) and Sheila (James's daughter), I marvelled at the human story of these two blacksmiths. I thought about their journey with the forge though the decades. These men had a huge sense of pride in their work, which was, in turn, very much part of their identity.

Nora and Sheila Cooney at the ruined site of the forge, summer 2008.

48. WHAT'S IN A PICTURE?

I personally like this photograph for a number of reasons. It is very creatively set up and tells a story – that of the Healy family and friends on an outing in Mushera Mountain. I was further intrigued to hear from Jane Quinlan (*née* Healy), who is in the picture and was about thirteen years of age when it was taken in 1932. She talked at length about the people in the photograph and how they came together for this outing to celebrate family:

Well what a day we had! It was in 1932. E.J. McCarthy was coming home and he said he wouldn't have time to see all the relatives, so someone had the idea to go to Mushera. You can see the two cars in the background. We had a Ford and the other family also had a Ford. My father Thomas John had a car very early on. He was, as they say, a man before his time. In general my family had an interest in progress. My grand-father John was head director of the Cork–Muskerry Tram. He was part of a delegation that went and spoke in Westminster to make a plea for finance.

I can always remember that day. I was meant to lead the Convilles. I was to take them through Rylane and up to Mushera. I was puffed up with importance but we got lost. I can remember my cheeks getting redder and redder with embarrassment. I hoped the ground would open up and swallow me.

We were looking for the Kingsmen Table – the site where many a Kerry farmer stopped at one time to rest whilst bringing butter to Cork. The site, which we eventually found, was at the base of the mountain. I remember the scenery looking out into Kerry and in County Cork.

At the centre of the photograph is uncle E.J. McCarthy who founded the Columban Mission in the States and whilst in university enrolled in the Student Action and campaigned a lot. He was an extraordinary man; after the Philippines he went to Burma, and the Japanese took over Rangoon at the time he was writing the history of the Columban mission. He was consequently interned for three years. He never regained his health after that ordeal.

It is also an extraordinary thing for me to look at the picture and see uncle Dermot McConville. He was a medic doctor and rose to the rank of Colonel in the army and went to Rangoon. He questioned where white people or British citizens were interned and discovered where his cousin E.J. was located. He took a platoon in to free E.J. Exhausted by the campaign and severe illness, E.J. moved back to London. He was sent to the Mater in Dublin and later to Los Angeles for health reasons and was sent to a chiropractor.

Years later in LA E.J. was killed by a car that mounted the pavement. He had survived Japanese internment and everything that went with it. He died after two weeks. There is a monument in Ovens church to his memory. We commemorated the fiftieth anniversary of his death last August (2007). You know I remember being in California and he'd talk and talk. We had great talks. I was married in 1946 and subsequently spent three years in California. I taught in the public-school system for two years. I was accepted for a Doctorate in English at UCLA but in the end I produced a son, Michael. He subsequently received his PhD at Utah State University.

Mushera Mountain 1932. Right to left: Mary Carroll, Mary Healy, curly haired girl unknown, Jane Healy, child with hat unknown, Denis Healy, E.J. McCarthy (with glasses), Dermot McConville, Nora McConville (lying out from the group, back left) Kathleen McCarthy, Joan McCarthy on fiddle and Bill Carroll on melodeon. (*Jane Quinlan & Healy family*)

Above left: Jane Healy's graduation photo from the 1940s. Jane went to school in Drishane and St Aloysius and later earned a Masters Degree in University College Cork. (*Jane Quinlan & Healy family*)

Above right: Jane Quinlan (*née* Healy), November 2008.

Back to the photograph, sitting on the left of E.J. was Cal McCarthy, and he was capped for Ireland in rugby in the triple crown and was also competed nationally in rowing. He went to Dublin and was involved in culture of all sorts. He got involved in the Young Ireland group. He developed an interest in the ideologies of such Irish patriots as Pádraig Pearse. He founded the Guinness Bagpipes. They were different times. After 1916, the effects of the Rising led him to write a history of the McCarthy Mors all the way down to his generation. He was my godfather and he only found out when he was seventy-one! Someone stood in for him at my baptism. He was a very funny man. I had a great bond with him. He lived in Ranelagh in Dublin. Uncle Cal's daughters were Kathleen and Joan, who are also in the photograph.

Nora Conville is pictured. She was Dermot's sister. She never married and was a teacher in England. Her father Robert had a milk emporium on Sheare Street in Cork. The McConvilles lived opposite the Gaol Cross in the 'American houses'. Those dwellings were a curiosity when they were built. Scher, a Jewish family who were dentists on Sidney Place in the city, were also popular residents of these houses. Scher was my dentist when I was young because I had another Uncle, Dan Donovan, who was his anaesthetist.

Bill Carroll, another man in the photograph, had a farm in Hayfield opposite Dripsey Castle. Every summer I would come down; Hayfield was a big old house with loads of passages and a large orchard. Bill brought horses to the Cork show. They were musical people; he had a love of Cork Opera House. He was in the civil service in Dublin. The Carroll family had a shop next to Singer's Corner in Cork City for selling the milk, which I visited when I was in Cork with my father. I always remember the big white cat in the window of the shop that was asleep all the time. Hannah, an employee, used to have a jar maybe full of whiskey to attract all the wasps during the summer months. On that point, James Scully was another worker on my farm in Clonmoyle and was born during the years of the Great Famine. I remember him telling us stories of the Famine and the collection of bodies around my locality all bound to Donoughmore Cemetery. He had tremendous knowledge and he was well read.

Bill's daughter Mary Carroll was a charming individual. She became a member of the French Drishane Order and was teaching English to Americans in Paris. She was in Paris when the Nazis overran it. She lived on her wits. Indeed, the war affected everyone. She later got married.

There were eight children in my family. I had one sister and five brothers. Many of them are in the picture as well. Mary Healy, my sister, was a great artist; she could draw before she could talk. She later married Denis Hurley of Woodhouse, Rochestown, Cork. My brother Michael later became a Columban priest. He was stationed in Shanghai and was under house arrest for being a priest during the Second World War. Many a time he witnessed killings of the public. It was very traumatic for him and for my family, who didn't know where he was.

My first cousins are also in the photograph. Mary McCarthy was from Clashanafrinn. She was one of two sisters. Joan is the violinist and is still alive. She later married the creamery manager Liam Stack in Ballinhassig.

Yes, the picture … it was a marvellous day; you could eat as much as you liked – the whole thing in the end was disrupted by midges. You could say they chased us home. We repeated the outing twenty years later and put all the names then into a bottle and buried it at the base of Mushera Mountain.

49. CHANCES AND CHOICES

The main road leading through the southern side of Inniscarra takes the traveller from Balyshonin through to Cloghroe (R579, Cork–Banteer Road). Along that stretch there are a number of key sites that for me reveal more about the character of Inniscarra as a place within the Lee Valley. First up is Blair's Inn. The premises were formerly known as Healy's Pub.

The Healys have been publicans in Cloghroe for over 130 years. My contact was Donal Healy, who on my visit talked at length of his roots and produced a whole range of documents and photographs that reveal the history of the family and their associations not only with Inniscarra but the city and wider county as well. There seems to be a vast set of complex interrelations in Donal's story, which is important to the identity of the family itself. Donal's great-grandfather was Daniel Healy (died 1897). He was a vintner and farmer and lived in Cloghroe. He married Ellen Callaghan (a widow). They had four children, two boys and two girls; Nan and Kitty, Daniel and Denis (who later became a priest and worked in Wichita, Kansas, USA).

Healy's Pub in 1971, with Thomas Healy (Donal's father), Mary Healy (Donal's wife), Thomas Healy (Donal and Mary's son) and Mary Healy (Donal's mother). (*Healy family collection*)

Daniel Healy (junior, son of Daniel above) married Mary Aherne from Ballygarvan, County Cork in 1908. They had six children: Eileen Frances, Patricia, Mary, Doney, Denis and Thomas. Eileen and Patricia became nuns – Eileen with the Mercy Order in Killarney and Patricia with the Presentation Order in Crosshaven. Mary Healy married Sonnie O'Reilly, a salesman with CAB motors on the Lower Road, Cork and they lived in Highfield Avenue.

Doney Healy had a shop and transport business on Barrack Street, Cork. Doney was married to Eileen Hawkes from Upton, County Cork. He was involved in setting up Lee Transport Co., an amalgamation of companies that were vying for the shipment of port trade coming in. He convinced them all to work together for the benefit of their businesses. His son Don continued his father's business and went on to develop the transport distribution centre in Glanmire and a business wholesaling salt (which was sold on in later years). Denis set up Healy Blue Bins and Healy Transport Co. in Ballinlough, Cork. He married Nora Dinan of Carrigadrohid. Her sister is Mary Kate Harrington of Harrington's Nurseries, Carrigadrohid. Today the sons of Denis Healy, Aidan and Denis, are continuing the family tradition of running Healy Bluebins and transport and warehouse companies.

Thomas Healy (Donal's father), publican and farmer, married Mary Carroll from Rylane. They had three children; Eileen, Kevin and Donal (my contact). He inherited the shop and Healy's Pub. Donal notes of his father, 'My father was a true gentleman, well known locally as courteous and kind. He was a great GAA man, a proud supporter of Inniscarra team and proud of his Inniscarra roots. Both he and my mother were great business people and passed on to me a tremendous legacy.'

Healy's Pub, *c.*1980.
(*Healy family collection*)

Donal remembers a lot of sporting occasions held in the area that brought crowds to the pub afterwards. In particular, Thomas, his father, was big into road bowling. He was part of the organising committee that ran the first senior All Ireland Ból Chumann championship final in Cloghroe in October 1954. Due to its popularity amongst the general public, the scór took place over two Sundays commencing at Cloghroe church and ending at the 'Yellow House' near Vicarstown. Local members of the committee other than Donal's father were: Jim O'Mahony of Berrings; Eamonn O'Carroll of Farran; Ned Healy of Ballyanley, and Percy McSweeney of Cloghroe. Other members of the committee from the city included: C. O'Connell; J. Waters; J. Cadden; C. Waters; T. O'Donovan; J. Barry; J. Dean; J. O'Shea; N. Healy, and J. Scully. For the record, Liam O'Keeffe, Waterfall, beat Ned Barry, also from Waterfall.

Of growing up in Inniscarra, Donal remembers:

I went to Cloghroe N.S. and in sixth class (the year was 1958), my teacher and Principal was Seamus O'Leary who lived at Canon's Cross. I went to Presentation Brothers Secondary School on the Mardyke, where a no-nonsense set of skills was instilled in us. Many of the lads in my graduating class of 1965 went to great careers: Aidan Horgan, President of the Past Students' Union; Jack O'Sullivan, President of Cork Constitution; Pat O'Sullivan, Major General and Chief of Staff of the Irish Army; Barry Galvin of Gavin's Wine and Spirits; Pat Keane of Keane's Jewellers, and Brian Bermingham, current Lord Mayor of Cork.

I remember a Brother David one day saying if there were any publicans in the class to stand up. A few others and I stood up and were duly sworn into the Pioneer Total Abstinence Association. My mother was delighted with that move and added her own incentive. If I didn't drink or smoke until I was over twenty-one, she'd give me £500. I kept my end of the bargain and so did she. It's ironic that later I had a career for over thirty years in Bulmers, promoting that brand.

In 1969, when I was getting married to Mary O'Brien at the age of twenty-two, I was able to use my mother's £500 to buy my first half-acre site to build a house. At that time I was working with Denis Coakley & Co., Seeds and Fertiliser Co., South Terrace/Penrose Quay (later Penrose Wharf Business Centre).

Donal's father Thomas retired from the pub in the early 1970s and Donal's brother Kevin inherited the farm and Donal inherited the pub. Donal's sister Eileen married Sean O'Sullivan, who had a farm on South Douglas Road at one time but now farms in Grange, Douglas, Cork. Interestingly, Donal married Mary O'Brien and later Kevin married her sister Ann. Both girls were from Killinardrish near Carrigadrohid.

As the seventies rolled on, Donal and his wife Mary focused on the development of the pub and in 1978 added squash courts to the Healy's Pub complex. To promote the new venture, they planned for Christy Ring and Eamonn Young to play an exhibition match but unfortunately Christy died in the fortnight leading up to the match.

Squash was a sport that had sprung up in the city and the Healys were one of the first to bring it to the county. Healy's Squash Club enjoyed great success, winning many Cork titles at both underage and senior-level grades. Donal notes:

> We made great friends through this initiative. We also had coaches Toby Featherstone Howe from Jersey and his partner Margaret Lucas, who now has a pottery in Farnanes. Two of my four children, Thomas and Karen [the other two were twins, Brian and Susan] were coached by Toby and Margaret at under seventeen and under nineteen.

In 1980, Donal and Mary sold the pub but kept the squash courts. However by 1993, squash was a dying sport and they sought an alternative use for the courts. In the year 2000, seven apartments were built on the squash court site. Healy's Pub eventually became Blair's Inn and is currently under the ownership of John and Anne Blair.

Donal Healy, November 2008. Donal is currently Chief Executive of Cork Business Association.

50. THE BLAIR LEGACY

The story of the Blair family of Blair's Inn touches many eras and places and also, in a sense, connects the Cork countryside to the city.

Of Scots Presbyterian descent, the Blairs arrived in Cork from Scotland in the mid-1800s. The current John Blair of Blair's Inn can take the story back to his great-great-grandfather John, who qualified in Glasgow in 1855 from the Apothecaries' Hall. That mid-nineteenth-century man went onto manage the Cork Chemical and Drug Co., which was a well-known pharmacy in the city. He later bought a chemist shop at No.7 Patrick Street from a Dr Atkins (who had established his shop in 1847). John Blair took a loan out from the Wright Lane & Lomney Company (who were also manufacturers of the popular Wright's Coal Tar Soap that is used for skin disorders). The loan was paid back in ten years and John Blair Dispensing Chemists grew from strength to strength. (No.7 St Patrick's Street is now occupied by the entrance to Marks & Spencer of Merchant's Quay Shopping Centre on St Patrick's Street.)

John had two sons, John and Richard. John became a doctor and set up a practice in Chester, England. His son Jim, as a seven year old, visited Cork in 1913. It was Richard who took over the family business in Cork. He was married to Ada George from St Helena, a remote island in the South Atlantic. The George family were part of the British establishment on the island and it is reputed that Ada's grandfather was part of the British contingent that guarded Napoleon Bonaparte. As for Richard Blair who married into the George family, his interests in pharmacy led him to serve as President of the Pharmaceutical Society of Ireland. In that role he attended the funerals of Michael Collins and Arthur Griffith. He also presided over the last National assembly of Northern and Southern Irish chemists before the group split in 1925.

In 1888, Richard had a son, John Duncan. He became a chemist and his first job was at Messrs Hayes Conyngham & Robinson, Rathgar branch (est. 1909). That firm had branches all over Dublin. John Duncan took part in the famous Leander Cup rowing race that was part of Cork City Regatta in 1909. The Leander Club was based on the River Thames in London. The race comprised of approximately twelve boats that raced in the river alongside the Marina. The cup was in the shape of a galleon. The event was a grand affair and built on links and associations made through the Cork International Exhibition held in the Mardyke in 1902/1903. Each participant in the race was given a replica cup as a souvenir. The Blairs' cup can be seen today in the restaurant area of Blair's Inn.

John Duncan served in the First World War in Mesopotamia (present-day Iraq). He spent the duration of the war between Egypt and Iraq. He was in the Royal Army Medical Corps and finished and retired from the army as a Major. His wife Emily's brother was Michael Mullins. Like many in Cork City centre at the time Michael joined up at the recruiting station at No.2 Patrick Street, now the entrance to Merchant's Quay Shopping Centre. He was a Private in the same medical corps as John Duncan. He died in the trenches on 22 November 1916 at around twenty-three or four years of age. He was buried at Pouchevilliers, Amiens, in France on the River Somme. The grave marker there notes that he was a Private in the Field Ambulance of the Medical Corps. His name is also recorded at the base of the Irish Memorial Park in the Round Tower at Messines.

As for John Duncan Blair, surviving the war, he came back to Cork City and moved to Victoria Road. Coming back as a British Major, he also arrived into an Ireland of chaos and joined the family business, Blair's, on St Patrick's Street. His association with the British Army never affected business; there was no vic-timisation but he did intentionally lay low for many years and never spoke of his experiences in war.

John Blair in 2007 at the First World War graveyard, Pouchevilliers, Amiens, France. (*Blair family*)

Recent turning on of Christmas lights at Blair's Inn with the Lord Mayor of Cork, Cllr Brian Bermingham. This is a rare but annual County Cork engagement for the Lord Mayor's office. From left to right: Duncan Blair, Anne Blair, Cllr Brian Berminghan, John Blair, Elma Bermingham and Richard Blair. (*John Allen of John Sheehan Photography*).

In time, he also became a prominent member of Muskerry Golf Club. He was President and Captain in the 1930s and subsequently was made an honorary life member. He came out on the Muskerry Tram and was great friends with Andrew O'Shaughnessy of Dripsey Woollen Mills. In Blair's Inn, there are a number of cups on display that John Duncan won at golf in the 1930s.

The son of John Duncan Blair was John Gordon. He was trained at Trinity College Dublin. He had a great bass voice and was a member of the Cork Operatic Society. He was a founder member of the Gilbert and Sullivan Group in Cork. He appeared on the old Opera House Stage in the 1930s, 1940s and 1950s and sang on programmes for Radio Éireann. He was also part of the formation of the 40 Club (or Chumann na Daihead), a society of business people who are also entertainers, which is still going strong in the city. In 1939, John Gordon joined the Irish Army and served in the army hospital in Mallow (now Cork County Hospital). There he met a nurse called Peggy O'Brien of the O'Brien family of drapers from Tipperary Town, who he later married. In their courting days during the Second World War, John and Peggy cycled on occasion to the Savoy Cinema in Cork City, a return journey of forty-four miles. The war hindered the movement of trains.

John and Peggy's first son was John (my contact) who was born on 31 December 1943 at Glenvara Nursing Home on Sidney Place. The family lived on the Main Street in Mallow over Hanifers's Pub opposite the Central Hotel. When John was three years of age, the family moved to Charlemont Terrace, and then later to Ballintemple. Another son, Desmond, was born in the ensuing years. John went to Christian Brothers College and then to Castleknock Boarding School in Dublin where his mother Peggy's brothers were educated.

On leaving school, John took a job in marketing and in 1968 was asked by his grandfather to take over the Blair establishment on St Patrick's Street. John obliged and helped in the rebranding of the business, shortening the name to Blair's Chemist. He was conscious there were other chemists on the street also vying for business; there was Lester's next to the Savoy and also Mac Sweeney's. During the 1970s, John developed an interest in civic matters. He began a campaign to clean up Fr Mathew. He joined a Fine Gael branch and he headed the poll in the local elections in 1974 in the south-east ward at the age of thirty. He was President of the Junior Chamber of Commerce and President of Cork Business Association in 1974. He was chairman of committee for the successful Lee Spree events that took place in the city, arising out of the Cork Film Festival and also during those years he contributed to the Land Use and Transport Study (LUTS), which looked at land use and attempted to alleviate the pressures on an increasingly gridlocked city. John ran as an MEP for Europe in 1979 but was unsuccessful and so returned to local politics in 1985.

Feeling the strain of the 1980s recession, John made the difficult decision to close Blair's Chemist and entered the pub business with his wife Anne (*née* Wyse from Tipperary). John O'Donovan, a friend of the family introduced him to Noel and Jean Elliott who had for a year previously had taken over Healy's Pub in Cloghroe. Since then, Blair's Inn has developed its trade and in particular its fine food repertoire, which has won multiple awards. John and Anne's sons Duncan and Richard are currently in the process of taking over the business.

51. THE WAYSIDE INN

It is where the local clubs meet – GAA, rugby, coursing, shooting, school fundraisers, even the crowd twinned with a village out in Brittany, the local Fine Gaelers and golfers plan for their loves, celebrate their victories and mark their sadness.

Jack Power, *Irish Examiner*, 24 April 2006.

In my fieldwork, I have encountered many local pubs with a myriad of family histories rooted in their community. They all vary in style, but there all have a sense of the picture postcard, a rural idyll. They hold weight and give character to their local places. The Wayside Inn always gave me that sense passing it. The building launches the viewer back in time; he is drawn into not only the culture of the Lee Valley but also Ireland's complex cultural heritage. When my research brought me to The Wayside Inn I was delighted to be able to explore it with the owner Kathleen O'Leary.

Kathleen and her son Jack O'Leary at the Wayside Inn, Inniscarra, April 2009.

Kathleen's grandfather was Dave O'Leary in Upper Cloghroe. He bought The Wayside Inn from the Kielys in the 1890s. He also farmed a small land holding nearby. He had a few cattle, hens and pigs and grew tobacco. Indeed, a number of people in Cloghroe tried growing tobacco before the First World War. Kathleen notes:

> My grandfather married Julia Ahern from Macroom town. I remember my father's first cousin John Ahern who taught in Kilnamartyra National School in Macroom. He dabbled in antiques – maybe did a little clock-making. I remember visiting him in my younger years on the way to the rounds in Ballyvourney. My grandfather died around 1940. He was buried in Ovens. My grandmother died in 1958. She was buried in the Old Inniscarra graveyard overlooking the River Lee. Her wishes were to be buried with her cousins, neighbours and customers.

Dave and Julia O'Leary had one daughter, Eileen, and five sons, Jeremiah, John, Tim, Connie and Dan-Joe. Kathleen's father Dan-Joe was the oldest. Tim was the youngest and he went to the City of Yonkers in New York State. John and Jer spent time working in England. Connie had a hackney car in Inniscarra but moved to Conna. He worked with the ESB for a time. Eileen lived in Cloghroe and married Denis O'Connell from Bridgetstown.

Kathleen says, 'Dan-Joe, my father, married Mary Elizabeth Lynch from Knockrour, Aghabullogue, on that farm where they found a Bronze Age hoard. They took them to the Museum. They also had a fairy fort on the land.' At The Wayside Inn, Dan–Joe inherited the cast-iron D. O'Leary sign that still hangs over the door. Dan-Joe ran the pub and also had a shop and petrol pumps. They were the only pumps between Cork and Kanturk and sold Lobitos petrol. Kathleen remembers the hand-pumped petrol pumps. When Inniscarra dam was being built, the lads with motorbikes got petrol there. Kathleen's mother Mary kept overalls, socks, handkerchiefs and other clothing needed by those working at the dam and living in the area. The O'Leary family assisted people in tough times. They put food on tab for families who struggled during the economic hardship of the 1950s and Dan-Joe grew potatoes. The family was self-sufficient; they had three cows and sold milk in the shop.

Dan-Joe O'Leary was very involved in coursing. He always kept greyhounds. His brother-in-law was Jack Lynch from Knockrour. He raced greyhounds at the old Cork Track on Western Road. Kathleen recalls that they had one good bitch called Steeped in Stout. She won a good few races. Kathleen and her sister Sheelagh accompanied their father to the tracks regularly. Indeed on Monday, Wednesday and Saturday nights, the nights of the races, several participants stopped in The Wayside Inn on the way back to North Cork. Kathleen remembers the great conversation in the pub every evening.

In 1979, Dan-Joe passed away and left the pub to Mary and family. Kathleen has been involved in running the pub since the mid seventies, marrying John Keating from Crosshaven in 1981. The fourth generation in the family is Jack and Kate (RIP).

So the O'Leary story is central to this pub's story, but walking around the lounge, the walls tell more of the local history; there are pictures of rugby, hurling, coursing, and bowls wins, Nobel Prize winners, Cork figures like Sean O'Riordain and Christy Ring, and former agricultural practices. The history on the walls promotes a greater understanding of the area and heightens the essential role of the pub in the community in learning and appreciating the past.

Left: Wedding photo of Dan-Joe and Mary Elizabeth O'Leary (Kathleen's parents), late 1940s.
(*O'Leary family collection*)

Below: The Wayside Inn, 1940s.
(*O'Leary family collection*)

52. IN THE HALF-LIGHT

I can remember that the weather was cold and that there was a December bleakness. The trees etched themselves in the horizon line as the half-light set in. The grey skies of dusk made the land in this part of Ardrum townland even gloomier. Several minutes later a blanket of darkness swept across the landscape. But in the midst of it all my two companions, Donal and Annie, and I encountered a revelation amidst a young forest – the ruins of a seventeenth-century fortified house, the extant towers carving their own meanings into the landscape and the half-light.

On Annie's copy of the 1830s Ordnance Survey map, the structure was marked as Old Court. I was intrigued to find these ghostly ruins. This was not the first major ruin that I have encountered in the valley but probably the first I met that I reckoned dated from the early 1600s. But it was not the date of the building that pulled me to explore further but the whole idea of seeing this piece of built heritage as an adventure. The more I pushed the trees back, the more I revealed the structure and its story.

At first glance, the site was a house with four corner turrets. The main block was gone – an empty space. The treasures of this house were also gone, along with its memories. But at one stage, the building had life, meaning, motion and warmth. The plaster on some of the extant walls reminded that people did live here and did aspire to comfort. The life cycle of the house is ongoing; it has gone through its construction, its dwelling and moved well into its decay phase. But this dwelling was also built to last and has even limped into our time, the twenty-first century. The ruin I encountered made an impression of me; it has an enduring presence. Of course, it has been there for over 350 years.

It was interesting to see the perishing, vanishing and petrified remains clinging to tree roots holding some of the walls in place. All the time the structure succumbs to water and the passage of time, which waits for no one or thing. There was also a sense of honesty to the place. By that I mean, part of the story of the ruin could still be told if one chose to read the landscape of the building and examine the falling stones.

My imagination was grabbed by the musket loops in the corner towers. Was there blood spilled here? Who guarded these towers? Who decided that it was important to have musket loops in the walls and why? I thought about the people whose job it was to stand there and protect this home if it was attacked. Those people were empowered with responsibility and indeed many ruins seem to ennoble the landscape, helping to convey its identity.

Local woman Annie Twomey explores the Old Court remains.

I examined the ruin closely; the former construction methods were showcased but it was a sadder shadow of its former greatness. There was beauty and art in the human detail. There was a kind of interplay of order and chaos – a rough elegance, a tension between the structure and its defensive meanings.

I began to think about the house in general, and its day-to-day practices. I thought about everything from how they orientated the house to the acquisition of wood for the floors. The holes in the upper levels of the guard towers suggested that the residents had an acute interest in being connected to and part of the surrounding landscape, by way of timber and stone.

These were just notes before I visited the library and the archives and tracked down a professional archaeologist with a specialist interest in the seventeenth century. The plot thickened. Welcome to Ardrum …

53. UNVEILING COURT SCULLANE

To me a ruin is like a picture frame but with the central image disjointed. It takes time to figure out the main elements. The Ardrum ruin offers insights into the material culture of an era from 400 years ago. Those insights comprise the class of person, the type of place created and the activities carried out. The house would have structured people's worlds – the household, labour, livestock, earth and plants.

After my first trip to the ruin, I was informed of a larger house that was built in the 1700s. It was remembered for its 365 windows and located perhaps half a mile west of the ruin. It was run by the Colthurst family, who eventually moved from Ardrum to Blarney Castle House and estate in the late 1800s. That was when the second house went into ruin and eventually the community took its stones for other purposes, such as local housing and other buildings.

So, my journey brought me to the Cork Archives Institute to see the Colthurst papers that are carefully stored in twenty boxes. No papers exist for the early 1600s, so the architect is unknown and any correspondence is missing, as well as drawings. In fact, the earliest reference of the grounds and lands is in 1677 when a lease from Charles II to the Colthurst family mentions the house and the fact that on the estate there were forty cottages with forty gardens. There was also 150 acres of meadow, 200 acres of pasture, 50 acres of wood and underwood, and 30 acres of furze and heath. A lease document in 1683 reveals that the name of the house was Court Scullane. Some of the lands were being sublet to John Meade and John Barrett. A lease document from 1684 noted that the Colthursts also had lands in Ballyvourney.

The leases reveal a lot but also present new questions, especially as the style of the extant ruin dates to the early 1600s. There are eighty years unaccounted for, with no leases present. One could easily say that the Colthursts built the house, but I'm reminded of my previous visit to Carriganmuck Castle in Dripsey and the history of the McCarthys in this region. Cormac Mór MacDermod MacCarthy was attending the English parliament as Baron of Blarney and because of the unsettled political climate in Ireland, he surrendered his lands and to the Crown and obtained a re-grant.

The problems arising from English colonisation and plantation in the late 1500s continued into the early 1600s. By the late 1500s, two Irish Chiefs, Hugh O'Neill and Red Hugh O'Donnell were waging all-out war against Queen Elizabeth. In 1600, O'Neill marched to the south of the country, reaching Inniscarra, five miles west of Cork. In 1601, the Lord of Muskerry, MacCarthy of Carrignamuck, raised an army to assist the Lord President of Ireland, Sir George Carew, in his fight to quash the rebellion by

Above left: Re-imagining the past; a possible view of Court Scullane in the 1600s, based on Kanturk Castle interpretative panels.

Above right: The ruins of the fortified house of Court Scullane with Rory Sherlock, archaeologist.

Hugh O'Neill and O'Donnell and any impending Spanish attach. The MacCarthys accompanied the Lord President in his march to Tipperary to find O'Donnell and then returned to Kinsale to engage in the battle against O'Neill outside the town. After these events, the country remained unsettled for a time and it appears that Carrignamuck residents engaged in some of the disturbances. They secured the usual pardon, one issued in March 1603 in favour of 389 Muskerry persons.

It is against this background that I would argue the ruin is set. The MacCarthys had lands, and apart from residing at Carrignamuck they also had Blarney and Kilcrea Castles. So there is a big part of me going towards the idea that the MacCarthys were involved in some part of Court Scullane's construction and that it was passed to the Colthursts later in time. The Colthurst family tree shows that they had roots in Yorkshire and are noted to have come to Ireland with nobility in the 1500s. Therefore they may have been granted land by the ruling monarch. A Christopher Colthurst is said to have settled in Cork and lived in Ireland until his death in 1641. Christopher's son John died about 1682 but is reputed to have been granted lands in the Act of Settlement of 1662. His son was also John, and he lived in Ballyanley in Inniscarra and was granted lands in County Cork in the 1680s. And it as at that point where the archive picks up the lease. I would propose that the McCarthys built Court Scullane sometime in the early 1600s and that the Colthursts took over the complex in the 1680s, building up the estate to 752 acres by the year 1830.

54. RETURN TO THE BEGINNING

The old ruin at Ardrum grabbed my imagination. It is part of the Lee Valley's cultural heritage but it also offers insights into societies elsewhere and the architecture of life itself. The social context of this ruined fortified house gives an insight into the identity of its past residents. Between the mid–1500s and 1700, there was great social, economic and political change in Ireland. People were witness to colonisation whereby religious and cultural conflict was present between the dispossessed Gaelic Irish, the Old English and the new Scottish and English colonialists. The plantation programme was a move to gain sources of revenue from Ireland through programmed colonial intervention and experimentation on the island. The programme was later carried out in the new English colonies in the Americas.

Kanturk Castle, North Cork, January 2009. Court Scullane at Ardrum would have been similar in design.

Helen Dodson, biologist, measuring the fallen masonry across the centre of the ruin at Court Scullane. Ardrum.

In the seventeenth century, there were fundamental shifts in power structures. There were new forms of land management and renewed investment in economy and infrastructure. The rural landscape was subject to intense activity and widespread enclosure took place. New agricultural estates were developed and industrial activity intensified to support those estates.

In terms of the existing population size before colonisation and after, it is difficult to gauge. In addition there are the issues of ethnic diversity and people's constructions of their identity. Those factors are difficult to assess but what is known is that in a sense place, culture and identity collided. There were tensions countrywide, and in Munster in the 1640s, rebellions between the older, rooted English families and newer English generations took place.

In terms of Gaelic society, it was largely structured around dozens of regional and local lordships, located in structures such as tower houses, crannog and earthen ring forts. Those were the symbols of Gaelic ethnicity, tradition, power and even resistance, as the colonisation process was carried out. However the bigger picture reveals that there was no defined sense of a Gaelic nation defending itself as a whole. There was pronounced individualism and regionalism emerging. Groups operated in an uncoordinated way and they were ineffective in disrupting settler life. In particular, there were Irish families that accommodated the Crown, such as certain septs of the MacCarthys, who did so in order to keep their lands intact. Religious adoption, political accommodation and strategic marriage alliances became ways of survival. Therefore several Irish families such as the MacCarthys were obliged to fight against Gaelic Irish families elsewhere in the country.

In the new plantation world of the seventeenth century, settlers were encouraged to build strong, defended houses and masonry castles, and to introduce English-style agricultural and industrial manufacturing practices. The Irish landscape turned into a model of English settlement, so that rich resources such as woodland, rivers and the land could be exploited in a much more organised and entrepreneurial way.

Old landscapes such as Ardrum can convey information not only about historical events, but also the complexity of people's lives, how they changed, moved and adapted. Court Scullane, the fortified house at Ardrum, was a symbol of conquest – a statement in the midst of a highly contested landscape between English plantation culture and Gaelic society. It represents colonisation and hostility, new and long-held, treasured landscapes. The building of the house was about conquering the land and manipulating the environment. The land was sublet and split into small plots. There would have been roads leading through the estate to the house, but they are all gone now. The house was intrusive on the landscape but also connected to it. The vast amount of stone required for the walls was ripped out of the ground in a chosen quarry site. It was highly labour intensive. There would have been an architect required, as well as engineers and stonemasons. In Cork City 400 years ago, Court Scullane was the Elysian Tower of its day. It probably took longer for the Court to be built than the Elysian because of the different technologies. The Elysian took three years to build in the twenty-first century. Perhaps Court Scullane took ten years in the seventeenth century? The house was a great feat of engineering for its day, containing a high level of contemporary architecture. It was based on an Italian Renaissance style – a mixture of country house and castle using symmetrical design. It had defensive features on the top but also had the well-dressed corner (or quoin) stones.

The Archaeological Inventory for South and East Cork notes that new ideas were coming in with the Elizabethan Planters and the opening up of the country to outside influences. The old-style tower houses gave way to a roomier, better-lit, more comfortable fortified house. There were defensive features but new innovations were provided for, including a wooden staircase in projecting blocks and far greater space for private rooms.

55. THE CONTESTED LANDSCAPE

The landscape's effect on those it passes through is powerful. And for tourists – for us – the experiences shadow departures, arrivals, unfamiliarity, fear, settling, unsettling, different perceptions surfacing in different contexts, small things standing in for huge events and historical reckonings, emotional and intellectual baggage reworked in new social and geographical spaces. We affect and are affected by the landscapes we move through. We return home but not to the same place.

Barbara Bender & Margot Winer, *Contested Landscapes.*

The human side of the ruin at Ardrum is another thing to think about. Issues such as the conception of the house, the arrival and takeover by the Colthursts in the late 1600s, their unfamiliarity with the region, their fears and the fears of the surrounding natives. Those latter issues humanise the landscape, adding a further layer to the historical data and the ruin. This way of thinking connects and energises our heritage with relevancy in our time so that perhaps one can then begin to fully understand the past and its rich legacies, especially in terms of identity formation.

A sense of place is important to the individual and communities. It can be rich, deep and enduring, with as many layers as those that constitute a human personality. Similarly, places can be full of internal conflicts – conflict over what its past has been, conflict over present development and conflict over what could be its future.

And so, in building a profile of life in the Ardrum house, there are many strands to think about. The phase of fortified house building was from the late 1500s to *c.*1641. In east and south Cork, fortified houses were built by the established merchant families like the Barrys at Castlelyons and Fitzgeralds at Ightermurragh, and also by city merchant families like the Archdeacons at Monkstown. The style of the fortified house structure was something new. It was designed in symmetrical fashion, one window over the next. Kanturk Castle is another impressive example, especially in its restoration. It has a big central block and turrets at each corner.

Archaeologist Rory Sherlock kindly came out to Ardrum with me on my visits, and he noted that Cork is one of the best counties in Ireland for fortified houses with around twenty-five identified so far. The Ardrum fortified house is an impressive size; twenty-nine metres in length by seventeen metres in width. It has two storeys and an attic, but it would not have been incredibly tall. There were ground loops (or musket loops) at ground and first-floor levels. There were few grand windows.

Interior view of Kanturk Castle.

In the wider environment, there were courtyards, which had dual purposes of formal gardens and defences. Portumna Castle, for example, had a formal approach. In the Italian Renaissance style, the idea of a court was forged. The name Old Court is shown for the Ardrum fortified house on the first edition Ordnance Survey Map in the 1830s. Two other examples are Coppinger's Court in West Cork and Burnt Court near Cahir.

Early castles were never pretty in aesthetics on the outside but inside because of their smallness, they were furnished with comforts. Contrasting with them, fortified houses were high status on the outside but lacking inside because of the vastness of the rooms. Many of the older castles had a public role and people were allowed entry as they were semi-public buildings. In the fortified house, there was a clear line at the front door and more of a private feel.

Despite the relative comfort, there would have been many threats to people's lifespans. Life was cold and hard and they spent a lifetime by the open fire; smoke inhalation would have presented a common type of medical problem. During a recent visit to Kanturk Castle, which Rory explains would have been similar in layout to the fortified house at Ardrum, I counted approximately twenty-six fireplaces.

In an age before the harnessing of turf and coal, wood was constantly required to service these fires. One needed a woodcutter, a wood 'getter' and someone to put the wood on the fire, all of which made the house and its association with timber looking like a type of factory, as the fires were probably all on in the winter months. Trees were constantly carved up and planted. And that's just one aspect of the house – what about guards, servants, gardeners, and rent collectors? Life back then was governed by the horse and cart so there would have to be stables, harness and tack makers, wheelwrights, wood carvers, water carriers, dressmakers, and wick makers for wicks in oil for light.

Compared to today, the years of the seventeenth century were primitive times. All people knew was work. Saving the harvest involved gathering it by hand. One of the stages of bread making involved crushing corn between two stones. It is amazing how today we can see or contact any part of the globe using the internet and mobile phones, but in a sense, it was this hard way of life that, over the centuries, inspired the globe to think of better ways to think, to live and survive.

Illustration reconstructing the entrance to the seventeenth-century fortified house. (*Kanturk Castle Interpretative Panel*)

56. DUELS AND DEBATES

Places have different meanings for their inhabitants according to the events and actions they witness, partake in and remember. When we roll on the clock in the history of Ardrum, more historical documentation comes to the fore and we see the estate of Ardrum transforming as tastes and styles change. Much of what is known about the eighteenth century in Ardrum is bound up with the actual family history of the Colthursts and passing references to the Inniscarra landscape.

In the early 1700s John Colthurst of Ardrum became head of the family. He was MP for Tallagh from 1734 to 1757 and was High Sheriff of Cork in 1738. His son John Conway Colthurst was the first baronet. He was MP for Doneraile from 1751 to 1760, MP from 1761 to 1768 and MP for Castle Martyr from 1769 to 1775. He was created a baronet of Ireland in August 1744. He was married to Lady Charlotte Fitzmaurice, a daughter of the Earl of Kerry. During the mid-eighteenth century, a second house was constructed on the Ardrum estate, perhaps a quarter of a mile east of the fortified house. The grounds surrounding the house, complete with a deer park, ornate garden features, orchards, ponds, barns, stables and other outbuildings, became a significant feature on the Inniscarra landscape. Traditionally, the house is said to have had 365 windows, one of which had to be closed up because at the time no private residence could have the same number (or more) windows as Buckingham Palace. Writing in 1750, Charles Smith in his *History of Cork*, notes, 'A mile north of Inniscarra on rising ground is Ardrum, a pleasant seat of Sir John Colthurst who was created a baronet on August 3rd 1744.'

The second baronet, John's son with Lady Charlotte, was John Conway Colthurst, who was born in 1743. He inherited Ardrum in 1775 and came to own large properties in Cork and Kerry. He also managed the Lansdowne estate. Ten years later, there was social unrest amongst tenants in the paying of land tithes to the Church of Ireland. Some members of the Protestant gentry supported the movement that became known as the Whiteboys' movement. The Whiteboys (Buachaillí Bána) was a secret Irish agrarian organisation that used violent tactics to defend tenant-farmer land rights for subsistence farming. Their name derives from the white smocks the members wore in their nightly raids. They sought to address rack-rents, tithe collection, excessive priests' dues, evictions and other oppressive acts. As a result they targeted landlords and tithe collectors.

As the campaign against the payment of tithes extended from parish to parish, the Whiteboys succeeded in making life difficult for Church of Ireland ministers. As a landlord, John Conway Colthurst was strict and enforced the payment of rents, but he did support the protection of the poor. About the year 1775 he was a founder member of the Farmers' Club, which met at Blarney. The aims of the society were to protect the poor from what they saw as the oppressions of the clergy and their agents in terms of tithes. They established rates for the payment of tithes, reducing the burden of this tax as much as possible. John Conway was particularly active on his own estates. In the parish of Ballyvourney, he encouraged a selection of poorer tenants to not pay the tithes. In response the Church of Ireland clergymen placed notices on him to attain the tithes. However, as time moved on, the Whiteboy unrest escalated and John Conway was accused of promoting the escalating violence. John discounted his involvement and became concerned with those who were spreading the rumours.

In early February 1787, a pamphlet was published by Dominick Trant entitled 'Considerations on the Present Disturbances in the Province of Munster'. Reading between the lines, John Conway Colthurst asserted that he was being referred to and went to Dublin to demand an apology from Dominick Trant. Dominick refused and John challenged him to a duel. On 14 February 1787, both men went to the border of County Wicklow, near Bray. John was accompanied by Councillor John Egan and Dominick by John Hely Hutchinson. John Conway Colthurst was deemed one of the best shots in Munster but on this occasion was shot in the chest by Dominick Trant.

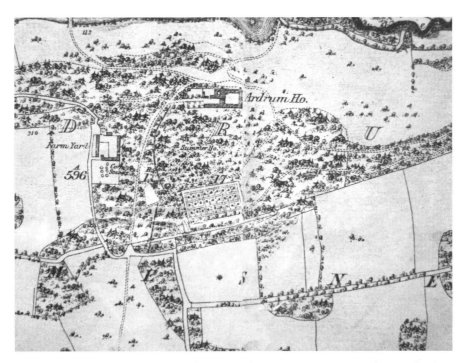

Section of second edition Ordnance Survey Map of Ardrum Estate, c.1836. (*Cork City Library*)

Former well folly, Ardrum, with
Annie Twomey and Donal Healy.

John's brother Nicholas Colthurst succeeded to Ardrum and the other estates. In time
Nicholas, like his predecessors, became High Sheriff of Cork (1788), MP for Johnstown,
County Longford from 1783 to 1790 and for Castle Martyr from 1791 to 1795. He
married Harriet La Touche, a member of an important Dublin banking family. Their
son Nicholas who succeeded to the title in 1796 also had an interesting background.
Born in 1789, he was educated at Eton and joined the British Army for the Napoleonic
Wars. He rose through the ranks to become a Captain of the Cork Militia or Captain
of the 68th Foot Regiment. Captain Nicholas was MP for Cork City from 1812 to 1829.
George Conway Colthurst was the fifth baronet, was born in 1824. He was educated at
Harrow and Christ Church College, Oxford. In the year 1846 he married Louisa Jane
Jefferies. When her father died in 1862 he succeeded to the Blarney estate.

The other interesting point that arises in the literature about the Colthursts in
the early 1800s is their own struggle in running approximately 32,260 acres of land,
which later became a factor in the decline of the Big House in Ardrum. Since the
late eighteenth century, rents and agricultural prices had been steadily increasing. But
when the demand arising from the Napoleonic wars in the 1810s stopped because
of the end of the war, the mortgages taken out to keep estates such as Ardrum going
were difficult to pay off. In 1829, it was noted that Sir Nicholas Colthurst, who died
that year, had left significant debts and an auction was held of all furniture, wines and
stock at Ardrum to try and clear the debt. However the rents continued to decline as
the century progressed. As a result the Colthurst landlords could not meet their mortgage interest and estates such as Ardrum were tailored to demand. Indeed by the late
1800s, the Colthurst family had moved to Blarney and the land in Ardrum was sublet
to several tenants: Major Westropp; Major General Meade; Captain Hereford (?); Mrs
Emily Bayley; Thomas Dixon; D. Douglas; D. Twomey, and R. Grey.

57. GRACEFUL AND ELEGANT

On my third fieldwalk of Ardrum, Annie and I walked to the site of the old ring fort, where in a sense the place name Ardrum or Ard Dhruim (Height of the Hill) began. From here one can see the physical journey of the River Lee and its extent. Looking west, one can see Shehy Mountains, where the river begins, and looking to the east one can see the water tower at Hollyhill in Cork City, where the river meets the tide.

In Ardrum, there are many signs representing change and continuity in the valley, and how each inhabitant used and uses the landscape for his living. Modern farming occurs alongside the ruins of another era: the towers of the seventeenth-century fortified house; the features of the eighteenth-century pleasure gardens; the elegantly arched Lady's Bridge, which spans the stream running through the townland; the old estate entrance gates and elaborate enclosure wall; the walled garden; the remnants of pedestrian gates that were associated with the Cork–Muskerry Tram that ran through the site; the old farm machinery, and the foundational remains of the outhouses of the Big House. There is so much memory here that has faded and reconstructing Ardrum is a book in itself. The multiple paths through the site also showcase Ardrum's rich natural heritage. However, I feel the perspectives of my guide Annie reveal much of the site's deeper sense of place. She notes:

> Ardrum has been a constant in my life. I have new memories every time I go there. It is not something in my past. Growing up in an idyllic place, we had freedom to roam and explore along the way, being immersed in nature and learning by observing. For instance, the crows come home from the north-west to roost in the trees around the great house – they signal dusk and nightfall and then they go out in the morning at dawn, hundreds and hundreds of them.

Ruins of Ardrum House in the 1970s. (*Donal Healy*)

Lady's Bridge, Ardrum.

My family, the Twomeys, have been intimately connected with Ardrum for generations. So I walk in the footsteps of my ancestors. The smell of the laurel when in flower evokes a far-off memory, a very early memory, which always fills me with happiness and brings a smile to my face, even though I cannot capture the scene associated with it. It is a woodland in Ardrum and there is an uplifting feeling connected to it. I remember playing beneath giant Douglas firs, but also recall the loss in 1973 of the old woodland around the great house, which was replaced with commercial conifer trees.

I was always aware that Ardrum was unique. Even on a map it stands out because of the amount of area devoted to woodland. It was the Ardrum demesne. Take the geography of the landscape for starters – it comprises of a valley that cannot be seen from any road. The woodland on the hillsides is interspersed with fields on the valley floor and there are so many different vistas. It is sheltered from the northerly wind and so it always feels warmer. The trees define it, even though a lot of them are conifers. Some of the older oaks and beech survive, living alongside Spanish chestnut, alder, hornbeam, ash, wild cherry and horse chestnut. Ardrum is cut off from traffic and noise pollution. It is tranquil and full of the sounds of nature; even at night the absence of light pollution aids the viewing of the night sky.

When I go to the site I bring a deep appreciation of what it offers me. It has defined me. It is home. It enriches the soul. I observe the seasonal changes, noting the trees that are in leaf first each year and how as a coniferous woodland matures the wildlife adapts – for example the squirrels colonise the mature trees and feed on the pine cone seeds.

From stories told by the older family members now deceased I can get a sense of what it was like. It is a private place in private ownership, so not a lot of people would be aware of it or its charms. In Ardrum, the landscape is elegant, grámhar, smiling, welcoming, consoling, embracing, old and wise.

58. INNISCARRA COMMUNITY CENTRE

Overlooking Ardrum is Inniscarra Community Centre in Ballyanley. I've passed the complex several times on my travels and for me it is another active and modern bastion of community life within the Lee Valley. I was impressed by its set-up. Its multiple clubs and societies bring people together and create a strong sense of place and belonging for those involved.

The centre's background is worth telling as it celebrates the long decades needed to establish a community centre in the area and the numerous people who brought their talents to bear on the development. The following was recounted to me by members of the community association. The need to make facilities available for the parish of Inniscarra was first mooted at a meeting of Berrings Macra na Feirme, a very vibrant club, in the early seventies. A meeting was held in the old Berrings Hall and a committee was elected. That was in February 1972. Eamonn Hegarty was elected chairman and John Cronin was elected as secretary.

Many meetings followed to establish what a centre might offer to the community and to deal with issues of location and the formation of the centre as a co-operative or a limited company. At that time, local farmer Bill Ellis was willing to sell some land in a central location in the parish, namely Ballyanley. Approximately ten and half acres were bought at a cost of £13,000. To obtain ownership deeds were required, so it was decided to buy the land outright. Now all the working group needed was money. Numerous fundraising activities followed including door-to-door collections with people giving what they could afford. A life membership began at £1 and became £5 after some time. That gave the people of Inniscarra a sense of ownership over the project. Great credit is due to the many men and women who walked the roads to make the vision of a community centre a reality. Clubs supported the concept as they needed grounds for training and a hall for indoor activities.

In 1974, when sufficient funds were raised, the contract was signed for the purchase of the land. Barretts of Ballintemple, Cork City, got the contract for the upgrading of the land on two pitches, to be known as number one and number two. The building of the centre began in February 1974 and was completed by July 1977. Michael O'Mahony, Berrings, was the contractor. During those years, the people of Inniscarra Community Centre became volunteer labourers as they picked stones and harrowed the ground. Volunteers also built the perimeter walls with Anco training centre providing local apprentices to plaster them. Equality was alive and well as there was also a female plasterer. John P. Hickey, one of the founder members, said pressure was put on as to who would put up most blocks per day.

Muskerry Rugby Club. (*Inniscarra Community Centre*)

By the late seventies clubs were developing around the centre. Inniscarra Badminton Club formed in 1977 and became one of the most successful in the country, providing officers at national level and competing in Division One. During 1977 and 1978, pitches were provided for soccer enthusiasts in the parish. Clubs such as Tower, Leemount, Dripsey and Strand United all trained and used facilities in Ballyanley. There was also the Cloghroe All-Stars. The 'Stars' played soccer and rugby and were established in Healy's Pub in Cloghroe. One night in 1978 a group of enthusiastic gentlemen were brought together by Donal Healy and Con O'Sullivan and Muskerry Rugby Club was founded. The club had its base in Ballyanley, where it rented the grounds from the Inniscarra Community Centre until they bought their own grounds from Bill Ellis. In 2004/5, the club came of age with the building of its own clubhouse within the complex.

In the seventies in Ireland, festivals were a great social occasion and Inniscarra had its own version in the Lee festival. The initial festival in 1974 was located on the banks of the River Lee behind Inniscarra Cycle Rest. Unfortunately the marquee that was erected was flooded in one of the worst Septembers on record. The final events had to be completed on the new but as yet undeveloped land in Ballyanly. The festival in ensuing years moved location to Ballyanly and became one of the staple fundraisers for the centre, as well as a great source of enjoyment every summer for young and old.

In 1978, a weekend harvest festival was initiated in the centre. It finished on Sunday night with well-attended concerts. Macra na Feirme clubs such as Berrings and Muskerry were instrumental in its success. As time progressed, it developed and moved towards an agricultural show and old-time threshing, an event which became synonymous with Inniscarra Community Centre under the guidance of Joan O'Riordan. The show still provides a great day out in late August, while keeping alive a tradition and providing funds for the centre at the same time.

In the late seventies a loan was secured from AIB South Mall of approximately £40,000 by Eamonn Ambrose, the treasurer. A second parish collection brought in a further £10,000. The very first structure, a pump house erected by John P. Hickey, has since been knocked down to make way for future buildings. The original hall measured 100 feet by 60 feet, which included two dressing rooms and a kitchen.

By 1981, an extension was required to accommodate all the clubs and activities. Once again local voluntary work built the new meeting rooms, one of which was named the Ellis Room. Christy McCormack, a local builder, did the block work on that phase. A £5 per month draw was well supported. About this time dancing became very popular at the centre on Sunday nights. Top names such as Dermot O'Brien, the Swarbriggs, the Dixies, Joe Mac, Linda Martin and Foster and Allen entertained people. Inniscarra Community Centre became a popular destination for the dancing public as the years progressed.

Community is about forging a connection and many of the events that supported the Inniscarra Community Centre down the years have created a great bond amongst the people. Fun days, discos, road races, bonfire nights, card drives, concerts, American tea parties and fashion shows have all contributed greatly to the life of the community centre.

Above left: Muskerry supporters at the Lee Festival, *c.*1988. Left to right: Mark (background), Keith Rothwell, Bill Ellis, John Arnott, Aoife Crowley, Brendan Crowley, Noel Lahiff and Karl Mitchell. (*Inniscarra Community Centre*)

Above right: Inniscarra people at the heat of the Over 60s Talent Contest. From left to right: Paddy O'Brien, Mrs Field, Michael Richardson, Maurice Wiseman, Sheila Cooney, and Joan O'Riordan. (*Inniscarra Community Centre*)

Between 1982 and 1983, two tarmacadam tennis courts were provided inside the main gate of the community centre. The cost was £4,000, a very modest sum, thanks once again to the voluntary labour supplied. While this enterprise was underway, a souterrain was discovered. It was a significant find and UCC were engaged to examine it whereupon a corpse was found. The corpse was taken away and later the experts informed the centre that it was 2,000 years old.

By 1985, the officers of the centre approached Bill Ellis once again for additional land to provide another pitch. The GAA was developing its own identity within the complex and required road frontage. Inniscarra Community Centre swapped land with the GAA and so began the GAA pitch.

The possibility of a pitch and putt course was now on the agenda. The existing grounds, as well as an extra strip of land bought, made this dream a reality. The greens were laid down in 1987 and the club founded in 1988. The club grew, and by 1991 a clubhouse was built for the members by completely voluntary labour. The building cost approximately £7,500 and a race night, run as a fundraiser, brought in £8,500.

By 1989, £200,000 had been spent on the development of Inniscarra Community Centre as it provided sporting and recreational amenities for the parish of Inniscarra and its hinterland. Demand was growing for an all-weather facility. At an estimated cost of £84,000, this was a project of greater stature – a costly and ambitious undertaking. The centre personnel were not daunted, and with a considerable bank loan and lotto funding, they undertook the project. A synthetic grass carpet with sand infill was laid down. Shortly after the pitch opened in 1996 the GAA club opened its own clubhouse within the complex.

By the mid-1990s, a number of sports called Ballyanley their home, with karate and athletics among those gaining a very high profile. By 1995, approximately £300,000 had been raised and spent on the purchase of around twenty acres of land, the building of the hall, and the extensions and development such as the tennis courts, the eighteen-hole pitch and putt course and drainage of soccer pitches.

However, in the pre-Celtic Tiger era of the nineties, costs were rising, volunteerism was declining, workers were tiring and money was scarce. While some clubs were gaining independence from the centre (e.g. GAA, rugby, pitch and putt) with consequent fundraising needs of their own, other clubs like badminton and tennis were finding the going tough. As a result, income to the centre was declining. By 1998, the debt on the centre was over £100,000. Activity on the scale witnessed heretofore was no longer sustainable. At this time of financial crisis, several individuals and businesses within the parish responded magnificently when approached for an interest-free five-year loan of £500. Much of the money was later paid back, while more was written-off by members, for which the centre was very grateful.

Above: Committee members of the agricultural show and threshing, September 1989. From left to right: Joe O'Riordan, Gerard Crowley, Jerome O'Callaghan, Johnny Herlihy, John Blair, Ricky Coleman, John O'Sullivan, Willie O'Brien, Joan O'Sullivan and Joan O'Riordan. (*Inniscarra Community Centre*)

Left: Inniscarra show organisers Ann O'Mahony and Eileen Collins. (*Inniscarra Community Centre*)

As the centre entered the twenty-first century, despite costs involved, committees felt that upgrading meeting rooms and showers was essential to encourage the use of the facilities and attendance at meetings. Approximately €20,000 was spent in this upgrade. The Ellis Room was completely refurbished. What must be remembered is that a community centre too has day-to-day running costs with little or no income to offset them, such as insurance, heating, and lighting. At that time the running costs ran at €40,000 per annum. Between 2003 and 2004, a series of meetings was held to put a strategy in place to offset the debt and move forward. A massive draw brought in a total of €80,000. Throats were not safe either as the next major fundraiser was a novel pub song contest entitled the 'The Voice of Inniscarra', which brought in £15,000. Celebrity status was attached to the singers from the various centres and the contest drew great support from the public as they cheered on their representatives.

In 2001, Inniscarra Camogie Club, founded in 1967 and based on rented grounds in Ballyanley decided to look into the purchasing of adjacent land to the centre to develop into a full-sized playing pitch. Land was purchased from Pat Cronin and with the dedicated work of a strong field and finance committee, the Inniscarra Camogie Club became the first club in County Cork to own its own grounds under the umbrella of Inniscarra Community Centre. Pairc Mháire Uí Cheallachain was opened in the summer of 2004. The Rugby Club too had enhanced their grounds and built a clubhouse. By now the complex was extended to forty-five acres of land.

In 2005, work in refurbishment took on a new impetus. Both the community and soccer pitches were re-drained. Re-sanding of the all-weather pitch followed. New goalpost and ball-stopping nets were erected. Whilst spearheading these improvements, Con O'Leary suggested the possibility of tarring the entire complex. The 'Great Tarmac Project' began. Once again, voluntary work was undertaken to make the tarmac a fantastic reality. Pathways, pedestrian crossings, lining and signage followed. The complex was now very much special-needs friendly, due to the perseverance of Pat Burton, who also founded a branch of the Special Olympics in the parish at this time.

The principal sources of funding for the works carried out at this time included the parish draw (£80,000), grants and lottery monies, club contributions (€78,000), a golf classic, the 'Voice of Inniscarra' song contest and the threshing/agricultural show.

In May 2008, a new lobby was created, a new stairway installed and a new lift fitted to accommodate people with special needs and the elderly. The state of the art toilet facilities were put in place. The cost of the 2008 project was €160,000. This was grant aided to the amount of €40,000. A small number of people took to the roads again to fundraise and within a few short weeks €38,000 was collected in the December fundraisers. In the words of one great community activist Dinny Buckley, the committee put 'its shoulder to the wheel and drove on'.

59. THRESHING OUR HERITAGE

When I first met the old-time threshing machine at Inniscarra Agricultural Show I was excited at the sense of pride taken in it by those involved and onlookers alike. Here was something very old that was made very engaging by the passion and enthusiasm of the organisers.

The organisation of the first old-time threshing event goes back to the early 1980s, when the then officers of Inniscarra Community Centre, chairperson John P. Hickey, secretary John Cronin, assistant secretary Rita Casey and treasurer Eamonn Ambrose, decided to celebrate the area's agricultural memories. The event was arranged to bring back happy reminiscences of yesteryear to older people of the parish and to enlighten the youth of the hard work done in years gone by. John P. Hickey purchased the old threshing set from Diarmuid O'Riordan, Vicarstown. The first corn grown for the day was grown at the farm of Con Desmond, Callas, and cut by John O'Callaghan.

The threshing at the beginning was a three-day event commencing with a dance on Friday night by Berrings Macra, a concert and entertainment on Saturday night, and threshing on Sunday, with numerous sideshows. On Sunday night Muskerry Region Macra held their competitions and dance in the hall.

Inniscarra's famous threshing machine with John P. Hickey, Pat Flynn, Dan Morrissey, and their respective children and grandchildren. (*Inniscarra Community Centre*)

I sat down with the stalwarts of the old-time threshing and talked about their passion and knowledge about how farming has changed. Dan Crowley is originally from Greenfield, Ballincollig. His father was John Crowley, a farmer from Ballineen, West Cork, and his mother was Margaret McCarthy from the same area. His grandparents were also farmers. John went to Presentation secondary school in Cork City up to Intercert and began developing an interest in farming in Ballincollig in his teenage years. On his family's land in Ballincollig, he kept cattle and rented the land for grain production. His first memories are of beef, sheep and tillage, and he ploughed with horses. He recalls, 'my family bought a tractor, a TVO, at the time of the Second World War; I was driving it when I was ten years old. We used it for ploughing and harrowing, sowing the corn.'

Dan Crowley subsequently bought a farm in Coolatubrid, Inniscarra, and for five decades his family have been farming there. In the early years there, he and his brother Denis did contract work with combines. In 1953 he remembers the first combine on the farm. He used to rent a lot of his land and hence did a lot of contract work with his combine from the mid-1950s onwards. Dan notes:

The Agricultural Vintage Commitee – Patrick Cronin (Gurteen), Pat Healy (Ballyshonin) and John P. Hickey (Coolatubbrid), pictured at Inniscarra Community Centre, March 2009.

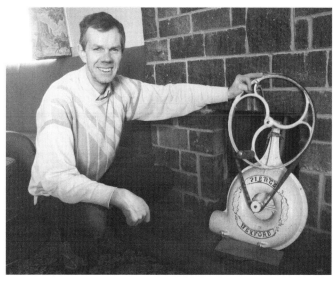

Above left: Dan Crowley, Coolatubbrid, Inniscarra.

Above right: Michael Hennessy of The Stirrup Bar, Whites Cross, with a Pierce fire fan.

Combines were new to farmers, they were very suspicious of the concept of the combine – people did not have to thresh any more. The combine did the work of the cutting and threshing and it took the people out of it. In the early machines, the combine trailer was very cumbersome. The combine was part of the ongoing mechanisation process. There was a massive changeover from horse to machine. Milking machines came in. At that time, there were huge changes as well with rural electrification.

John P. Hickey is originally from Rathmore, County Kerry. He came to Cork to work as a psychiatric nurse in Our Lady's Hospital. He always had an interest in farming and when he retired at fifty-five he started a small farm of sheep and sucklers at Coolatubrid/Springmount, Inniscarra. He recalled to me the old threshing ways and what manual work it was.

John remembered when the horse reaper and binder (a machine that cuts grain and binds it in sheaves) came in, pulled by two horses. The other machine that made a difference was the horse-thresher machine, which was powered by two horses, and allowed the small and large grain to be separated at the one time. He remembered John Desmond, a cattle dealer from South Berrings, and his workhorses, which he got from Kerry. He talked about the social occasions in particular, such as the threshing dance in the kitchen. There was a big social scene attached to it. Drink, in the form of porter in kegs or barrels, was part of the tradition. The occasion was, as he notes:

> …like a feast coming to the end of the years; it was a tradition attached to the joy of goodwill that the harvest was saved. Harvesting was a very intensive business. Grain was bagged and stored in the loft. The whole event was a neighbourly thing – the coming together of a community.

Pat Healy from Ballyshonin, the next man I chatted to, reminded me he is known as 'Pat the Farmer'. He has been farming since the early sixties. He recalls ploughing with horses. He walked with his cattle and horses for sale to the fairs. He got up at 4 or 5a.m. and walked to the market locations. He walked four hours to get to Mallow and two hours to get to Coachford, but found it was the walking home that was the hardest after a long day at a fair or mart. He noted the advent of the tractor and trailer, and how much they improved the hard effort of transport. There were other changes as well, he explains:

> A bulk tank replaced the creamery run, so visits there were done away with for the most part. At the creamery you met your neighbours. There were three within Inniscarra parish – Kilcolman, Dripsey and Ballyshonin – and all had local shops and merchant stores adjacent. As machinery came in, fields had to become bigger to accommodate. Wastage of ground was not an option. Ditches were removed from fields to let bigger machines work as much of the land as possible. The disadvantage was that shelter for cattle was taken. In addition, the run-off of water that was kept back by ditches was free to run, hence more flooding of the nearby roads.
>
> Farming was more relaxed back then – regulations are ruining it today. There is more factory farming today, all mass produced and computerised. There's no mixed farming; it's either milking cows or dry bullocks now. Buildings have changed. Stalls have gone. Cows used to have their own space. At one time cows could find their own stalls and had names – now they have tag numbers and lots of paperwork attached to them.

Patrick Galvin is from Gurteen, Inniscarra. His interests are in the vintage. He is a painter/decorator by trade but over several years he developed an interest in old cars. Around 1990, he bought an Austin A43 (1968) and started going to shows and vintage rallies. In 2000, Brian Smith of Gurteen and Patrick organised a national vintage rally in Inniscarra. It was sponsored by Feeney's of Dripsey and McCann's Huntsman of Tower. It was a great success and as a result vintage was added to Inniscarra Agricultural Show.

60. KNOWLEDGE AND WISDOM

I first met George Williams of Carrignaveen Stud whilst researching a cousin of his, Bill Williams, who owned a shop and garage at one time in Lower Dripsey. When I contacted George he mentioned his own history and experiences. George Williams has lived a very active life, has made a great contribution to the sense of place where he lives, and as a result he is bound up with the history of his locality.

George is the fifth generation of Williamses in the area. He informed me that his branch of Williamses were originally from Clew Bay in Mayo. Several members moved and settled in Kinsale for a bit, working as pawnbrokers before banking came into being. A branch of the family then came to Inniscarra and set up a post office and shop. His father, Edmond Thomas Williams was born in Carrignaveen House. George's mother was Anna Eliza Williams from Coolcower near Macroom. He had two brothers, James Arthur and Sam, and a sister, Audrey.

George was born in 1927 and raised in Carrignaveen House. A Nurse Lucey, a Jubilee nurse, came to the house from the Tower area to deliver him into the world. Growing up he remembers her on a bicycle doing her visits. She has grandchildren currently living in Tower. George recalls:

As a young fella, I remember the shop. We used to do deliveries by horse and cart; we delivered flour, meal and coal around the vicinity. We kept cows, made butter and sold it in the shop. The post office had five postmen who took off from here at 6a.m. The post was sorted in our dining room. The postmen were Neil Lucey, 'Brick' Riordan, Jack Murray, Paddy O'Leary and Jack Buckley. I remember Jack Buckley who walked to the sub post office in Berrings to deliver the post.

I went to St Nicholas National School in Cork. By my time, the Protestant school in Blarney had closed. I travelled to Cork on the Muskerry Tram. The nearest station to us was a mile away in Cloghroe. In the mornings on the Coachford to Blarney there were no seated carriages for people; at that hour of the morning, the train transported goods such as milk churns. The churns held warm milk and heated our hands. We got on the seated carriages at Blarney Station. In the evening there were seated carriages from Cork to Coachford. I remember travelling with the Woods family of Faha.

The site of present-day Jury's Inn was the terminus; in fact I remember if a butcher was late with a carcass bound for the Blarney area, he could trot out the road on his horse, catch up with the tram and throw in the carcass, such was its slow speed. For cyclists, if the wind was right, they could hold onto the side of carriage and get a lift for some of their journey.

George's parents, Edmond Thomas Williams and Anna Eliza Williams. (*Williams family collection*)

Above left: Staff of Ocean Insurance Company at a company picnic in Inniscarra in 1944. Back row: George Williams, Frank. Middle row: Jim Heapy, Eileen Cavanagh, Olive Pritchard, and Nora Daly. Front row: Betty Kiely, Douglas Whitaker, Douglas Matson, Sheila Murphy and dog Barney. (*Williams family collection*)

In later years, my two brothers, sister and I worked in Cork. We went in on bicycles as the tram closed in the early 1930s. I started off in insurance, in Ocean Insurance, 28 South Mall. I went to Midleton College and one day the headmaster came in and said there was an insurance job going. Another fella Whitaker and I pretended to be interested, so that we could get the day off to go to Cork. I really had no interest and I made no effort at the interview. The other fella got the job. When I met Whitaker in later weeks, he told me that the job was great. I reapplied and the second time round made an effort. I was four years with that company. Then a vacancy arose in London Insurance, 77 South Mall, at the corner of Pembroke Street, now part of the Imperial Hotel. I took on that job, and got the junior inspector's job, which involved getting out and meeting people. For that, they gave me a company motor car. I spent twenty-seven years in the insurance business altogether. I retired on April Fool's Day 1971 to pursue the dream of breeding horses.

In terms of my interest in horses, it started at a young age. My father's first cousin was Bill Williams who had a brother Jack, who worked in Beltham Stockbrokers. Captain Holpoid of Ballinatray in East Cork was a client of Jack's. He trained horses and had a vast amount of land. He had a gallop for training horses for the Curragh. One of his horses, named Vourloper, suffered tendon trouble in training. The Captain sold him onto me. I got him ready and won three point-to-points with him in 1954.

So began my semi-professional career in horse training. During those years, the post office was turned into stables. There are thirty-five stables in the complex now. There was ten acres originally; there is now an extra fifty acres plus some rented land. I got a trainer's licence and worked from there. I was delighted when Captain Christie won the Gold Cup in 1974. A horse called Another Dolly won the Queen Mother's Champion Race around 1978. Mon Capetaine, a famous stallion, was stationed at the stud. He was the sire of Captain Christie and Another Dolly. The stallion was a champion sire, bred in France by French champion Wild Risk out of a mare, My Prince. I bought him from Ted Walsh.

I married Gilliam Williams who was from Southampton. We had two children, James and Kim. James now runs Carrignaveen Stud. My son is the sixth generation of Williamses to live in this house.

Left: George and a three-year-old horse, Carrignaveen Stud, Inniscarra, May 2009.

Below left: Pigeon Hill point-to-point, *c.*1950. George Williams rides Funny Bunny, pictured here with owner Lavender Rose. (*Williams family collection*).

Below right: Christie's Boat, Dam of Captain Christie, plus stallion Mon Capetaine and Johnny Buckley (right) – lived in Vicarstown plus who worked with George for many years. (*Williams family collection*).

61. ETCHINGS IN THE LANDSCAPE

Before I left George Williams at Carrigaveen House, he brought me to the nearby site of Cloghroe Station, where I met the O'Leary family. There, Eleanor, Terence and family showed me what has survived of the station. At the Cloghroe site, the passing route can still be made out. The station house and ticket house have been taken down due to health and safety reasons. The O'Leary family showed me pictures of the former station house, ticket office and platform through old postcards and colour pictures from a number of years ago. The family also showed me where the track passed over stream dykes; the land was not level there, so culverts were created.

Alongside its material history, this train forged unlimited memories for those that participated in its journey. Its construction in 1887 brought something different to the Lee Valley, something modern; it brought industrial progress, which, pitted against the beauty of nature at the time, won out in the 1880s. It brought a conquest of the landscape. It gave residents of the valley new views of the countryside. It transformed people's attitudes to the landscape and it certainly created a privileged position for those that travelled on it.

As a sleek machine, the train in its early days must have been a technological marvel. Standing at the Cloghroe Station, I thought about Charles Stewart Parnell fighting for the case for the train in Westminster, the community pushing for it, the commitment to a large investment, the sanctioning of the plan, the hard work involved in laying the tracks. On the former track bed, I considered the first day the train ran on its track. It was a new spectacle connecting the countryside to the city and changing the city–countryside relationship.

Surely for the city resident, the train presented a feeling of release in the open country; away from business the focus was on the fields, the sky, trees, country cottages, ruins. Perhaps for the countryside resident, the city was a larger space of people, so perhaps anxiety was present. However, for both the sense of travel probably created anxiety and mystery.

I like the romantic idea of the slow steam train chugging through the undulating landscape. I like the idea of people engaged with the countryside, the fleeting effects of light through the windows creating a changeable atmosphere, the train windows framing new worlds for the traveller and creating familiar mental pictures for the regular passenger. There is that tension between the Lee Valley and huge iron machines pulling passengers and goods cars. In addition, the railway compartment and the railway station both raised the issue of social class, but in the end all travelled on the same medium.

The Cork–Muskerry Tram was not alone in its transformation of values and attitudes. There were several three-foot narrow gauge systems that once existed in Ireland. In County Donegal an extensive network existed, with two companies operating from Derry; the Londonderry & Lough Swilly Railway, which one of Phil Coulter's pieces immortalises ('Lough Swilly Railway') and the County Donegal Railways. Well known was the West Clare Railway in County Clare, which saw diesel locomotion before closure. The Cavan & Leitrim Railway operated in what is now the border area of County Cavan and County Leitrim. Some smaller narrow gauge routes also existed in County Antrim and in County Cork.

As for the Cork–Muskerry Tram, its career ended in 1934 as a slow, cumbersome machine, its route affected by the quickening pace of the world. But for me the site still holds a lot of its energy and identity through the present family the O'Learys, who have harnessed the memory of the station here for their present and future. They have collected memorabilia related to the site and many stories to tell their own children, part of the future generation of the Lee Valley.

Above left: Cloghroe station, *c.* 1900. These postcards were sold in the Williams's Shop at one time. (*George Williams*).

Above right: Former station house at Cloghroe, in front. (*O'Leary family*)

Left: Former ticket house, Cloghroe station. (*O'Leary family*)

62. STRANDS OF TIME: THE CHURCH OF IRELAND CHURCH IN GARRAVAGH

My trek in the valley has brought me on several occasions to the old ruined Inniscarra Church of Ireland church in Garravagh (Garbhach, 'Rough Land'); I enjoy walking the riverbanks here. I have my own memories there. When I was at Coláiste Chríost Rí, my geography teacher Charlie O'Leary brought my class here for Leaving Certificate fieldwork. We cycled out from the city and explored the meander of the river at this point. We measured the flow at the concave and convex sides. Here the river carves a route through soft sandstone, which is visible along the adjacent main road.

Ruined Inniscarra Church of Ireland church, 2009.

Various threads of Irish history are told here. Hugh O'Neill and his men rested in the area on their way to the Battle of Kinsale in 1601. A memorial stone at the entrance to the ruined church complex (and Dripsey GAA grounds) records Hugh Maguire, Chief of Fermanagh, who was killed by English forces in the area on 11 March 1600. In addition, at the time of the Lee Hydro-Electric Scheme in the mid-1950s, a seventeenth-century sword was discovered in the river and given to the Cork Museum. It is reputed that O'Neill stayed with monks at Inishleena, or Inis Luinge, meaning the 'Island of Encampment'. Legend has it that St Senan set up camp about AD 530 and built an abbey before going downstream to Inniscarra.

The ruined church and graveyard is iconic-looking in its appearance, a relic of a once golden age in County Cork's past. In terms of the historical narrative, William Maziere Brady in his *Clerical & Parochial Records of Cork, Cloyne & Ross*, published in 1863, notes a reference to a priest in Inniscarra in the year AD 1291. O'Hynovan is the recorded name. In the year 1591, the Protestant Church in Inniscarra was headed up by William Feld or Field, who was formerly a priest in Holy Trinity or Christchurch in the walled town of Cork. In 1615, the vicar was Richard Alley. He was also curate of Aghabullogue in 1615. In 1634, Edward Johns was vicar at Inniscarra and Benjamin Hearice was the curate. In September 1640, Phelim Fitzsymons was a prebendary of Inniscarra. A prebendary is a post connected to an Anglican or Catholic Cathedral or collegiate church and is a type of canon. Prebendaries have a role in the administration of the Cathedral. In July 1664, Patrice Thompson was vicar of Inniscarra. Thomas Wilcox took up the post in 1669. George Synoe appears as vicar between 1671 and 1673. Roland Davies took up the vicarship in 1673 when Synoe died.

Dives Downes, on his tour of Cork and Inniscarra in September 1700, notes:

> I saw the church of Inniskarra; it is in repair; the walls were built with stone and clay. The north wall is supported by two buttresses. There is a handsome altar rayl'd in; a pulpit, desk, and three large good pews. The churchyard is not well fenct. This church stands near the River Lee, on the north of the river, four miles from Corke, to the west. This is in the diocese of Cloyne.

Roland Davies, apart from his Inniscarra station, became Dean of Cork in 1710 and passed away eleven years later. Robert Carleton succeeded him at Inniscarra and as Dean of Cork. In 1735, Christopher Donellan took up leadership at Inniscarra. Donellan was born in Dublin, and on 11 November 1719, when sixteen years old, entered Trinity College Dublin. He was a Fellow there from 1728 to 1735. In 1742, Dr Donellan obtained a certificate for certain improvements on the adjacent glebe house in Inniscarra. He died in 1750. By his will, dated 7 July 1750, he gave £600 to the Charter School Society to erect a school at Inniscarra. The Charter School system was established under a royal charter of King George II and aimed to educate Protestant and Catholic children alike. By 1750, there were forty-eight Charter Schools operating in Ireland. In addition, many poor Catholic children were taken away from parents who could not look after them to be educated as Protestants. Boys were apprenticed to such trades such as bookmaking, carpentry and farm work, while girls trained for domestic service. The Charter School at Inniscarra was in the townland of Gurteen overlooking the Lee Valley. It was a mixed school and in the year 1788 housed twenty-six girls and fifteen boys. It was a two-storey building built of red sandstone with walls three feet thick.

Dr Christopher Donellan gave £280 14s 6d to trustees (the Bishop, Dean, and Archdeacon of Cloyne), the interest to be given to some widows of the diocese, having children. This bequest became the basis of the present Widow's Fund of Cloyne Diocese. He gave £200 to the Hospital of Incurables, £200 to Mercer's Hospital, and £200 to Swift's Hospital. Christopher Donellan also left money with which the steeple of Inniscarra church was built, and a bell was put up in 1756. The following inscription is still visible on a tablet on the wall of Inniscarra church, 'This steeple was erected and bell put up by a legacy of the Revd Christopher Donellan, DD, late rector of this parish, under the direction of the Right Revd the Lord Bishop of Cloyne, AD 1756.' Marmaduee Phillips succeeded Christopher Donellan from 1750 to 1770. Phillips was author of *A Sermon, preached before the House of Commons, on the Anniversary of the Irish Rebellion* (1745).

Henry Agar succeeded Philips on his death in June 1770. In 1785 the Protestant population was twenty-two. In 1799, George De La Porr Beresford took over at Inniscarra. Under Beresford, a new Church of Ireland parish church was built in 1818.

The current interior of the ruined Church of Ireland church is overgrown and roofless. A plaque on the wall near the door records Tirry Matthew Jones of Donoughmore, who died 7 December 1717. An ornate railing surrounds a chest tomb of Major John Galway, who died on 8 March 1836. A chest tomb in the north-west corner is unreadable. A George Vesey is recorded on a plaque in the altar area.

The adjacent graveyard is enclosed by a stone wall and is still in use. A large collection of eighteenth-century and nineteenth-century headstones exists to the south of the church ruins. The earliest noted date is 1770. The oldest family names from the nineteenth century that I recorded in the wider graveyard were Barrett, Corcoran, Delanymour, Forrest, Harrington, Lee, Leest, Mahony, McCarthy, and O'Donoghue. Just north of the ruined church are five gabled mausoleums, one of which has the Colthurst name. In the most easterly section lies the largest with near identical pedimented gables. All five have suffered from vandalism. The memory here is fading.

63. THREADS OF TRADITION: INSIDE ST SENAN'S

You pilgrim who comes from afar, welcome,

The church is a museum of beauty from the past and present,

You can enjoy it to the full but this church is also something more,

For believers this is a sacred space, a house of God,

Many generations have come here and there are still many people coming with the greatest joy and their deepest sorrow at turning points in their life or just passing by,

May it be a place of quietness also for you where perhaps you come nearer the source of all life.

Inscription at door, church of Our Lady, Bruges.

On a trip to Bruges in Belgium, I came across the above quote at the entrance to the church of Our Lady and I thought its commentary widened the perspective of the visitor; churches are not just bricks and mortar, there is something deeper at work – they are a landscape full of commentaries about human nature and national and international belief systems. The past co-exists with the present and is built into a way of life that sustains it. Throughout the Lee Valley, I have been drawn to sites like standing stones and church sites because they are tangible memories. You can observe them, touch the stone. They add to my own fascination for the rural landscape of the Lee Valley, with its myriad of complex human interventions.

Exterior, St Senan's church, Inniscarra.

Above left: Interior, St Senan's church, Inniscarra.

Above right: Plaque on the tower of St Senan's church.

I was looking forward to visiting the Church of Ireland's St Senan's church for months, having passed the site so many times and admired it from the road. At the outset, St Senan's church, located at Canon's Cross, replaced the nearby, now-ruined Inniscarra church in 1819. The Protestant community chose to refresh and develop their community by constructing a new church.

The commemoration tablet on the tower wall reveals, 'This church and tower was erected AD 1819, with a loan from the Board of First Fruits, Rt Revd Wm. Bennet, Lord Bishop of Cloyne, Hon. Revd George Delapoer Beresford, Rector, Revd Wm. Townsend, Curate, Sir Nichs. Conway Colthurst, Bart. Philip Rubie, Esq., Church Wardens, G.T. Beale, Arch.' The plaque anchors in time all the people mentioned and the building of the church, and it commemorates an occasion that drew great pride, marking it for the future passerby.

St Senan's is the first active Church of Ireland church that I have discovered in my travels through the valley. Many others I have encountered are ruins and rebuilding the memory was difficult. But St Senan's is a complete building that oozes identity – it is a living sacred space. It has history but also much more, it has active traditions; its bell is rung to call people to the church and it has a service every second Sunday.

The church was built in 1819 at a cost of £923 1s 6½d to accommodate 120 persons. Its design consists of a nave and chancel (chancel not added until 1893), a plain bell tower and a small vestry abutting on the north wall. As I sat in the rustic pews, I compared St Senan's to other heritage structures I have encountered. I was drawn to the roof and the glass, the plaster, the pine floors, the carved altar – the sheltered and bright interior. The building was intact and in a sense the fabric of its identity was complete.

The church's exterior environs have overlooking Magna Carta and yew trees and the interior has wooden floors. The wooden pews made me think about how rooted the building was in nature, with its stonework and timberwork. Ideology as well as theology is expressed in the church through the method of construction, shape, design, and orientation. In the interior, tangible memories remain in the form of the organ, the Good Samaritan depicted on the stained glass, the plaques remembering the deceased, the chalices, the pews, the carved eagle, and the carved pulpit.

The organ came from Christchurch in Coachford, a building that is now a family home. On that church's closure, the organ was stripped and rebuilt in St Senan's. It is worked by hand-pumping. It is still going and was recently serviced. At the base of the altar, which also came from Christchurch, the memory of Warren Allman Crooke, who died on 22 March 1886, is recalled. The colourful, mullioned stained-glass window in the east section of the church over the altar recounts the Good Samaritan. It was erected by the children of Richard Barter MD, the founder of the Hydro at St Anne's Hill, Blarney, who died in 1876.

St Senan's church remembers and honours the past. It has antiquity but also functions in the present. The structural and decorative elements comment much about religious beliefs and goals, human nature and memory, local identity, and the dynamics of social change. Perhaps what struck me most about St Senan's was how it reflects tradition's ability to structures our feelings, expectations, fears and realities.

Above left: Close up of the stained-glass window in memory of Richard Barter.

Above right: St Senan's graveyard, Inniscarra.

64. THE VICTORIAN WAY OF LIFE

I've always been interested in the Victorian way of life. In Cork City, I love the decorative architecture of the numerous bright red-brick buildings from the Crawford Art Gallery to the Victoria Buildings on the McCurtain Street to the terracotta design terracing at places such as Summerhill South. There are many other sites of interest that I been enticed to photograph over the years. Very little has been written on the art and architecture and the human side of Victorian Cork. Hence, the story of Richard Barter's hydropathic establishment gives an insight into the values and attitudes of community leaders in the mid to late nineteenth century.

At the outset, the cultural composition of the Cork of the nineteenth century was deeply influenced by developments in other Western European cities at the time. The romance arising out of revolutions, such as those that occurred in the 1780s in America and France, bred ideas of human purpose. Society sought for the ideal model of civilisation. New ideas emerged and old conventions were questioned. A great debate ensued on every creed, doctrine and institution. The study of 'natural philosophy' grew. This was a term applied to the objective study of nature and the physical universe that was dominant before the development of modern science.

A more thoughtful, vigilant, and moral-driven society emerged. Responsibility and philanthropy were maintained but there was more freedom to use the senses and intellect, to enjoy art and to be openly curious and critical about science. All aspired to change the static views of pre-nineteenth-century society. There was increased industrialisation and subsequent population growth in cities such as Liverpool, Bristol, London, Dublin and Cork. In Cork, large parts of the city were levelled to make way for new municipal buildings and public spaces. The city underwent a physical and moral facelift. There were also a growing number of philanthropists, who established a variety of civic institutions for the working classes such as charities, mechanic institutes and savings banks.

The concept of educating the general public was deemed a key component in improving the social conditions of British and Irish citizens living within large urban settlements. Public health laws, poor law acts and municipal reform acts were numerous in the nineteenth century, and aimed to show that 'cleanliness was next to Godliness'. It was those ideas that Richard Barter supported and brought into the Cork countryside. His Turkish baths opened in 1856 amid a turbulent time in post-Famine Ireland, an Ireland of emigration and poverty. Barter's project, at a basic level, provided a steam bath followed by a shower and massage, which cleansed the body.

 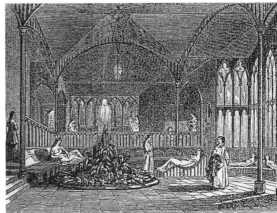

Above left: View of St Ann's Hydropathic Establishment. (*Guy's* Directory of Cork, *1886*)

Above right: An interior view of the Turkish Bath at St Ann's. (*Cork City Library*)

St Ann's Hydropathic Establishment survived for just over 100 years, closing in 1952, and since then its story and its elaborate set-up has slipped away from memory. Richard Barter was not alone in his pursuit of scientific knowledge in the mid to late 1800s. For the working and middle classes, science was rapidly becoming a fundamental aspect of leisure, self-improvement and political ideology.

In Cork, the Royal Cork Institution and later the Cork Mechanics' Institute provided lectures, evening classes and publications on science for those who wanted to learn more. The great debates and theories of modern science found their way into the hearts of many Cork citizens. But Cork scientists were not alone in their plans for using science for social reform. In 1851, there were approximately 700 public institutes of various sizes promoting science in Britain and Ireland.

Richard Barter was a working scientist and developed the so-called 'improved' Turkish bath. Barter's revised bath was based on the belief that saturating the atmosphere with moisture or steam interferes with the free transpiration from the lungs and skin, and thus impedes the process that nature provides by cooling the body. *The Irish Builder* for 1870 (vol. XII, 1870, p. 170) reveals more on the science but also how Barter, in the context of living in Victorian times, drew deeply, like many other business men, on history, nature, geometry, theory and on modern fashions in creating an inspiring set-up. *The Irish Builder* notes:

> The new building is situated upon a terrace below the main building, and for style of architecture and beauty excels anything of the kind ever seen in this country. The baths occupy a

space of 180 feet by 36 feet, and consist of two complete sets, one for ladies, and the other for gentlemen. The structure is divided transversely, a cupola surmounting the building upon the outside, at the point of division. The entire building has an exceedingly classical and imposing effect externally and internally, and is built in a substantial and permanent manner. The division walls of the sanatorium have piers of Caen stone carved, and styles panelled in red Cork marble, the capping of the top rails being polished Sicilian marble.

The flooring throughout is laid in red marble, also giving a beautiful effect to the building … These noble rooms are decorated in the highest style of architectural ornamentation. Much use has been made of mirrors and stained glass in the construction of the building, which, combined with the rich tapestry, gives it internally quite an Oriental appearance. In the centre of the cooling room a marble fountain plays into a plunge-bath of large dimensions. Special arrangements have been made in the hot room for its illumination by gas … The architectural beauties of this magnificent establishment are due to Mr R. Barter.

Richard Barter. (*Cork City Library*)

65. INTERTWINING MEMORIES

Often we assign too much stability to memory, as if it were fixed; memory moves and changes. We add and remove layers, concealing, exposing and colouring, intertwining reality and fiction.

Oonagh Hurley, 'Site 46' Exhibition, Crawford College of Art and Design, June 2009.

From the rich setting of St Ann's Hydropathic establishment, the view of the present-day landscape reveals many cultural memories of Inniscarra parish and beyond – the growing housing estates of Tower, Blarney and the famous Castle and further south, the water tower on the top of the ridge in Hollyhill, Cork City. All those sites present different meanings for the viewer. The commercialisation of heritage in Blarney Castle and the Celtic Tiger housing boom in Tower catch my eye.

In the trees behind me lie the ruins of Richard Barter's aspirations for health and science education. The clock tower evident in the late-nineteenth-century picture stands in ruins. The clock faces are gone and the extant timbers of the tower are held in place by rusted iron posts.

Several years ago I visited the ruined Hydro site. I got a tour of the extant building and took pictures but at that time I had very little context. So I was excited to retrace my steps and search the site with a knowledge of how it came into being. An advertisement in 1886 in *Guy's Postal Directory of Cork* revealed that the building once had a circulating library, reading room, covered tennis courts, three grass tennis courts, theatre, American bowling alley, and billiard room for both ladies and gentlemen. It promoted itself as a residence for invalids and accommodation for tourists to the region. There was 'daily communication' from Blarney, both by rail and sedan car. Later the Cork–Muskerry Tram stopped here. As I read these notes from my visit to the library I thought about how these once-grand aspects lay at my feet as physical rubble within the overgrown ruinous landscape.

Light streamed through the glassless windows of the ruin. The frames of some sash windows remained intact complete with slide slits intact for moving windows up and down. Fallen masonry blocks corridors and nature now forbids entrance to large parts of the complex, keeping its secrets intact. Trees are growing through walls, pushing the yellow slob bricks and the mortared limestone and sandstone structural building pieces to one side.

Dr Richard Barter, who established the famous hydropathic baths in 1842, died on 3 October 1870 at the age of sixty-seven. His son Sir Richard Barter (1837-1916) and his wife Anna carried on the Hydro at St Ann's. One of the second business threads of the Barter family was the development of the dairy farm at St Ann's. On Richard's succession to his father's work, he devoted his life to modernising St Ann's dairy farm and gardens. The *Farmer's Gazette* in 1883 described Richard's dairy farm as one of the largest and most successfully conducted in the country, affording as it does, ample evidence of the advantages to be gained by pursuing dairy farming in accordance with approved modern practice. Richard had an average of 100 cows and 80 calves at any given time. Richard received his knighthood in 1911 in recognition of his services to agriculture.

Dr Richard Barter's second son Henry (1847-1875) was a Captain in the Indian Army. He died from yellow fever on the boat returning for leave in Ireland. He left a widow and a newborn son, Richard Harry Barter (1875-1944). Sir Richard and his wife Anna took a keen interest in their nephew. From 1894 until 1904, he worked as a bank clerk at Coutt's Bank in the Strand in London. In 1904, he went to live at St Ann's and he started a course in Medical School at Queen's College Cork (now UCC). He qualified in 1911. He was subsequently appointed resident physician at the Hydro.

Five years later, in 1916, his uncle Sir Richard died, with his wife Anna passing away a year later in 1917. They left no children. They are remembered in the side altar stained-glass windows in St Senan's church in Inniscarra. On their nephew Henry's death in 1944, he was buried in St Senan's, amid other Barter family gravestones.

66. ALONG THE MEMORY SHORE

It is said that places are full of internal conflicts; over what a place's past might have been, over present development, and over what could be a place's future. The story of St Ann's Hydro seems embedded in many histories compiled on the Inniscarra region. Pictures of the site are in every local historian's archives, as well as retellings of its history.

In particular I was interested to find out more about the families who worked at the site and the way of life at St Ann's. My research brought me in contact with a number of individuals whose own lives have been tied up with the site and its place in the region. My first contact was Zwena McCullough, who grew up on the site of St Ann's. Her father was Dr Hugh Quigley who in 1945 came from Glasgow to Cork on holiday with his sister. He visited the Hydro, fell in love with it, and subsequently bought it, along with the farm and part of the nearby woods. Dr Quigley hired Kenneth Besson from Dublin (formerly of the Hibernian Hotel) to run the hotel side of the business.

In the closing years of the 1940s, the Hydro complex began to make a profit. However, in the early 1950s, international circumstances in the guise of the Korean War forced the closure of the Suez Canal, which had a huge impact on the Irish economy and fuel sources. Petrol became scarce. As well as that, the European continent opened up after the war and people could go abroad on holidays again. Rising costs and fewer customers resulted in the closure of the Hydro in September 1952. Many of the interior fittings were sold off at an auction held by Marshes. In time, the principal baths in the lower gardens were dismantled. Around 100 staff were let go (seven of them were working on the farm). The seventy-six bedrooms were never to be filled again.

Above left: Hugh and Alice Mary (Babs) Quigley. (*McCullough family*)

Above right: St Ann's Hydro, Tower, Blarney, *c*.1945. (*McCullough family*)

Above left: Ruined clock at the present-day site of St Ann's, June 2009.

Above right: Zwena McCullough standing adjacent to the old boiler of St Ann's.

The 'model' farm continued until 1962. At that point in time, the land was let and part of it sold. Attached to the Hydro, there were magnificent vegetable gardens and orchards. The Hydro had 200 acres of land on deep, dark soil, which was also well drained. The farm supplied milk, butter, cream, cheese, poultry, beef, pork, fruit and vegetables. The Hydro was almost completely self-sufficient. Vegetables and fruit were taken fresh from the gardens each day as well as dairy products from the dairy.

My chat with Zwena on the past fifty years led us through the site of the farm. Alongside the present-day road through the old complex, we viewed the old coal boiler that ran the central heating, which was saved by Zwena. She remembers elements of the disused Hydro buildings when she was growing up. In the north of the complex, there was a water tower that had corners of brick or was quoined with brick. In the tower was a reservoir and a drying room and boiler (the boiler wall was three bricks thick). Walking through the site, Zwena pointed out the remains of the coal house and the covering of the surviving weighbridge. The inscription on the weighbridge reads 'Pooley & Son, Patentees, Liverpool and Glasgow, Clyde No.2'.

Evidence for the installation of new medical baths in early twentieth century can be seen in another ruined building with pipe work intact. The oratory is also in ruins and the building that was once a theatre space. We passed the original gates to the complex from the Tower–Blarney road, which were re-used and originally casted by Richard Perrott & Son. The original battery house was converted into a cottage in the 1960s. The Hydro was the first place in Munster to have its own electricity. A hydro-electric station was built on the River Shournagh, one of the Lee's tributaries, and the charge was sent to the battery house for distribution. We passed the old dairy building (now restored into a tool shed for the allotments). The milk from cows would have been cooled and separated; the skimmed milk was given to the pigs and calves and the cream was sold to the creamery. The milking parlour and calf houses have been dismantled over the years and are now are part of the allotment facilities.

A plaque on old stables notes that they were built in 1923. Horses and carriages met the trains at Blarney station to transport visitors. When I met up with local Inniscarra author Madge Ahern (prior to meeting Zwena) she informed me that her great-aunt Elizabeth Byrne ran the provision of the horse transport to the Hydro. The business had been in the Byrne family for many years. Elizabeth also put on day trips in summertime for Hydro residents. On Sunday there would be morning and afternoon outings. A very popular one was over to Tower, up the old Kerry Road (which gave one a commanding view of the countryside), from Inniscarra and Ballincollig right back to Donoughmore. A left turn brought one down to the village of Cloghroe and by Ardrum Wood. Madge's father, Mr Coleman, was also involved in leading the tours. He would take the road leading from Cloghroe church to the Vagabond Rock and Leemount Cross along the Lee Valley. A chat with Maire Geary of Cork revealed that in the 1930s her father Patrick O'Sullivan (originally from Ahiohill, West Cork) was involved in taking visitors on tours of the area.

On my walk with Zwena of the contemporary Hydro site, she showed me the old orchard, which for the past ten years has been an allotment area, where some sixty-plus people grow their own vegetables. Here history is repeating itself in terms of drawing people to St Ann's. The site had a reputation and wove a route into the way of life of the area, which it is again doing. Richard Barter brought innovation and opportunities to the area, and I feel that these are being brought again.

Zwena's sister Olwen runs the successful B&B Maranatha, a Victorian residence built in the 1880s by the Barter family on the St Ann's property. The decor is very authentic; there is a feeling of being back in the old world with the values of Richard Barter. An inscription on a silver vase notes the people's thanks to Barter for bringing them hope and inspiration, 'Presented to Richard Barter Esq. MD by the Tenantry of the Cloghroe estate as a tribute of gratitude & esteem for his uniform kindness to them and his very judicious management as agent for the past 17 years, May 1858.'

67. TOWARDS A RIVER OF MEMORY

The Lee Valley is just one of several river valleys in County Cork, which are all different in their topography, their shapes and forms. There is, for example, a tangible difference between the cut-up landscapes of Gougane Barra and Inniscarra. The rolling fieldscapes are impressive in Inniscarra, but the raw, glaciated landscapes are as impressive in Gougane Barra. Both areas differ in topographical nature and both landscapes stretch beyond the borders of their respective named boundaries, Uíbh Laoghaire into West Cork and the rugged Bantry coastline, and Inniscarra to merge with mid-Cork to the north of its territory.

In building up a profile of the latter places, I have travelled through them and tried too to think outside the veil of history, facts and figures. But I find this manner of thinking trickier. It was only with the passing of the River Lee project and travelling around the county for the 'Discover Cork: Schools' Heritage Project' that I have been exposed to the bigger picture of human survival and the human connection to landscape itself.

Many times I have been drawn to stop and look at the new scene presented to me. It's like some sort of discovery. I'm drawn to stop and photograph. I'm pulled into the story. It's like the landscape itself can talk to me. That may sound surreal, but I feel there is something in the landscape that is engaging us. Landscape, just like memory, is attractive and powerful.

Looking from Agharinagh to Kilgobnet townlands, Dripsey.

The landscapes of the Lee Valley have affected me in different ways. Landscape has affected my mood and, over time, my personality, tweaking who I am and my pride and passion. I get excited and inspired by some vistas, and feel sad or switch off at others. But that's just my view. Each viewer has different tastes, come from different backgrounds and see things differently. The landscape as an entity, with all its changes, rules and structures seems not to be static; the more I travel the more I learn how to see, read, understand and appreciate what I see.

My journey down the Lee Valley has opened up my imagination. However, such is the location of the Lee Valley. I have encountered a multitude of views, close-up and wide-pan shots. It is rather random and messy. For example, the lush fieldscapes of Inniscarra seen from a distance are large, with the bigger picture of the parish presenting a grand and at times tamed scene. However, the underlying curvature of the land can still be seen. Further west along the valley the glaciated landscapes seem raw, rough, persistent and enduring. And yet, when you add in the human component, you can see the vulnerability and frail nature of both the landscape and human elements.

It is amazing how in the twenty-first century even the most extreme landscape environment can be modified. But as the story of the Lee Valley unravels through my own travels and engagement with the valley's landscape and people, I can see how the landscape, in an indirect partnership, has shaped people over time. Attempts to structure landscape become a negotiation down to the smallest stone used on a dry-stone masonry wall.

One of the threads running through my journey is the concept of time. Sites from various periods are scattered throughout the valley. At all times I struggle to grasp the past, especially an era I wasn't born in. The past fits uneasily in my mind. The more real-life stories I reveal, the more I struggle to accept the past's values and technologies. I am very respectful of the power and magic of the past in the construction of the present attitudes and values but at times, for me, the past seems like some kind of black and white romantic journey.

However, what keeps pulling me back to reality is the concept of identity and how all the people I have met use the past to reinforce who they are. Their personal stories frame their past experiences, and indeed those of others. So perhaps the first positive thing for me about time is that it seems to be one of the major foundations of identity.

The second important aspect is that through thinking about the element of time, one is exposed to a complicated web of social relations. Every generation seems to be informed by its own past and present, but their sense of place is constantly being reinvented, due to their evolving needs for survival.

The third aspect I've noticed about time is that arriving into an area wishing to attain the memories of a place, there is a marked difference in the responses of the

The River Lee near the Church of Ireland church, Garravagh.

young and the older Lee Valley residents. Most working individuals in the present are captivated with everyday preoccupations. Although valuable, the past is some-what irrelevant to their present. Contrasting to that, many older people, perhaps tired of life's action, seem to have a need to evoke nostalgia and the past.

The older people I have met look for precision. They go through old papers, old letters and they tell what they remember, but for the most part do not try to write it down. It's like the past does not seem to impose itself. In fact, they are free to evoke it whenever the individual wishes. The past does not compete with today's world.

The fourth aspect that is emerging for me about time is that reminiscing also seems to have had a great deal to do with social nature; bonds between people, formed in a shared experience. Many a social occasion is designed to evoke reminiscing. In addition, many times in the midst of an interview, the narrative may go off on a tangent and tell another story as the person is interrupted by a relative who adds to the past being told.

These ideas haunt my own journey down the Lee but also add a great deal to what each Lee Valley resident is saying. My writings are, perhaps, attempts to come to grips with the underlining questions of how cultural heritage is passed on. What are the processes? What are the foundations? How are identities formed? For me, these questions are important parallels to the memories I collected in my journey in the Lee Valley.

These are my ideas, ideas for contemplating the past and the present, indeed perhaps even ways of looking at the future and exploring our local heritage, environment, society, and the very essence of our identity in the Lee Valley.

To be continued...

BIBLIOGRAPHY

Ahern, M., c.2000, *Inniscarra Looks Back, Through the Avenues of Time* (St Colman's Press: Cork).

Andrews et al., 2006, 'Their finest hour: older people, oral histories and the historical geography of social life', *Social and Cultural Geography*, vol.7, no.2, pp.153-176.

Bender, B. & Winer, M. (eds.), 2001, *Contested Landscapes, Movement, Exile and Place* (Berg Press: Oxford).

Berger, J., 1973, *Ways of Seeing* (British Broadcasting Corporation: London).

Berque, A., 1997, *Japan, Nature, Artifice and Japanese Culture* (Pilkington Press: U.K).

Bielenberg, A., 1991, *Cork's Industrial Revolution, Development or Decline* (Cork University Press: Cork).

Breen, C., 2007, *An Archaeology of Southwest Ireland, 1570-1670* (Four Courts Press: Dublin).

Buckley, J., Greene, A., Long, T. & O'Donoghue, S., 1990, 'Aghabullogue Hurling Team 1890 Cork's First All-Ireland Champions', Coachford Historical Society, (Cork).

Cadogan, T., 1998, *Lewis' Cork* (Collins Press: Cork).

Cadogan, T. & Falvey, J., 2006, *A Biographical Dictionary of Cork* (Four Courts Press: Dublin).

Cody, B.A., 1859, *The River Lee, Cork and The Corkonians* (J. Barter & Sons: Cork).

Coleman, J.C., 1950, *Journeys into Muskerry* (Dundalgan Press: Dundalk).

Cooney, G., 1999, 'Social landscapes in Irish prehistory', in Ucko, P. & Layton (eds), *The Archaeology and Anthropology of Landscape, Shaping your Landscape* (Routledge: London) pp.46-65.

Creedon, C., 1985, *Cork City Railway Stations, 1849-1985: An Illustrated History* (Quality Print: Cork).

Crookshank, A., 1972, 'A Sketch of Irish Landscape Painting', *Eire*.

Cullen, L., 1971, *Six Generations* (Mercier Press: Cork).

Devoy, R., 2005, 'Cork City and The Evolution of the River Lee Valley' in Crowley, J.S., Devoy, R., Linehan, D. and O'Flangan, P. (eds.), *Atlas of Cork City* (Cork University Press: Cork).

Exhibitions by Oonagh Hurley, April Curtain, Mairéad Geary, Sinead Hehir, Louise Hogan, *Site 46 Exhibition*, Crawford College of Art, June 2009.

Feeney, P.J., 1996, *Glory O, Glory O, Ye Bold Fenian Men, A History of the Sixth Battalion, Cork's First Brigade, 1913-1921* (Self-published: Cork).

Feheny, J.P.M., 1996, *The O'Shaughnessys of Munster, The People and their Stories* (Iverus Publications: Cork).

Fehily, D.B., 1988, *Cork Harbour & City Water Supply Scheme* (Report prepared for Institution of Engineers of Ireland).

Fitzgerald, J., c.1899, *Legends, Ballads and Songs of the Lee* (Hand-written: City Library).

Forsythe, W., 2003, 'The Finances of the Colthurst Estate in the Nineteenth Century', *Journal of the Cork Historical and Archaeological Society*, vol. 108, pp.31-40.

Gillman, H.W., 1891, 'Carrignamuck Castle, County Cork: A Stronghold for the McCarthys', *Journal of the Cork Historical Archaeological Society*, vol.1, pp.11-33.

Gillman, H., 1895, 'History of a Townland in Muskerry, with Glimpses of Country Life', *Journal of Cork Historical and Archaeological Society*, Cork, vol. 3, pp.14-15.

Gillman, H.W., 1897, 'The Problem of the Souterrains', *Journal of the Cork Historical Archaeological Society*, vol.3, pp.1-9.

Greene, A., 1990, 'Magourney Church and Graveyard', *The Coachford Record*, Coachford Historical Society, (Cork).

Guy, F., 1875-1900, Postal Directories of Co. Cork.

Halbwachs, M., 1992, *On Collective Memory* (University of Chicago Press: Chicago).

Harrison, F., 1986, *The Living Landscape* (Pluto Press: London).

Hart, P., 1998, *The I.R.A. and its Enemies, Violence and Community in Cork, 1916-1923* (Clarendon Press: Oxford).

Healy, J., 2001, *Aghabullogue, Coachford, Rylane, When We Were Young Together*, Coachford Historical Society (Cork).

Healy, J.N., 1981, *Castles of County Cork* (Mercier Press: Cork).

Hill, J., 1998, *Irish Public Sculpture* (Four Courts Press: Dublin).

Hirsch, E. & O'Hanlon, M., 1995, *The Anthropology of Landscape: Perspectives on Place and Space* (Clarendon Press: Oxford).

Homo Faber, *150 years of Engineering in UCC* (Interpretative Panels in Department of Civil Engineering UCC).

Hoskins, W.G., 1955, *The Making of the English Landscape* (Hodder & Stoughton: London).

Hughes, T.J., 2006, *Wales Best One Hundred Churches* (Poetry Wales Press Ltd.: Brigend, Wales).

Ingold, T., 2000, *The Perception of the Environment, Essays in Livelihood, Dwelling and Skill* (Routledge Press: London).

Irish Tourist Association, *Topographical and Cultural Surveys of Aghabullogue 1944* (Files of Cork County Library).

Irish Tourist Association, *Topographical and Cultural Surveys of Inniscarra 1944* (Files of Cork County Library).

Kerrigan, P., 1995, *Castles and Fortifications in Ireland, 1485-1945* (Collins Press: Cork).

Lewis, S., 1837, *Topographical Dictionary of Cork* (Collins Press: Cork).

MacLaughlin, J., 2007, *Donegal, The Making of a Northern County* (Four Courts Press: Dublin).

Meinig, D.W. (ed.), 1979, *The Interpretation of Ordinary Landscapes, Geographical Landscapes* (Oxford University Press: Oxford).

McLaughlin, Jenkins, E., 2003, 'Walking the low road, the pursuit of scientific knowledge in late Victorian working class communities', *Public Understanding of Science*, vol. 12, pp.147-166.

Manning, C., 1995, *Early Christian Monasteries* (Country House Press: Dublin).

McCarthy, K., ongoing, 'Our City, Our Town', *Cork Independent*.

McCarthy, K. & O'Donoghue, S., 2008, *Generations: Memories of the Lee-Hydro Electric Scheme, Co. Cork* (Lilliput Press: Dublin).

McCarthy, K., 2006, *In the Steps of St Finbarre, Voices and Memories of the Lee Valley* (Nonsuch Publishing: Dublin).

McCarthy, K., 2003, *Discover Cork* (O'Brien Press: Dublin).

Mitchell, F. & Ryan, D., 1986, *Reading the Irish Landscape* (Tower House and Country House Publishing: Dublin).

Murray, P., 2007, 'Re-discovering Seamus Murphy', *Irish Arts Review*, Spring 2007, pp.68-73.

Nora, P., 1989, 'Between memory and history: les lieux de memoire', *Representations*, vol. 26, pp.7-25.

O'Connell, D., 1987, 'Sir John Colthurst and the Muskerry Whiteboys', *Corkman*, 13 March, p.16.

O'Donoghue, B., c.1990, *Parish Histories and Place Names of West Cork* (Kerryman Ltd: Kerry).

O'Donoghue, S., 1996, *The Flooding of the Lee Valley* (Tower Books: Cork).

O'Donovan, J., 1957, 'Concrete Production and Control of the Lee Hydro-Electric Power Scheme', *The Institution of Civil Engineers of Ireland*, pp.83-185 (O'Donovan family collection).

O'Keeffe, T., 1997, *Barryscourt Castle and the Irish Tower House* (Gandon Editions/Barryscourt Trust: Cork).

O'Leary, S., 2000, 'St Ann's Hydro', *Journal of the Blarney & District Historical Society*, Vol. 5, pp.2-30.

O'Shea, D., 1954, 'River Lee-Hydro Electric Scheme', *Engineers' Journal*, Vol.7, No.1.

Power, D. (ed.), 1992, *Archaeological Inventory of County Cork, Mid Cork* (Government Publications Office: Dublin).

Schama, S., 1995, *Landscape and Memory* (Vintage Books: New York)

Schratz Hadwich, B., 1995, 'Collective memory-work: the self as a resource for research', in Schratz, M. & Walker, R., *Research as Social Change: New Opportunities for Qualitative Research* (Routledge Press: New York), pp.38-64.

Sheehan, T., 1972, 'The Mills of Lovely Dripsey', *Evening Echo, 20 January 1972* p.5.

Sheehan, T., 1972, 'Recalling One of Cork's Great Men of the Century', *Evening Echo, 20 January 1972*, p.5.

Sheehan, T., 1972, 'O'Shaughnessy Touch Brought Weaving to its Highest Peak', *Evening Echo, 20 January 1972*, p.5.

Sheehan, T., 1979, 'Dripsey Paper Mills', *Cork Hollybough*, p.17.

Shorter, A.H., 1971, *Paper Making in the British Isles: A Historical and Geographical Study* (David and Charles Ltd: London).

Southern Industry, 1888, 'A Visit to the Dripsey Woollen Mills', *Cork Examiner, 11 December, 1888*.

Thompson, P.R., 2000, *The Voice of the Past* (Oxford University Press: Oxford).

Tilley, C., 1994, *A Phenomenology of Landscape, Places, Paths and Monuments* (Berg Press: Oxford).

Tuan, Y.F., 1977, *Space and Place* (University of Minnesota Press: Minneapolis, MN).

Tuan, Y.F., 2004, 'Sense of place: Its relationship to self and time', in Mels, T. (ed.), *Reanimating Places, A Geography of Rhythms* (Ashgate Publishing Limited: UK), pp.45-56.

Toren, C., 1995, 'Seeing the ancestral sites: Transformation in Fijian notions of the land', in Hirsh, E. & O'Hanlon, M. (eds.), *The Anthropology of Landscape, Perspectives on Place and Space* (Clarendon Press: Oxford) pp.163-183.

Twomey, D., Cronin, M. & O'Donoghue, P., 1993, 'Coachford Creameries', *Coachford Record*, Coachford Historical Society, Cork, vol.2, pp.15-25.

University College Cork, 2006, *Stories in Stone – Interpretative Plaques*, Ogham Stone Corridor, UCC.

Walsh, H.N., 1939, *How to Make Good Concrete* (Concrete Publications Limited: London).

Wertsch, J.V., 2002, *Voices of Collective Remembering* (Cambridge University Press: Cambridge, New York).

Wylie, J., 2007, *Landscape* (Routledge Press: London).

Zerubavel, E., 2003, *Collective Memory and the Social Shape of the Past* (University of Chicago Press: Chicago).